POLYGENDERED and PONYTAILED

The Dilemma of Femininity and the Female Athlete

Dayna B. Daniels

Women's Press
Toronto

Polygendered and Ponytailed
By Dayna B. Daniels
First published in 2009 by Women's Press, an imprint of Canadian Scholars' Press Inc.
180 Bloor Street West, Suite 801
Toronto, Ontario
M5S 2V6

www.womenspress.ca

Canadian Scholars' Press Inc./Women's Press gratefully acknowledges financial support for our publishing activities from the Ontario Arts Council, the Canada Council for the Arts, the Government of Canada through the Book Publishing Industry Development Program (BPIDP), and the Government of Ontario <through the Ontario Book Publishing Tax Credit Program.

Library and Archives Canada Cataloguing in Publication

Daniels, D. B
    Polygendered and ponytailed : the dilemma of femininity
and the female athlete / Dayna B. Daniels.

Includes index.
ISBN 978-0-88961-476-5

    1. Femininity (Philosophy). 2. Women athletes. 3. Sex discrimination in sports. 4. Masculinity in sports. I. Title.

GV709.D353 2009   305.43'796   C2009-900247-7

Book Design by Aldo Fierro

Cover photo © iStockphoto.com/stock-photo-2461006-top-of-the-key-ready-to-drive-for-a-layup.php

09 10 11 12 13 5 4 3 2 1

Printed and bound in Canada by Marquis Book Printing Inc.

Canadä

ONTARIO ARTS COUNCIL
CONSEIL DES ARTS DE L'ONTARIO

Canada Council   Conseil des Arts
for the Arts   du Canada

To those who inhabit the bodies of women ...

—With thanks to Adrienne Rich, *Of Woman Born*, who once described herself as "the inhabitant of a female body ..."

To all the girls and women who believe enough in themselves to learn that their bodies are strong and skilled, that movement is fun, and that sports and physical activities are exciting, empowering, and are worth fighting to play despite the resistance, name calling, and stone-age beliefs about women and their bodies that have been used to keep the playing fields off limits to us.

Table of Contents

Acknowledgements

As with most other book acknowledgements that you have read, this one will also acknowledge that many people need to be recognized in the effort of writing this book. What is different for me is that I do not know most of the people who have to be celebrated in the quest for girls' and women's equality in the world of sport. Some are from the distant past. Some are from a more recent past. Some are currently working in all levels of sport and physical activity advocacy to break through the many barriers that still exist for girls and women in this realm. Some of these people may not even have been born yet, as the quest for complete equity in sport and physical activity for girls and women will not be achieved until socially constructed obstacles, biases, and prejudices are torn down and sport is recognized as a healthy, fun, and worthwhile human endeavour that is important for all people.

One specific person that I would like to acknowledge is a man whose name I do not even know. He showed up in my schoolyard one Saturday morning in 1958. It is important to remember that, back then, children played unaccompanied in schoolyards and parents did not worry about predators endangering their children in the way that we do today.

In any case ... the playground was my baseball stadium. I was there from sun-up until someone called for me to come home for dinner, often when it was nearly dark. I played baseball all the time and I was good. The neighbourhood boys and the occasional other girl would rotate in and out of games all day. I was going to play first base for the New York Yankees when I grew up.

One day this man approached us as we were playing ball. "Who wants to play Little League?" he called. We all ran over to him. This was it! This was my first step on the road to the House That Ruth Built!

The man began talking to us. Then he saw me with my pigtails sticking out from under my baseball cap. "You can't play," he said. "You're a girl."

That was it? What about skill? Desire? Drive? Obviously none of that mattered. Boys who were much poorer, slower, and weaker ball players than I was were allowed to stay and I was told to go home. *Just because I was a girl.*

I have to thank that nameless man for providing me with one of my most enduring memories and for introducing me to the world of gender. As I grew, I would learn that this was a place where often little other than having a penis or not having a penis was the only criterion for entry into or success within many endeavours that I would encounter in my academic and professional lives.

I would also like to thank the numerous female physical educators who, from the late 1800s until today, have struggled to find ways to make games and sports accessible to girls in schools and universities. These women have recognized not only the health benefits of physical activity, but also the fun and empowerment that can be had through playing and competing in activities that have become institutionalized as masculine.

Every school physical education teacher and coach I ever had was female. Our classes, except for the obligatory dance units, were segregated by sex. Except for some equestrian competitions, every referee, umpire, and judge I ever had for a playday or in a competitive situation was female. As a physical education major in college, every instructor I had in my primarily sex-segregated physical activity classes was female. Nearly all of the instructors I had in my theory-based classes were female. Most of these women were second- or third-generation physical educators, taught by the women who created the curricula and structures for girls' physical education in the early years of the 20th century. They possessed a love of sport and physical activity. And they acknowledged and accepted the cautions that were drilled into them—and that they, in turn, drilled into every one of their students—about the need for ladylike behaviour, even while we got sweaty and dirty on the pitches and in the gyms.

I was in college when the Association for Intercollegiate Athletics for Women in the United States and the Canadian Women's Interuniversity Athletic Union were struggling to support national championships for women's sports, and organizations such as the National Association for Girls and Women in Sport worked to train and register female officials for women's competitive events. I thank all of the people who worked to bring about these opportunities and who fought against the loss of female-controlled sports as their organizations were amalgamated with and swallowed up by the men's organizations, forcing women to start their fights for teams, championships, and coaching positions all over again.

I want to thank the women who began and continue to work and volunteer for the Canadian Association for the Advancement of Women and Sport and Physical Activity, the Women's Sport Foundation in the United States, and the International Working Group on Women and Sport who have influenced the development of sport and physical activity across the globe. I want to thank Billie Jean King for publishing *WomenSports*, the first magazine dedicated to girls and women in sport.

My list of thanks could go on: to the women who work in countless organizations that support or fight for girls' right to play sports ... to the parents who have baked dozens of cookies for the bake sales that supported girls' sports in schools and organizations that automatically supported the boys' programs ... to the female athletes who fought to get their sports recognized by local, national, and international governing bodies and went to the courts to challenge biases that kept them from participating ... to the activists and athletes who began fighting in 1968 (and continue to fight) to get rid of sex testing, and who lobby for maternity rights and day-care provisions for women in all areas of training and competition ... to the female coaches who pace the sidelines and get paid thousands of dollars less than their male counterparts ... to the fans who wouldn't miss a game—many of whom have never had the opportunity to fulfill their own heart's desire to be an athlete. To all of the people who know that all sports are for girls and are willing to pay a price, whatever form that may take, to make sure that never again will a young girl hear the words "You can't play. You're a girl."

I would especially like to gratefully acknowledge Rebecca Conolly, Beth McAuley, and Colleen Wormald, my editors at CSPI/Women's Press, and the many reviewers of this manuscript. Their meticulous readings of the text and their insightful commentaries eased revisions and contributed to a stronger final version. Appreciations also to Eoin Colquhoun and Sarah Faulkner of the University of Lethbridge Pronghorn Athletics Program for their assistance in locating sport photographs, and to Canadian Interuniversity Sport for its permission to reprint the cover photograph. Thanks to my colleagues in the Department of Kinesiology and Physical Education at the University of Lethbridge: to Michelle Helstein for many discussions on gender and intersectionality, and for her suggestions for finding valuable references to support this work; and to Jennifer Copeland and François Billaut for information and resources on strength development and physiological differences between women and men. I want to recognize my long-term colleague Wilma Winter for years of support and encouragement that became a motivation for me to carry out much of my research and scholarship in women, sport, and gender.

I feel much gratitude to the people who have supported me through the ups and downs of my career and in creating a manuscript, but more importantly through the ups and downs of my life: my birth family and my extended family, most especially Wendy Bedingfield, Mary Swenson, Shirley Fleming, and Gwendolyn Jansma. And to Rachel Bedingfield, the woman/athlete who has inspired me since she was a young girl because she always stood up for her right to play and now fights that fight for others.

Blind to the Obvious

Dayna B. Daniels

As I walked toward my home on a cold Friday night
The moon on the snow cast a wondrous blue light.
As I looked up at my house another blue shone
And I knew he was sitting with the TV turned on.

What manly sport had him in its thrall?
I knew the answer as I stepped into the hall
And heard the anthem every Canadian knows.
It means that hockey is the sport that he chose.

"Hi, honey," I called as I closed the front door.
"Uh huh," his reply. I expected no more.
When he's into his sports it is always the same,
Nothing else matters. There is only the game.

I putter around and get something to eat;
Check the messages on the phone; fix him a treat.
I sit down to join him as soon as I'm able
Shocked to see the remote lying on top of the table!

I think to myself "This must be some game,"
To put down his clicker is nearly insane.
I've learned not to argue. This is his turf.
Every time out is a reason to surf!

But something is different. He's so intent on the screen
Watching the Canadian and U.S. teams.
They fly over the ice; pass the puck, shoot and score.
Three-three in the second. What fan could want more?

"These guys are awesome!" he said never looking away
From the big screen TV where the game was in play.
 "This game is fantastic! The best of the season!
It's a world cup final," the apparent reason.

I watched for a while before I said:
"I'm really beat and I'm going to bed."
"But the score is tied going into O.T.,
I have to see who wins! You know me!"

I climb up the stairs happily shaking my head,
Put on my nightgown and get into bed.
I smile to myself as I drop off to slumber.
He never noticed the braids that bisected their numbers.

Preface

This is a book about words. It is about the meanings given to particular words and the changing meanings of words across time, place, and culture. It is an investigation of the power of words to uplift us and to constrain us. Words are powerful. They can represent concepts that have the power to cause us to assume tacit permission for engaging in certain actions and certain warning about doing things deemed inappropriate. Our interpretations can be built on a foundation of socialization or of rebellion against the expected.

One interesting factor about words is that their meanings can be different for people of different genders, socio-economic classes, races, ethnicities, and sexualities who seemingly live in the same time and place. Words come into our language as new expressions are needed to represent new concepts and things. Words become obsolete or are driven from language as their meanings and uses become passé or offensive. And, most importantly, we can change the meaning of words.

The particular focus of this book is to examine and challenge the meanings of and to suggest changes for the specific words "gender" and "femininity." Ultimately, the goal of this book is to present a new construction of these concepts that informs who we are as individuals. I refer to this new understanding as "polygender."

My quest is directed at analyzing gender and its meanings in the lives of female athletes, and their personal associations with femininity. "Femininity" describes the socially constructed conditions of gender for people assumed to be female. One of my purposes in writing this book is to challenge social and scientific explanations of this concept that we call gender. My desire is for the reader to set aside whatever notions she/he has regarding gender as she/he conceives it and to be open to using a new lens through which the pictures of femininity and masculinity blur, fade, and metamorphose into a new way of accepting ourselves: being polygendered. I believe that we are all, to some extent, polygendered. We are all a mix of those characteristics, interests, behaviours, and appearances that have traditionally been used to sort females and males into exclusive

1

categories called feminine and masculine. I don't believe that gender is a natural or rigid binary state where we are all relegated to one or the other end of a polarized way of being.

TO BE OR NOT TO BE ... POLYGENDERED

There are many researchers[1] who believe that the terms female, feminine, male, and masculine are not as simple to define as we might suspect. They do not represent a rigid polarization or a two-sex-only model of human categorization. On a personal level, and one that I suspect most readers can identify with, I grew up in a world that identified me from birth as a girl. As I grew up there were not a lot of problems with this label, except that there were a lot of "girl" things that I did not like. I hated dolls and wearing dresses, and the colour pink. And very early in life I developed a passion for sport—most definitely a "boy" thing.

If femininity and masculinity are opposite factors, how could aspects of both of these things be so central to the person I saw myself to be? I had little awareness that my interests and skills ebbed and flowed between feminine and masculine territories. This was also true for most of my girlfriends. At times it was true for many of the boys I knew. The primary difference was that other boys (and some parents) were quick to tease or punish boys who showed any supposedly feminine interests or behaviours. I could not see it as a child, but as an adult I came to understand that this thing we call "gender" is a continuum, and that just about everyone possesses qualities that are artificially divided into "feminine" and "masculine." In other words, we are all polygendered, and slide back and forth along this continuum throughout our lives as our personalities develop and our interests change.

For me, the most personally troublesome aspect of this hybrid feminine–masculine or polygendered way of being was related to sports. Growing up in the immediate pre-Title IX (the 1972 amendment to the Education Act in the United States that prohibited discrimination based on gender in any school receiving federal funding) decades proved to be problematic for a young girl whose biggest dream was to play first base for the New York Yankees. Girls were encouraged to play various activities, roller skate, and ride bikes, but the "sports" we were limited to were dance, gymnastics, swimming, figure skating, and tennis,[2] activities with strong feminine components. Even these had a very restricted competitive side. My love of baseball, basketball, and other "boy" sports became challenging as I grew older and was expected to transition out of being a tomboy into something that was more appropriately and obviously feminine. My resistance to that expectation was strong. Sports were a very important part of the person I saw myself to be. My lifelong study of sport and gender and the conflicts between them arose from my childhood experiences, which are some of the driving forces for this book.

A TYPICAL TOMBOY STORY

Sports have been an important part of my life for as long as I can remember. Even before I was old enough to understand what I was seeing, I watched the Gillette fights on an Admiral black and white television set with my parents on Friday nights. Baseball was my first love. I would play it, watch it on television, and listen to it on the radio. I would skip school on the opening day of the minor league season and somehow get into the bleachers to watch a game. I had a baseball card collection to be reckoned with (and that I could probably retire on if it was still intact!). In the summers, besides riding my bike everywhere, I would go swimming and, of course, play baseball. I would also play tennis and pretend I was competing at Wimbledon or go horseback riding and dream of making the Olympic equestrian team. During the school year, I would play on as many school teams as I could: soccer and field hockey in the fall, volleyball and basketball in the winter, and track and softball in the spring. Outside of school, I would go bowling, ice skating, tobogganing, and canoeing.

When I wasn't playing sports, I enjoyed exploring in the undeveloped areas near our suburban house. I would catch pollywogs (tadpoles) and turtles. I loved to climb trees and walk along fences. I had a very active imagination and I would create great scenarios of being an explorer, a cowboy, or an astronaut.

It's pretty obvious that all of this adds up to being a real tomboy.

This did not necessarily make my parents all that happy, but I also did many stereotypically girly things. I loved to read, play board games, and do puzzles. I took piano and acting lessons. Although I didn't like dolls, my stuffed animals were perfectly happy to come to occasional tea parties. I had some girlfriends who were generally my non-sporting companions, and we played hopscotch and had sleepovers.

When I was young, the tomboy side of me was generally acceptable and accepted, especially as it was tempered by my gender-appropriate activities, long braids, and, with much coercion, appropriately feminine dress. As I got older, however, my interest in playing sports and being outdoors never waned. Even though I no longer collected pollywogs or baseball cards and climbed trees far less frequently, the tomboy aspects of me, especially my interest in sports, somehow shifted from being okay and the occasional source of parental pride to being something problematic.

In high school, the girls who played on sports teams were never considered quite acceptable enough to be a part of the in-crowd. The most popular girls did have an avid interest in sports, but it was for the boys who played football, basketball, and baseball. The only exception to the popularity quotient of female athletes was for those girls who were cheerleaders, in addition to being on a sports team or two outside of football season. Strangely, the girls on the tennis, swimming, and synchronized swim teams were not marginalized from popular circles. But then, they were not considered to be real athletes (by the boys or girls, including the rest of the female athletes in the school). "Real" athletes were those on the team-sport teams.

As I got older, being acceptable/accepted as a tomboy transitioned into something far less desirable. This was not a particularly slow process, and the negativity and pressure to change escalated as I reached high school. Initially, the criticism seemed to be directed toward "boys won't like you if you're too good at sports" and then to something more sexually ominous. Even back in the 1960s when homosexuality was, in general, deeply closeted, I received a clear message from my mother, from many female teachers who were "concerned" about us tomboys, and from many female physical education teachers and coaches that sports and lesbianism were inherently connected. And it was clearly underlined that that was a bad thing. Personal conflict over my own sexuality was deeply embedded in my love of sports and the negative messages about lesbianism that came with being a female athlete. It was years before I was able to sort this out for myself. The overriding picture painted by these warnings was that gender roles were not to be violated.

Studying physical education as an undergraduate student provided me with many more examples that further solidified the female athlete = not feminine = lesbian connection. There was an obvious suspicion that many of the female physical education majors were probably lesbians, but an unspoken acceptance that none of the male majors were gay. Where I went to school, and in other colleges where friends had gone to study physical education, the female majors had strict controls for dress and deportment placed upon them. We had to "dress appropriately" in the physical education building, unless we were dressed specifically for physical activity courses or team practises. Generally, this meant no jeans or sloppy clothes that made us appear in any way masculine (in other words, not acceptably feminine), and in no way that could be defined as anything other than heterosexual. These cautions seemed to be directed more forcefully to those of us who were members of team-sport teams as opposed to members of the gymnastics, tennis, or swim teams. The femininity factor of both the sports and the athletes was one obvious difference among us, although sexuality concerns were strangely directed to only the team-sport athletes.

We had to wear skirts or dresses for varsity team away games. We had lectures on "PA" (professional attitude/appearance) that were lightly veiled cautions about the negative reactions to female physical educators who were likely to be seen as masculine and, possibly, lesbian. Our requisite presentation of self as feminine physical education majors and professionals seemed on a par in importance with our academic performance. Whether we were lesbian or straight, we were forced to see this inherent (and negative) link between the sportswoman and a masculine label that was never to be overlooked either personally or professionally. The messengers of these cautions were often female faculty members, who themselves demonstrated a personal discomfort with the standards of professional appearance that seemed at odds with who they were as obviously polygendered women, regardless of their sexual orientation.

For over 35 years, I have seen the reality of these cautions manifested in myriad ways. Once Title IX was passed and there was an explosion of girls' and women's sports participation, the problems related to beliefs about sports, masculinity, and lesbianism became even more solidified rather than diminished. High school and post-secondary girls' and women's teams that had, prior to Title IX, been coached almost exclusively by women began to be coached in exponentially growing numbers by men.[3] The stated reasons for this were that men were more experienced or better coaches, but, in many circumstances, male athletic directors did not want lesbians (real or imagined) in their programs. I personally sat on many hiring committees for the coaches of women's teams and heard innuendo and oblique questions that failed to disguise the attempts to learn the sexuality of various female applicants. These same inquiries were never made of male applicants for either the women's or men's teams.

In high school and post-secondary institutions in the Unites States and Canada, the message remained generally unvocalized and yet blatantly clear. No matter how many female teachers and coaches there were in the physical education departments, no matter how many girls and women participated in sports programs in or outside of school, no matter the growing level of excellence in women's sport performances at all levels (including the Olympics and World Championships), the message only seemed to get stronger: sports were for men, and the masculinity of sports themselves made women trespassers in this male domain.[4] This trespass went beyond girls and women who wanted to participate in gender-normative activities for boys and men. It extended to the vilification of many female athletes. If they wanted to play these sports then they must also be masculine. This masculine gender categorization was rarely stated outright, but was implied in many ways. And it was always cast in a negative light. The gender line between masculine and feminine was supposedly clear and never to be crossed.

In 1984, I developed and began teaching a course called Women and Sport (which later was changed to Women and Physical Activity to broaden its scope). The focus of the course has changed over the years, but embodiment, including primarily feminist-based theories of gender and sexuality, has always been a central focus of the critical analysis of women and sport used in the course.

In the 25 years that I have been teaching this course to undergraduate students in two Canadian universities, there have been two obvious changes in the attitudes of the students. The female students have gone from being quietly and politely supportive of the feminist theoretical foundations used to study and critique women's sporting involvement (so as not to be labelled as lesbians or to offend the male students in the class) to being assertive in their belief that they belong on the playing fields and will not be bullied by lesbian labelling or by their male student colleagues. The male students have gone from eye-rolling attention to the materials to a greater acceptance of women in sport in general, but also to a far more critical and negative perspective of how women should look and behave on and off the field.

The basic understanding of my students has generally been that female athletes must appear to be feminine in their appearance and behaviour, and heterosexual, to be accepted as athletes at all. Unfortunately, and in contrast to their defence of women as athletes, the female students themselves buy into the visual requirements of the feminine female athlete. Although extremely proud of their participation and success in sports such as rugby, basketball, soccer, and ice hockey, the women echo the concerns regarding their appearance and identity as feminine. They participate in intentional self-surveillance of their outward appearance both on and off the playing field in an attempt to justify their place in the world of sport even though they are women. Depending on the sport, the femininity requirements become more specific and strict—not simply in the eyes of my undergraduate students, but particularly in many forms of the media.

The favoured argument against women's sporting equality is one made repeatedly by men in my sport sociology classes: women will never make the NHL. The fact that none of the men who have stated this have ever been good enough for the NHL is never seen to make this a poor argument for denying girls and women equal citizenship in the sporting world. The argument is always the same—biologically, women are not strong enough to compete with or against men. The best athlete will always be a man. This argument is even used to protest against women playing "men's" sports only against other women. This isn't real sport, so don't even bother!

THE GENDERING OF SPORTS

The fact that sports themselves are as gendered as the people who play them is an interesting consideration. It establishes a double bind for women who choose to participate in "men's" sports and for men who want to participate in "girls'" sports. Notice the adult/child distinction that is often applied to the gendered nature of these activities. Sport is often seen as a more organized or sophisticated category of play. Play is something that children do. Adults are supposed to be grown up and to have left childish things behind them. That many men aspire to play manly sports or to watch other men *playing* manly sports as adults is often a point of critique from pundits and opponents of the monopolized capitalist industry of professional sport. Referring to the traditionally normative sports for boys and men as "men's" sports while infantilizing non-normative activities as "girls'" sports attempts to remove sport from the realm of play and to deterritorialize[5] it so that adult males, but not females, are justified in engaging in sport as a career or pastime.

The infantilization of the culturally normative activities of girls provides space—often positive space—for girls and women to participate in certain physical activities. This distinction between girls' and boys' sports feminizes the girls' activities. It sends notice to boys to steer clear and to accept ownership of "real" sports as exclusively their own. This distinction has a more confusing effect on girls. They learn that it is okay for them to participate in physical activity, but they do not learn, as equivocally as boys, the restrictions regarding their participation. This may cause girls problems as they get older and come face-to-face with the compulsory demands of femininity, which more definitively include no masculinity.

The position of male/masculine privilege in sport extends to all males, regardless of their athletic ability or even their level of interest (or lack thereof) in sport. This is why the "women will never play in the NHL" argument is called upon so frequently and so matter-of-factly. Even though the men making this comment will never play in the NHL (or the CFL/NFL, the parallel argument for football fans), the fact that the possibility existed for them in a far-off dream of their childhood makes it a possible reality for all boys and for no girls.[6] Even though Manon Rhéaume played in the NHL farm league and Hayley Wickenheiser played very successfully in a professional men's ice hockey league in Finland, these are dismissed as anomalies or publicity stunts. If women can be good enough athletes to really play men's sports, then the fairy-tale structure of men's exclusive sporting superiority will never end in a happily-ever-after conclusion. This also calls into question the gendered designation of certain activities and behaviours as feminine or masculine, belonging exclusively to females or to males. It supports the idea of a polygendered continuum for all of us.

There are a number of problems with many of the discourses that separate femininity and masculinity (or gender) and the apparent sex of the female or male person. One argument against women's participation in sport always reduces to the least common denominator—Olympic or professional team-sport levels. This argument goes as follows: no woman will ever be good enough (meaning strong, fast, powerful, or aggressive enough) to make a professional team (meaning male-stream professional teams such as in Major League Baseball, the NHL, NFL, or NBA), except maybe as a publicity stunt, such as Manon Rhéaume and the Tampa Bay Lightning organization. Therefore, why should they play—or even be given the opportunity to play—at all? As far as the Olympics go, the men will always be faster, stronger, and have better times ... therefore the women's events are not really important.

The exception might be women's beach volleyball, which has become one of the favourite spectator sports at the Olympic Summer Games and receives a large percentage of the overall broadcast time for women's sports. The fact that beach volleyball requires incredible strength, power, flexibility, stamina, and skill is often overlooked by spectators who like the beautiful bodies in the skimpiest of uniforms.

Another belief that women will never be good enough as athletes is underlined by the conclusion that any woman who might be good enough is likely to really be a man or wants to be a man. Beginning in the 1960s and ending with the games in Nagano, Japan, female athletes competing at the World or Olympic levels had to "prove" that they were female.[7] Female athletes who come out as lesbians or who are assumed to be lesbians (an interpretation of mannishness or masculinity) are denied or lose lucrative endorsement contracts. The demarcation between femininity and masculinity and what these designations really mean seems to be clearly understood by many in the world of sport, but not by the girls and women who want to play the games!

The argument that women will never be able to compete with or against men is frequently raised as a reason to keep women out of sport. In general, the activism and advocacy directed toward increasing girls' and women's involvement in sport has little or nothing to do with competing with or against men. This is a specious argument as it does not take into consideration the age or skill level of the participants or the specific sport or activity. It also ignores the very real argument that not all men are able to compete with or against all other men or even some women.

"Men's" sports often divide participants by height or weight in order to overcome the obvious differences in abilities that arise from physical parameters. Boxing, wrestling, and martial arts have weight classes so that a flyweight never has to get pummelled by a heavyweight. A 185-pound man might make a good quarterback on a football team, but he would not last more than one or two plays as an offensive lineman. These divisions provide space for all men who choose to participate to find an event or a position where their chance to succeed is enhanced. It is true that these distinctions have some differences in social value as, for example, the heavyweight boxing champion of the world has greater status than the flyweight. But the masculinity of the flyweight or of the quarterback is never called into question because of his size, weight, or skill relative to other men.

This flexibility is rarely extended to women and provides numerous opportunities to impugn the femininity and/or sexuality of many female athletes. Most men will never be good enough athletes to have a professional sports career or to compete at the World or Olympic levels. However, this is never presented as an argument to keep boys and men from participating in sports. The importance should be in the fun and social and health benefits that are achieved through involvement in physical activity, not the development of the masculinity of the participants.

Prior to puberty, there are few physical or physiological reasons to separate children in sporting activities. If children could participate together in physical activities, then the gendered nature of those activities would diminish or disappear. Parents would see that soccer and T-ball are simply sports that their daughters and sons like equally well and at which they may be equally skilled. There would be no need for boys' soccer and girls' soccer or separate T-ball leagues. As long as all the children could have good coaching in the skill development and the fitness characteristics needed to play successfully, the natural divisions between children would occur among skilled and less skilled youngsters, not necessarily between girls and boys.

One "problem" that might arise if all prepubescent children participated together in sport is that many of the girls would be better than many of the boys. At certain stages of anatomical and physiological development girls tend to be taller, heavier, and more developmentally advanced than boys. In general, girls also have greater flexibility and balance. As long as they are given equal coaching and playing opportunities, these factors would advantage girls over boys in many games and sports. The socially constructed notion of the natural superiority of boys over girls in sport would disappear. Children would develop very different ideas about what it means to be a girl and what it means to be a boy relative to sports participation, although this might not sit well with all parents. This is not to suggest that playing sports together would eliminate gender or gender bias in our culture. There are far too many other influences that guarantee their existence and influence.

One of the important aspects of childhood participation in sports, regardless of whether in a single-sex or mixed organizational structure, is its effect on the lifelong involvement in physical activity that is needed for health and well-being. Participation in physical activity needs to last throughout a person's life, far beyond the normative span of involvement in competitive sports and the gendered separation of individuals on the playing fields of schools and clubs. The importance of the elimination of polarized gendered thinking in this aspect of involvement in sports and physical activities cannot be underestimated for the health of all individuals.

Following puberty, the interests and skill levels of athletes should be the primary separator of participants. Although, in many cases, males would be advantaged over females, this has a lot to do with cultural valuing of specific sports that favour masculine-defined traits. If we valued different activities more highly, or devalued the socially constructed boundaries of masculine and feminine in favour of celebrating the skills and abilities of people regardless of sex, this argument would be seen as a sham as well.

CHALLENGING THE SPORTING STATUS QUO

One of the oldest arguments that maintains the segregated and gendered nature of sports states that sports will make women more masculine and consequently unattractive to men. Dudley Sargent, a leader in physical education from Harvard University in the early 20th century, wrote that success in sports could be achieved only by taking on masculine characteristics (Cahn, 1994). This was a direct critique of women's participation in sports that were defined as masculine. This is the primary argument that I will challenge in this book. I believe that femininity and masculinity are false as exclusive or essential categories, and are certainly not dichotomous indicators of the natural state of females and males.

Through the writing of this book, I hope to accomplish an analysis of gender and how it impacts on girls' and women's sporting choices and opportunities. The associations of femininity, masculinity, and sexuality to sport are complex and impact females and males very differently within this most dominant of social and socializing institutions. I trust that this analysis will have an influence on how gender is perceived and applied in a larger scope in our culture, but tackling sport is a large enough piece of cultural analysis for one text!

The hybrid feminist–queer–culturally theoretical picture I will present of the dilemmas associated with the embodiment of females, femininity, sexuality, physicality, and sport needs to be painted with brushes from numerous other disciplines. The integration of arguments presented from various disciplines means that the arguments are not developed as specifically as they might be within the individual disciplines of history, psychology, sociology, cultural studies, and so on, and thus might not satisfy experts from within those fields. However, the strength of this book lies in its ability to highlight, present, and link important moments and arguments from across these disciplines. This book provides a compelling argument for the current cultural advantages and barriers that impact girls and women in their quest for fun, health, excellence, and personal fulfillment through sport and physical activity.

What I will propose here and attempt to defend sufficiently enough to elicit serious thought, if not total and outright acceptance, is the notion of the polygendered state of all humans; that we possess and exhibit traits that have been linked exclusively with either femininity or masculinity, but which have changed and transitioned over time. I will use female athletes as the clearest and most positive model for such an embodied and polygendered state of being.

The roadblocks that keep many girls and women who are involved in sport and physical activity from striving for or reaching their desired level of excellence often come from hegemonic and compulsory femininity demands. The constructed and limiting effects of gender could be easily demolished by the acceptance of a polygendered norm of existence. Ultimately, I would prefer to see the elimination of gender as a classification of people that has outlived its perceived necessity. As this is unlikely to happen in the foreseeable future, a more precise understanding of gender and its conflation with sex as dangerously and damagingly applied to limit the potential of all people in myriad ways must be put forward. I hope to present a position of the human condition in which all individuals can say "I am proud to be polygendered!"

Chapter 1

GENDER: NATURE OR NURTURE/FACT OR FICTION

> Throughout the history of Western culture, three beliefs about women and men have prevailed: that they have fundamentally different psychological and sexual natures; that men are inherently the dominant or superior sex; and that both male–female difference and male dominance are natural. Until the mid-19th century, this naturalness was typically conceived in religious terms, as a part of God's grand creation. Since then, it has typically been conceived in scientific terms, as part of biology's—or evolution's—grand creation. (Bem, 1993, p. 1)

Most people would say they have a fairly good understanding of the notion of gender. It is likely, though, that if you were to do a casual investigation of your family and friends, then you would find a lot of variation in the interpretation of gender. Some people would identify gender as being the same as a person's sex—so either female or male.[1] Others would define gender as the femininity or masculinity of a person. Still others would interpret gender as both the sex of the person and the appropriate feminine/masculine designation that is naturally linked to it.

My point is that gender is not a clear-cut category of being and, as such, it is a problematic aspect of the lives of most people as they negotiate their life path from childhood onward. For over a hundred years, even scholars and researchers from fields as far-reaching as anthropology, psychology, history, biology, and sociology have all speculated upon and written about women and femininity. In their work, all have "claimed the mantle of science and objectivity but their contradictory theories on the feminine character were inextricably bound to their particular academic disciplines, historical contexts, and personal perspectives.... Theories on the sources of femininity and what feminine attitudes should be varied greatly" (Tarrant, 2006, p. 134). Gender is not a simple concept to understand or explain, yet its control over aspects of our lives is powerful.

As very young children, we take our bodies and our identities pretty much for granted, but still quite seriously. We are not yet encumbered by the socially constructed conception of girls and boys that will mould us into the contemporary designs required of feminine women and masculine men, although it will happen very soon! These constructions "serve not only to remind us how most of us become alienated from our bodies in adult life; they also point out how differently the childhoods of girls and boys come to be structured by discourses of femininity and masculinity" (Messner, 1994, p. 353). The social designations of feminine and masculine and their seemingly natural attachments to female and male bodies cause girls and boys to inhabit their bodies differently even when engaged in the same activities. Thus, the activity of play becomes as gendered as the bodies that are participating in the games.

How people learn, display, negotiate, perform, change, and resist gender differ in the lives of different people and between different groups of people. I am particularly interested in how contemporary notions of gender impact on girls and women who are athletes, aspire to be athletes, or simply want to engage in physical activities for enjoyment and life-long health. The complexities of the intersections of gender performance, femininity, and sexuality are in many ways unique to the female athlete. "Western culture emphasizes a feminine ideal body and demeanor that contrasts with an athletic body and demeanor" (Krane et al., 2004, p. 315). To understand this complexity, an investigation of gender (in my interpretation, this is the same thing as femininity and masculinity), sexuality, and sport itself is needed. How these social constructs interact, are interpreted, and are applied to the female athlete is complex. I feel that it is very important to unravel these complexities in the hope of providing girls and women with all of the opportunities they want and need to participate in sports and physical activities, and that they deserve for a healthy and active life.

At its most simple, this book is an investigation and critique of contemporary understandings of gender—the factors that determine those qualities that are known to identify something called the femininity or masculinity of persons. At its more challenging, this work is the presentation of an argument that might be compelling enough to encourage readers to shift their perspectives on gender to see women and men in a way that not only recognizes but also celebrates the breadth of human potential, rather than seeing a narrow requirement of how we are expected to look and behave in the socio-cultural world in which we live. I hope to compel readers to understand and accept the lived life as polygendered. This blend of feminine and masculine is a fairer and more realistic version of all people than a categorization that allows each of us only half of the potential that is available for personal expression.

My primary interest is in looking at the representations of female athletes through the lenses of femininity and sexuality, which are the direct applications of our knowledge and understandings of gender. Myriad femininities are displayed by women worldwide. In North American culture, there is a more dominant form of femininity that is seen through the media, fashion, and other consumer-targeted campaigns directed at girls and women. This pervasive and exclusive display is presented as the only acceptable or desirable feminine presentation. This popular culture femininity becomes hegemonic—the only acceptable way for women to present themselves. It privileges women who are able to conform to it. But what about the girls and women who do not, cannot, or choose not to present themselves in this way?

"Different bodies are afforded differential values in comparison to the ideal feminine body; for example, Black, queer, and disabled coding of bodies are considered inferior to this heterosexual, White ideal" (Krane et al., 2004, p. 316). The reason I have chosen to look at female athletes is because they are, in many ways, viewed and evaluated (often judged) through the same cultural filters as all other women, including the biases just indicated. As athletes, however, they represent females who prize and utilize characteristics that are often deemed to be masculine and, therefore, the presumed domain of men.

One outcome of this designation of sport = masculine is its impact on the female individual who has learned the social importance of accepting herself and demonstrating herself to be a feminine person. This narrow restriction on the meaning of feminine can have a negative impact on her understanding of herself as a gendered individual, but one who wants to engage in activities that she believes she will enjoy even if they are understood to be identified as masculine. This has an enduring impact on the choices of girls and women relative to choosing to rebel against traditional femininity by engaging in particular sports. Most individuals, especially young girls, will not consciously analyze who they are as females or their femininity compliance. However, the outcome of their choice to be an athlete is likely to become obvious to them the longer they remain in the realm of sport.

THE PECULIAR PROBLEM OF WOMEN AND MOVEMENT

Many philosophers, sociologists, and feminist scholars have investigated how contemporary understandings of femininity and masculinity, within their historical time frames, have privileged and/or constrained women and men of various races, ethnicities, socio-economic statuses, and sexualities. Many of these analyses have included how an understanding of the uses and comportment of the body has been an integral part of women's restricted and oppressed rank within various communities.

Maurice Merleau-Ponty (1962) and Simone de Beauvoir (1952) wrote about embodied experiences and how our sense of self is intricately tied to our mastery of physical movements. Young (1980) used perceptions of embodiment to analyze sports and the involvement in sports, or lack thereof, of girls. She supported the concept that feminine embodiment requires a limited use of space and effort in the execution of movements, which would make the successful participation in sporting activities nearly impossible for girls. She referred to this learned behaviour as "ambiguous transcendence," "inhibited intentionality," and "discontinuous unity."

These terms indicate that girls learn to consciously restrict the motion of their bodies and the space they take up in movement. It involves a considered thought process that limits anatomical movements and subsequently causes uncoordinated actions. The expression "throwing like a girl" arises from such commonality in the discontinuous unity of bodily movements and the restricted spatial action of overhand throwing by girls, so as to appear to be a natural condition of the female body. The awkward movements of females reproduce a visual display of feminine use of ambient space and represent the "I cannot" sense of self defined by Merleau-Ponty (1962).

In his work, Merleau-Ponty (1962) posited "I," "I can," and "I cannot" as expressions of bodily intention and mastery. The concept of "I," relative to movement, supports a sense of self through which bodily expression is accepted as appropriate. In general, boys learn this sense of "I" and demonstrate "I can" intentionality in their movements. Although many boys execute a throwing pattern, for example, that exactly parallels "throwing like a girl," the expectation of the "I can" by both the boy thrower and those observing his actions renders the "feminine" nature of his movements invisible.

Many girls and women often move with "I cannot" intentionality to their actions, even after they have had instruction in the proper method of skill execution. They may believe that it is not possible to do appropriate sporting actions because they have been told that girls cannot do these things, or because they have observed so many girls and women move in uncoordinated and spatially restricted ways. In the "I cannot" movement patterns of females (holding the arms and legs close to the midline of the body, taking up less space, and demonstrating hesitancy in dynamic movements), which are in definite contrast to the "I can" intentions of boys' movements (free flowing and expansive), there is a culturally ingrained belief that feminine and masculine movement forms are as natural to girls' and boys' bodies as other aspects of personality and behaviour that are understood to be feminine and masculine.

Because these movement differences are traditionally interpreted as natural, the encouragement and teaching that boys receive relative to sporting movements is much greater than that for girls. Even when girls are encouraged and become successful in a sporting activity, they continue to receive mixed messages regarding how they need to look and what movements are appropriate for them (Messner, 1994). When girls are appropriately skilled in sporting movements, the feedback to their actions often takes the form of "you throw/run/play like a boy!" This backhanded compliment functions to keep the intentionality and success of sporting movements out of the realm of the feminine, even when performed by females.

Positioning natural and learned human movements within the dichotomous constructs of femininity and masculinity functions to extend the anticipated personality and behaviour displays, which are believed to be gender related and gender appropriate, to those created activities, such as sports, that further privilege males/masculinity over females/femininity. Sports and physical activity become labelled as masculine, which problematizes not only the participation of girls and women in these pursuits, but also restricts quality human movement acquisition and execution to masculine individuals.

This is explained more generally by de Beauvoir through a more global conception of the condition of female existence defined by a "feminine essence" (de Beauvoir, 1952). According to de Beauvoir, cultural, historical, social, and economic constraints situate and limit human existence. "We reduce women's condition simply to unintelligibility if we 'explain' it by appeal to some natural and ahistorical feminine essence. In denying such a feminine essence, however, we should not fall into that 'normalism' which denies the real differences in the behavior and experiences of men and women" (de Beauvoir, 1974, p. 275–276; as summarized by Young, 1980, p. 138–139). Accepting (and celebrating) female and male differences does not assume an inherent feminine essence. We must examine the socio-cultural biases that exist in patriarchal, white, Western culture that inform our belief systems about females and femininity as a constructed condition of difference from males and masculinity.

The situation in which female athletes find themselves is one that muddies the gender pool because they are "supposed" to be feminine individuals, but are displaying masculine movements and behaviours, often within supposedly masculine endeavours.[2] Because of this, female athletes can be simultaneously celebrated for their accomplishments and vilified for achieving "masculine" success.

Female athletes provide us with an everyday challenge to traditional beliefs about sex roles and the binary construction of gender. Their lives are often lived in the public arena in ways that most other women's lives are not. They can be media stars, but in a different way from rock stars or movie celebrities. They can be role models, but again different from politicians or other newsmakers. Female athletes force us to see gendered lives in ways that challenge those that are traditionally accepted as natural or inviolate.

Female high-performance athletes, Olympians, and professional athletes seem to occupy a significantly different cultural space to the majority of women because they are so infrequently seen in the media venues that highlight athletes. This limited exposure places female athletes in a different category to athletes in general (assumed to be male) and even from other women, who are generally less likely to be celebrated for their physical activity achievements. This sets up "us/them" relationships not only between female athletes and male athletes, but also between female athletes and a majority of other women.

As with other categories that separate particular individuals from the majority, critical binary extremes are applied to highlight these differences:

"good/bad, civilized/primitive, ugly/excessively attractive, repelling-because-different/compelling-because-strange-and-exotic. And they are often required to be *both things at the same time*" (Hall, 1997, p. 229)! Hopefully, female athletes will force us to see that femininity and masculinity are not the rigid and sex-linked characteristics that many have long held them to be, and that muddying the gender pool may be a very good thing indeed for both women and men in and outside of sport.

Femininity and masculinity represent collections of traits, behaviours, interests, and appearance factors that are understood to belong to females and males, respectively. How women and men acquire these collective differences is not clear. Current arguments in the social and natural sciences vacillate between biologically essentialist positions, learned social positions, and combinations of all possible influences.[3] What is problematic, however, regardless of the ontological assumptions one supports, is that girls/women and boys/men engage in many of the same activities, have the same interests and behaviours, and share multiple physical and behavioural traits that obviously do not support a female/feminine, male/masculine exclusivity, either biologically or culturally.

The overlap in human sex-based similarities is often ignored as many biological and sociological norms would, of course, be demonstrated in all humans experiencing the same socializing influences. The overlaps do become problematic when privileged conditions of the masculine (within patriarchal structures) are usurped by females who then are seen to be non-normal, if not abnormal, or not real women.

SEX, GENDER, AND SEXUALITY

As this chapter's opening quote from Bem (1993) suggests, throughout Western civilization there have been certain assumptions about women and men, the sexual division of labour, and the apparent inborn sex roles of human beings. These beliefs paint the picture we have of two distinct, biologically occurring sexes and genders. The truth about the origins of gender is not as clear-cut as that of sex, which is also not as completely straightforward as most of us have been taught. Even now, in the 21st century, there is considerable debate about the biological and cultural origins of gender as a defining marker in our lives. Research from sociology, cultural studies, queer theory and feminist perspectives, psychology, biology, and medicine has put forth varying and often contradictory information regarding the origins and compositions of sex and gender (Fausto-Sterling, 2000).

It will be beneficial to clarify the meanings of sex, gender, and sexuality that will be used in this book. Sex, gender, and sexuality are separate and distinct aspects of human beings. Over many decades, sex and gender have become more and more conflated to the point that most people understand these terms as different words that mean the same thing, or as having a cause and effect relationship. However, one's sex does not naturally determine one's gender, and one's gender may not have any indicators of one's sex or sexual orientation.

The following definitions and explanations of sex, gender, and sexuality inform my understandings, analyses, and applications of these concepts to my arguments for accepting a polygendered state of being.

A BRIEF UNDERSTANDING OF THE MEANINGS OF SEX

Sex refers to the biological components that make up human beings. In general, this refers to being female or to being male. Most people might remember their grade school science, which taught us that females have two X chromosomes and males have one X and one Y chromosome. The belief that there are only two sexes and that they are based on these chromosomal distinctions is widespread, but biologically incorrect. In reality, sex can be defined in many ways, including "genetic sex; chromosomal sex; gonadal sex; internal phenotype sex; external phenotype sex; sex of rearing; and finally the sexed identity of child and sexed identity of adult" (Hester, 2004, p. 218).

Individuals can therefore be classified into many more than two distinct sex categories. Most people from these "alternative" categories do not necessarily look different from those with an XX or XY chromosomal make-up. The frequency of intersex individuals is more common than a number of abnormalities with which we might be more familiar.

"Intersex" refers to individuals who are born with ambiguous genitalia or both female and male genitalia. Intersex births can be as frequent as 1.7 per 100 births, which is more common than "cystic fibrosis (one in 2,500 'Caucasian' births), Down's syndrome (one in 800–1000) or Albino births (one in 17,000)" (Hester, 2004, p. 217). The existence of intersex individuals challenges our belief in only two sexes. The frequency of intersex births challenges the notion that these differences are, by definition, abnormal. The frequencies indicated above mean that tens of thousands of children are born every year who do not fit the normative categorizations of XX female or XY male. This common deviation from the norm might cause us to question the naturalness of other factors that are based on this binary distinction; most specifically for the purpose of this book, gender.

Differences in biological sex markers are often not determined until children reach puberty and begin to develop secondary sex characteristics that are generally assigned to the "other" sex, or they do not develop other reproductive signifiers such as menstruation. Often individuals are unaware of their non-XX or non-XY chromosomal composition or abnormalities related to XX or XY designations until they seek medical attention, generally for fertility-related assessments.

Female athletes have actually provided us with some interesting data in this area. From the mid-1960s until the 1998 Olympic Winter Games in Nagano, Japan, all female competitors in the Olympics and at many World Championships were tested to determine whether they were actually female [4] (some sports continue to force female competitors to undergo testing). The International Olympic Committee (IOC) Medical Commission began this process by calling the procedure "sex testing." It was later changed to "femininity testing," and in its most recent incarnation was called "gender verification."[5] The inability to settle on what the Medical Commission was actually testing (sex? femininity? gender?) or could possibly hope to "test" in a scientific way shows some of the problems related to this endeavour.

The testing, which was originally introduced to supposedly discover males masquerading as females, revealed that not all female competitors were XX; some were actually XY females or had other genetic differences. These athletes were not attempting to deceive their sports organizations or gain any advantage over the other competitors. They grew up believing that they were female. Some female athletes who "failed" the sex testing chose not to compete because their genetic abnormalities would be publicly revealed and cause them to be disqualified. Other women were forced to withdraw by their countries or sport federations to supposedly avoid embarrassment (Carlson, 1991). This topic will be discussed further in Chapter 3, as the reasons for the testing being used in the first place were due to issues surrounding the "femininity" of certain female athletes.

Some infants are born with normative XX or XY chromosomal designations, but with "abnormal" or indeterminate genitalia. In these cases, a decision is often made (generally by medical personnel guiding the parents) to alter the genitalia. Surgery is performed to "normalize" the genitals, thus determining a gender, but not a sex, of the infant. Surgical reconstruction of a vagina or a penis, which will not be visible to the vast majority of individuals who come into contact with the person, allows the parents to state that the child is a girl or a boy, regardless of the chromosomal make-up of the infant. This is done so that people will know how to treat the baby and react to it as it grows up according to some social construct of how we are to properly engage with girls and boys.

I am not an expert in this aspect of biological science and I would encourage the reader to study some of the vast literature that exists in this domain.[6] The reason I have included this simplistic overview of sex and sexual differences is to illustrate that if the sex of individuals cannot be easily categorized into two distinct and universal classifications, then, very likely, neither can the assignment of social behaviours, roles, appearances, interests, and other aspects that make up what we have come to call gender.

A BRIEF UNDERSTANDING OF THE MEANINGS OF GENDER

Gender refers to a collection of characteristics including personality traits, interests, behaviours, and appearance factors that culturally and socially define a person as feminine or masculine. There is an assumption that female persons are or must be feminine and that male persons are or must be masculine. This would imply that the biological make-up of people determines gendered characteristics such as interests and abilities, and that these characteristics are sex-linked. There is some support for the idea that certain feminine- and masculine-defined qualities are more likely to appear in females or in males (Butler, 2004). However, the research and literature in this area are inconclusive and often relate to specific reproductive capacities. In addition, a binary gender divide does not explain many of the transgender realities that are increasingly being seen in North American culture.

Many of the factors that comprise or define femininity and masculinity change from culture to culture and from generation to generation. Factors that change so rapidly are unlikely to be biologically or physiologically based. There is a strong argument for gender being primarily a culturally created and administered definition for the behaviours and interests of females and males. This does not eliminate the possibility that certain gendered behaviours are biologically based, but then it might be more correct to label these as biological or sex-based, rather than as gendered.

During the latter part of the 20th century, general knowledge about sex and gender conflated these two areas of embodiment into a single, indivisible unit of femaleness or maleness. There is such a strong cultural belief about the relationship between gender and sex that Peper (1994) coined the word "gendex" to verbally illustrate this understanding of the integration of gender and sex.

Caudwell (2006) wrote, "A fixed gender/sexual identity is problematic" (p. 146). A fixed identity reduces the choices of all individuals to understand themselves in a variety of ways. Feminist, queer, postmodern, and cultural theorists, sociologists dealing with the gender-bending cultural influences of the rock music industry and the growing lesbian, gay, queer, transgendered movements, and some medical and psychology researchers concerned with identity or with intersex individuals and the "problems" associated with such medical and social uncertainties as not having a clearly female or male body, work to keep the realms of sex and gender separate.

The power of the media and various backlash movements (particularly to feminism and lesbian and gay rights movements) have provided compelling information about or resistance to various cultural changes, and have helped to keep the terms "sex" and "gender" interchangeable and biologically essentialist or natural. In turn, this has helped to keep socially embedded notions of femaleness and femininity and maleness and masculinity intrinsically linked in the minds of most North Americans.

In the 21st century, there is still resistance to recognizing the separate domains of sex and gender. It is a simple and unifying organizing principle for ideas about family, education, occupation, sex roles, sexuality, and other social constructs to be based on a belief system that supports femininity and masculinity as consequences of being female or male.

Many contemporary realities confound this simplistic social organization. In *The Gendered Atom: Reflections on the Sexual Psychology of Science*, Roszak critiques science as an often non-objective and likely unintentionally biased endeavour. He writes, "There is a collective unconscious made up of cultural elements that are absorbed into the personality in the cradle, and not before" (Roszak, 1999, p. 8).[7] Ignoring this position has caused many scientists to hold dear to the notion of the inherent masculinity of men. Roszak further defers to Maslow's contention that he "began to see connection between the psychology of objectivity and the character traits of stereotypic masculinity. Like other men, male scientists could also be burdened by 'the inflexible, neurotic need to be tough, powerful, fearless, strong, severe'" (Roszak, 1999, p. 12). If leaders in science and education feel threatened by any sense (misconceived or misinterpreted) of femininity in themselves, it is possible that conscious or unconscious rejection of the value of anything deemed feminine might negatively impact the scientific questions that they formulate or their analyses of collected data.

Women have successfully moved into almost every aspect of the public realm. Occupations that have traditionally been seen to be masculine endeavours and that, at times, were legally restricted to men are now open to women. Many men are taking on more active parenting and domestic roles, which have traditionally been seen as the exclusive domain of women. Some young people are identifying themselves as transgendered, and the recently de rigueur (but now passé) identification of heterosexual men who show a greater appreciation for stylish dress and fashionable living (traditionally feminine attributes) as "metrosexuals" further demonstrates the fluidity of gender constructs. This plasticity removes gender from a cause and effect relationship with sex.

The conflation of gender and sex continues to be a barrier to the study of femininity and masculinity and the application of this concept to various human activities, including sport and physical activity. Peper's (1994) term "gendex" linguistically illustrates the interconnectedness of sex and gender role construction that is primarily accepted in contemporary North American culture. Putting the gender aspect first in this term reminds us that roles are based more on socialized gender *constructs* than on biological *determinants* (Peper, 1994).

A BRIEF UNDERSTANDING OF (SOME) MEANINGS OF SEXUALITY[8]

Sexuality refers to the emotional and physical attraction that an individual has for others. Similar to the rigid binaries of sex (female or male) and gender (femininity or masculinity), sexuality is often polarized into only two possible categories: heterosexual or homosexual—although these terms have only entered the scientific language and social vocabulary in the last 150 years (Fausto-Sterling, 2000).

Heterosexuality, the sexual attraction of females for males and vice versa, and its linked position to reproduction, is considered by many to be the only "normal" or proper expression of sexuality, as long as the sexual contact is with an appropriate person of the "opposite" sex. An analysis of sexual practices over time and between cultures, races, classes, and spiritual beliefs will reveal that sexuality lies along a continuum and that acceptable and desirable practices and partnerships have moved along this range of possibilities throughout Western civilization (Fausto-Sterling, 2000).

Sexuality is more complex to define than either sex or gender. Strong social and religious traditions inform our ideas about what is normal, natural, and deviant sexual practice. I will include a discussion of sexuality in later chapters only insofar as notions of the femininity and masculinity of female athletes impact on assumptions about who they are as sexual beings.

A FOCUS ON GENDER

In this work, I focus more on gender than on either sex or sexuality. My belief that gender is socially constructed means that it can be changed relative to understanding and practice. As defining or changing one's sex is beyond the scope of this book, I will not be examining biological sex except as the sex of female athletes has been challenged by sex testing. However, much of my analysis is grounded in the literature that I have studied on intersex conditions and the impact that these biological differences have on individuals' lives. This leads me to further question the construct of gender as a dualistic or essential outcome of biology.

One implication of the existence of intersexed individuals is that they "expose the limits of the gender dichotomy" (Hester, 2004, p. 217). I do not believe that gender is the expressive state of one's sex[9] any more than I believe that sex is the identifiable body underlying the gender. The presence of intersex individuals and the fluidity of gendered norms strongly support the notion that the requisite dualism of these human characteristics is not as concrete as some might have us believe. It further supports a notion that individuals can possess characteristics that are considered to be feminine or masculine, as neither of these states is based on a concrete structure that defines a biological entity.

Intersex individuals also challenge the very idea of the necessity of gender at all, and some contemporary researchers do support a post-gender body as the future (Butler, 2004). I would like to support a position where gender and the restrictions it places on human experience (including sexuality), potential, and quality of life are eliminated. However, this does not seem to be a likely possibility in the short term. So instead, I propose the idea of individuals being polygendered: having the culturally defined characteristics of both femininity and masculinity that provide people with the ability to express whoever they are in a manner that is most comfortable and appropriate to them. The rest of this chapter will present the hows and whys of the problems of gender and the particular difficulties for those of us who have been socially assigned to the role of "feminine."

A CLOSER LOOK AT GENDER

In her book *The Lenses of Gender*, Bem (1993) presents a strong argument for the concept of gender directly contributing to the inequality that exists today between women and men. She describes three underlying principles ("lenses") that support inequality based on an understanding of gender that is considered natural and essential to the human condition. The "lenses" through which North American culture traditionally views gender are androcentrism, gender polarization, and biological essentialism (Bem, 1993, p. 2).

In this next section, I provide a brief description of these three lenses. Later chapters deal more specifically with how these lenses help to define constructions and restrictions of compulsory heterosexual femininity to which all women are expected to conform, but to which female athletes have a particular relationship. The details raised in this introductory material will be used to examine sport and the participation of women in what is traditionally considered a masculine endeavour. Viewing sport through these lenses and examining the impact of the structures of and opportunities in sport for women is an important foundation for the acceptance of a polygendered existence.

Androcentrism

Androcentrism (from the Greek *andro* meaning male and *centric* referring to the centre or the norm) defines male experiences as the norm of all human experience. It is considered neutral and defining of the human condition. Under the concept of androcentrism the male is defined as human

26

and the female as "other" (de Beauvoir, 1952). Everyday use of language supports this position, as "he" is often used as the neutral term for both males and females whereas "she" only ever refers to the female.

The placement of males and maleness at the centre of all human activity places what is female and everything related to femaleness, including femininity, in a position of inferiority and undesirability. What is therefore seen as central to the human experience can also be defined as being not female or feminine. Human characteristics have been defined as female/feminine or male/masculine based on sex roles and sexual divisions of labour that have a foundation in the biological reproductive contributions of females and males. The structure of social institutions was originally based (and often continues to function) on an artificial and androcentric belief system that came to increasingly influence all aspects of cultural tradition and organization.

Androcentrism is the underlying structure that supports the political notion of *patriarchy*, which the feminist movements of the 19th and 20th centuries identified as the structure that keeps women in an inferior position to men. "Patriarchy is the power of the fathers: a familial–social, ideological, political system in which men—by force, direct pressure, or through ritual, tradition, law and language, customs, etiquette, education, and the division of labor determine what part women shall or shall not play, and in which the female is everywhere subsumed under the male" (Rich, 1976, p. 40). The concept of patriarchy does not mean that all males are superior to all females. Androcentrism, however, functions to privilege male desire and masculinity over femininity.

A patriarchal social organization not only defines who is superior and can hold positions of power, but also how people go about attaining and maintaining such privilege. The androcentric social institutions and cultural forms upon which North American forms of democracy and human rights are based are so entrenched in our collective understanding of "society" that they seem completely natural, or even essential to human existence, and are accepted as such. Over the past century, sport, as a cultural form, has become one of the social institutions that is organized and structured on hegemonic patriarchal influences.

Patriarchy does not mean that all men have power or privilege in society. Issues of race, class, ethnicity, and religion were no more a part of the mindset of the male Greek citizens who established our ideas of democracy (except as conscious omission) than was the place of women. Citizens could only be Greek men who had status or power within their communities. Men who were not of the proper race and class were often slaves. They were treated as property and had no greater status than women.

In North America today, patriarchy is still mostly represented by white men of a certain class, status, and education. Androcentrism, however, instills in all males a sense of privilege that is reproduced in areas such as politics, education, media, and the paid labour force that teaches males to feel a privilege that they have not earned and may never acquire, and sense of superiority over women that they have not earned and may never obtain in any sense. Sport also fits into this privileged state.

This sense of androcentrism, expressed as male entitlement, underlies the idea that certain sports are not appropriate for women. Even though many males have less physical capacity to participate in certain sports than many women, and even though those men may have no personal interest in participating in those particular sports, there is still the accepted belief that certain activities are the domain of all men and no women. That women might want to participate in such masculine activities is seen, at the least, as a trespass into a male domain. At its most problematic, these women may be seen as really wanting to be men. The notion of the mannish female athlete, which came to be understood to mean a lesbian in the later years of the 20th century, is one strategy that has been used to question the femininity of female athletes and to keep them out of sports that are culturally normative for males.[10]

The ancient Greeks, who we celebrate as the "fathers" of democracy, were hardly democratic in their ideas or practices when these related to women or others to whom they felt superior. It is interesting that from the Greek language we have the word "misogyny," which translates into hatred of women (*misein* = hate; *misos* = hatred; and *gune* = woman). There is no word describing hatred of men, a concept that was probably unimaginable to these Greeks! The practice of humiliating male athletes by referring to them with epithets that imply femaleness or femininity is one means by which misogyny is maintained in the cultures of some sports. Vilifying women in this way further establishes that females, or anything recognized as feminine, have no place in sport (Daniels, 2005a).

Gender Polarization

Gender polarization can be defined as the organizing principle upon which many cultures and their social institutions have been created and function relative to the natural, seemingly natural, or assigned roles of females and males. For the majority of Western civilizations, these separate realms have been based on biology because of the differing roles and responsibilities of reproduction and child rearing. Many aspects of gender polarization have been codified in law and have, until the recent past, restricted women from voting or holding public office, attending schools, owning property, engaging in certain professions, serving in the military, or playing certain sports. Gender polarization places sex (and the assumed sex of the individual) at the centre of every aspect of human experience.

According to Bem, gender polarization operates in two ways. "First, it defines mutually exclusive scripts for being male and female. Second, it defines any person or behavior that deviates from these scripts as problematic—as unnatural or immoral from a religious perspective or as biologically anomalous or psychologically pathological from a scientific perspective" (Bem, 1993, p. 82). The cumulative effect of these two processes creates a seemingly natural connection among the supposed sex of one's body, the gendered personality, and the requisite sexuality of the person.

Where androcentrism places what is male at the centre of what is "normal" and important in being human, gender polarization constructs a barrier that ensures that women will never enter into this realm without the consequence of being seen to be abnormal in some way. Even activities and endeavours that have been created by human beings, and which in and of themselves have no natural origin, often have a male/masculine or female/feminine designation placed upon them. Learning to read and write, fighting for one's country, having the right to vote, and most sports participation have been entrenched in the male/masculine domain.

Box 1.1

One of the strongest examples of gender polarization in sport is the construction of the Olympic Games. The first games of the modern Olympic era were held in Athens in 1896. There were no events for women and no female competitors. The founder of the Games, Baron Pierre de Coubertin, was intensely opposed to women's involvement in sport.

Even though the complete exclusion of women as athletes from "his" games happened only in 1896, the effect of his misogynistic beliefs impact the Olympic Games to this day. At the second modern Olympic Games in 1900, women were eligible to compete in golf and tennis. These were exclusively country club activities at this time, in which only upper-class white women were able to participate. Many women, however, were intensely interested in a larger program of sports and events at the Olympics, including track and field. All attempts to have women's athletics included in the Games were vehemently resisted by de Coubertin. However, women had such a strong desire to compete that in 1921 Alice Milliat, a French sportswoman, established the Fédération Sportive Féminine Internationale and created the Women's Olympics (Leigh, 1977; Kidd, 1994).

The Women's Olympics were held every four years from 1922 through to 1934. These Games, which included track and field events for women, so enraged de Coubertin, the IOC, and the International Amateur Athletic Federation (IAAF) that they struck a deal with Milliat. If she would change the name of her Games to the Women's World Games, the IOC would institute a 10-event track and field program for women in the 1928 Olympic Games in Amsterdam. Milliat agreed. However, the IOC went back on its word and offered only five events for women. This segregation of women from a fair program of events caused some of the best female track athletes to boycott the Amsterdam Olympics.

In order to keep Milliat from expanding the track and field program in her Women's World Games, the IAAF took over as the organizing body for track and field events worldwide and subsequently undermined the Women's World Games altogether. The number of events for women in track and field gradually increased over the first century of the modern Olympic Games, although it took until 1960 for the 800-metre race to be reinstated (it was dropped after the 1928 Games) and until 1984 for the women's marathon to be added to the program. The impact of de Coubertin is still felt today, as women work to get other events and sports added to the Olympic program.

For generations women were publicly prohibited from engaging in male-designated activities, although there is strong evidence to show that, out of the public eye, or more openly for females of "lesser" race or class, girls and women engaged in many culturally normative-defined masculine activities. To this day we still acknowledge these male realms by specifically indicating that women have been "allowed" to enter them through language that continues to designate women as *other* in these male activities. Police*woman* and *female* athlete are two examples of necessary authorizations that dictate that police officers and athletes are "naturally" men.

Challenges to the structural and other social outcomes of gender polarization are not as recent as common-sense understandings might support. They have been occurring for over 150 years through various feminist movements or other activist or professional endeavours. The second-wave feminist movement of the late 20th century questioned the naturalness of the different and accepted realms of females and males, but activists in the mid-19th century and researchers in the early decades of the 20th century had confronted these ideas as well. Terman and Miles, two of the earliest researchers of the femininity and masculinity of personality, included the following in their book *Sex and Personality*: "The enfranchisement of women and their invasion of political, commercial, and other fields of action formerly reserved to men have afforded increasingly convincing evidence that sex differences in practical abilities are also either nonexistent or far less in magnitude than they have commonly been thought to be" (Terman & Miles, 1936, p. 1).

In North America, there is evidence of men increasingly challenging contemporary states of gender polarization in the late 20th century, as some males chose to cross over into the traditional female/feminine realm. Fathers wanted to participate more in parenting and began to sue for custody of their children in some cases of divorce. Professions such as nursing, elementary-school teaching, or modelling, for example, began to attract males. These men faced the same sorts of gender polarization as women who chose traditional male endeavours, but movement in this direction was less common and, possibly, seen to be more preposterous.

When females were seen to be trespassing in male domains there was some degree of understanding and a grudging acceptance of their actions. Positions of power and potential access to more wealth and/or status were possible in moving "up" to male professions. The male nurse or elementary-school teacher was not only seen to be moving "down" into a female realm, he was giving up a place of privilege. Contempt for females who attempted to usurp male power and position was common, but their attempts were seen as somewhat understandable because who would not want to rise above the second-class status of woman? Men, however, faced ridicule for wanting to assume "female roles," and their intelligence or sexuality was often called into question for choosing such an inferior or undesirable path.

One significant difference between women attempting to enter male domains and men attempting to enter female domains is that as more men entered traditional female occupations, a "glass elevator" often carried them up the administrative ladder and past their female counterparts. Conversely, women in traditional male occupations and increasingly in female occupations being entered by males found their advancement constrained by a "glass ceiling" that kept them subservient to managers and bosses who were generally male, even in female-dominated occupations.

One noteworthy outcome and direct by-product of gender polarization, which began to be discussed and researched in the late 19th century, was the notion of gender inversion. If one's gender is intrinsically linked to one's biological sex then the factors that are identified as being feminine or masculine would naturally occur in females and males, respectively. Any person who deviated from these gendered norms was considered to have a personality or psychological disorder, which became identified as gender inversion.

Male homosexuals, female suffragists, and early feminists would have been labelled as gender inverts for their non-gender-conforming activities. Questions regarding their femininity would have arisen for women who were engaged in public demonstrations, wearing pants or bloomers, or with an interest in cultural aspects that were considered masculine, such as politics, education, and sports. These women would have been seen to be deviating from normal gender scripts and therefore as biologically or psychologically abnormal. It was not the sexuality of these women that was challenged (as became common from the mid-20th century), but their gender—their "womanness."

Contrary to what might be assumed today, the association between gender inversion and sexual inversion or homosexuality was not made until much later, when the study of sexuality became a popular focus of medicine and psychology in the early decades of the 20th century. In 19th- and 20th-century science, prior to the appearance of the science of sexology, it was thought that women were completely lacking in any personal sexual motivation. A female required a male to become sexually aroused. "... autonomous ... sexuality was inconceivable except as inherently masculine" (Bem, 1993, p. 86). Therefore, females engaging in masculine activities—even those engaged in same-sex relationships—

were seen to have a gender abnormality, not a sexual one. Eventually, due to the work of sexologists and psychologists such as Ellis and Freud, inversion became a pathological condition of sexual desire rather than gender. However, this focus on sexuality rather than gender did nothing to modify the assumed essential natures of femininity and masculinity.

Another significant issue that will be discussed in detail in subsequent chapters is how the ideas of gender inversion (initially) and lesbianism (more recently) became an almost standard practice of suspicion directed toward many female athletes. If sport is male/masculine then women who want to participate in sport must want to be men. This thinking became even more twisted when a sexual interpretation was added to this presumption: if female athletes really want to be men, then they must also desire women in a sexual way. Thus, female athletes must be lesbians. This circular illogic has had an amazingly enduring history and continues to deter some girls and women from participating in some sports and keep many lesbian athletes, regardless of their sport choices, deeply closeted. Of course, there are lesbians in sports, but the overwhelming majority of female athletes are not homosexual. That the notion of female athlete = lesbian continues to be a prominent designation is a direct result of both androcentrism and gender polarization.

One might ask how gender polarization functions relative to those sports that are seen to be culturally normative physical activities for women. It functions in exactly the same way as it does for men's sports, but with one addition. Boys and men who desire to participate in girls' sports and physical activities, such as figure skating or dance, are suspected of being gay or, at the very least, sissies (Adams, 1997). They may be even more vilified than female athletes because, as explained above, moving "down" into feminine activities is seen to be a repudiation of privilege—a traitorous action!

One additional point that will be addressed further in later chapters is the lesser valuing of culturally normative feminine activities. Synchronized swimming, rhythmic gymnastics, cheerleading (considered a sport for girls in many high schools when gender-equity challenges are made), and other primarily feminine-designated activities have less social value than those activities considered to be masculine. Many culturally normative activities for girls are often not even recognized as "real" sports.

This lesser social valuing of "female" sports is demonstrated in a number of ways, most of which highlight the invisibility of girls' and women's sports, especially those that parallel professional men's team-sport leagues. Outside of the Olympics, women's sports are infrequently seen on television or covered in the sports sections of newspapers (Duncan & Messner, 2005; Duncan, Messner & Williams, n.d.). The concept of professional team-sport leagues for women is not well accepted, and many of these leagues have started, failed, and started again over a period of decades. They often have little funding and even less media exposure. Both of these conditions are based on the belief that people do not care about women's sports. When these leagues fail because of their poor funding and invisibility in the media, the response from critics is to support their own self-fulfilling prophecy that people do not care about women's sports and *that* is why the leagues struggle or fail. They, of course, accept no blame in the demise of the leagues, which is based partially on the lack of support and exposure that is needed to help potential fans and supporters to learn about and support the teams.

This lesser valuing is an outcome of the gender polarization that functions to keep even normative women's sports on the outside of male-stream sporting and media practice. Through the mid-20th century there were numerous amateur, professional, and quasi-professional team-sport leagues for women—mostly in basketball and baseball. They were extremely popular with spectators. Following World War II, as North American attitudes became very conservative and family oriented, women's sports and women's sports leagues were cemented into a second-class status with which, in many respects, they continue to struggle today.

The gendering of sports and the social value attached to that gender is interesting when one considers the differing values of an activity over time and place. In the United States, prior to 1976, gymnastics was primarily considered a girls' sport. There were exceptions to this (e.g., in communities where German turnverein organizations existed), but in the early years of televised sports the broadcasting of gymnastics events was primarily reserved for women's competitions. In 1976, Peter Kormann, a U.S. male gymnast, won a bronze medal on the floor-exercise event at the Montreal Olympic Summer Games. This was the first Olympic gymnastics medal won by a U.S. male since before the entrance of the Soviet Union into the Olympic movement in 1952. Following this, gymnastics became a legitimate sport in which American boys could participate.

The growth in men's gymnastics over the next few years was so great that the U.S. men temporarily surpassed the U.S. women in their success in international gymnastics competition. Today, there is equal appeal for girls and boys to enter gymnastics and the gendered and valued nature of

34

the sport has equalized (within gymnastics itself, if not between gymnastics and other sports), even though there are still gendered differences in the events in which women and men compete.

Interestingly, the gendered nature of specific sports varies by geographic location and local sporting history. For example, in certain places high-school volleyball is considered a girls' sport and it is assumed that the only reason boys would play volleyball is because they could not make the basketball team. Field hockey, which is traditionally considered to be a men's sport in many places in the world, is almost exclusively a women's sport in North America. Field hockey was brought to the United States from Great Britain early in the 20th century so that an exclusively female team sport could be introduced into the women's colleges in the U.S. East.

The gendered nature of sport assignment can readily be seen by looking at the characteristics of field hockey. Field hockey is a team sport in which the players physically interact with one another on the field; there is physical contact between players' bodies and between players' and opponents' (if not team mates') sticks. In addition, the ball is one of the hardest used in any sport (and I have permanent bumps on my shins to attest to this!). The sport is extremely physical and speed, power, and stamina are needed by players in all team positions. These characteristics are not only common to most men's team sports, but they are usually defined as masculine. Even so, field hockey is recognized as a girls' sport in North America and is, de facto, feminine! The gendered nature of sport, including the feminization or masculinization of activities and participants, is completely created and non-essentialist.

Biological Essentialism

Bem's third lens through which we can explore gender is that of *biological essentialism*. This concept can be used to maintain an inequality between the sexes (and also between various races) by presuming a naturalness to both androcentrism and gender polarization that has allowed legal and medical discriminatory practices to be perpetuated. Biological essentialism provides for the defining natures of females and males to be based on natural or reproductive functions only. This further translates into a sex-based (and also race-based) "biologically ordained" (Bem, 1993, p. 11) division of labour for all aspects of socio-cultural structure.

Arguments for biological essentialism appeared in the mid-19th century as three significant social shifts began to occur in North America. One of these shifts centred on women. The women of concern were primarily white, upper-class women who began the first wave of feminism. Efforts by these women to access higher education and get the vote were seen as significant threats to the social order of the day. In addition, as upper-class women began to be university educated and to seek careers outside of the home they began having fewer children, which led to the second social shift from which biological essentialism arose.

Beginning in the latter half of the 19th century, large numbers of immigrants arriving in North America were seen as potential threats to the control of the nation by white men of power and privilege. White women, particularly those of privilege, were having fewer children. Immigrants who saw North America as a haven of refuge and safety began having large numbers of children. The growth in non-white or other "less desirable" ethnic populations was deemed to be a potential threat to the social order.

The third shift that occurred in the United States, but less so in Canada, was concern over the number of former black slaves who were seeking education and jobs and who were also producing large numbers of children. Sexism and racism became grounded in efforts to maintain a social order that had not been challenged in North American culture prior to the Industrial Revolution. In an attempt to maintain the social order, medical and biological theorizing about women and men became common. The science of gynecology was "established" by the medical profession and provided men (because all recognized or accredited medical doctors at this time were male) with the opportunity take over all aspects of female reproduction that had formerly been the domain of midwives and female lay healers.

Menstruation, pregnancy, and menopause were pathologized because they were different from male biology and little understood. Controlling the reproductive functions of women was a significant way to keep them under the control of men and to ensure their inferior social status (Sayers, 1982). Science and cultural ideology became entwined (Roszak, 1999) in a way that would impact women's social standing and personal freedom for the next 150 years.

Education was targeted as a primary threat to the reproductive capacity of women. In the mid to late 19th century, the concept of "vital force" or "vitalism" was a popular way to control women's educational and sporting endeavours (Lenskyj, 1986). Vitalism proposed that there was a limited amount of energy available to the human body to carry out its basic functions and sustain life. From this, it was proposed that through the process of education females would use up so much energy in the brain that there would be insufficient vital force for the development of the uterus.[11] This would obviously have a negative effect on the female's capacity to have children or to have healthy children. The fact that university-educated women were having fewer children was seen as significant supporting evidence for this concept. The fact that women might have more knowledge about their bodies and increased information on how to control conception never entered the equation.

The anti-feminist beliefs of biological essentialism were strengthened in 1873 with the publication of an article by Edward Clarke, president of Harvard University, entitled *Sex in Education* (Bem, 1993; Sayers, 1982). In his article, Clarke supported the conservation of energy principle and argued that the education of women was extremely harmful to their reproductive capacity. He implied that not only could classroom activities and studying be detrimental to females, but that physical activities should be curtailed during menstruation because a woman's reproductive organs required the most vital energy at this time. For the brain or muscles to take up this energy was harmful. In addition to reinforcing the biological essentialist argument that women's reproductive functions, and therefore the healthy continuation of the human species (note this refers primarily to Anglo-Saxon humans), was a woman's primary role, women's place in androcentric society was a also fortified, if not undermined.

It is important to note that Clarke commented not only on classroom activity, but also on the negative effects of physical activity on girls and women. As women were increasingly attending high school and post-secondary institutions they began to demand not only the educational opportunities of boys and men, but also greater access to sports and physical activities.

In North America at the end of the 19th century, Victorian standards of womanly comportment meant that only gentle, moderate, rhythmic physical activities that were seen to be beneficial for women's health, particularly their reproductive health, were appropriate (Cahn, 1994). Rough-and-tumble play was discouraged, especially among white, upper- and middle-class girls for whom such activities were seen to be at odds with their womanhood. However, as these same women were entering colleges and professions that had previously been closed to them, they viewed sports as a vehicle for women's emancipation. The relationship of femininity, womanliness, and sports became an unforeseen and, possibly, unintentional victim of biological essentialism that would have a far longer lasting impact on girls and women than restrictions on social, political, educational, and professional advancement.

Biological essentialism not only functions to keep females in an inferior social position to males, but also requires different behaviours of the sexes. Un-ladylike behaviour, however this may have been and continues to be defined by parents, teachers, religious leaders, and even peers, is quickly criticized (if not chastised) in young girls and teenagers. Various games and sporting activities are often included in the realm of un-ladylike behaviours, but not in all venues. In private spaces, such as the home, rough-and-tumble play might not be discouraged or punished. In public spaces, however, where the behaviour of the daughter reflects on the parents, different behaviours might be expected.

Girls can experience confusion about their being active in sports and physical activities in general and the appropriateness of certain games and sports for them specifically. They are often encouraged to be active, but cautioned about the nature of acceptable activities. These differences are often not well defined or understood, but there is generally some internalization regarding those activities that are deemed to be appropriate for boys, but, at the very least, cautioned against for girls.

Girls who like the rough-and-tumble nature of boys' activities are often labelled tomboys. Mixed messages accompany this label. At times, there is pride and positive attention gained by being a tomboy; at other times, girls learn that being a tomboy can have negative consequences, whether real or implied. The reasons for these differing reactions to tomboy behaviours are often not explained and therefore not necessarily well understood by the tomboys themselves. They are often defiantly resisted by the tomboy herself, whose sense of personal identity may be more tied up in being an athlete than in being a "girl"!

Even today (a time when girls are encouraged to enter sporting activities), when the tomboy reaches puberty she is likely to receive increasingly negative reactions to her "masculine" sporting interests and behaviours. Tomboys know that there are common-sense assumptions about the differences between girls and boys. They have learned this as well as (if not better than) many other children through family, peer, and school interactions. The tomboy begins to learn, or is faced with pressures to accept, that the differences between girls and boys go beyond the obvious biological ones (Carr, 2005). Tomboys have chosen to reject many of these differences. No matter how skilled the tomboy may be at the culturally normative male activities in which she engages and for which she has been accepted by her male and female playing cohort in the past, she learns that she is an intruder in these games and sports and that there are negative consequences to her trespassing on this masculine territory. These increase and become more strategic as she ages.

Biological essentialism developed into an area of study known as *sociobiology*, which underlies the development of theories and controversies that support and challenge the differences between the sexes and the subsequent social status of females relative to males. Sociobiologists support the concept that sexual discrimination is natural and results from a universal genetic programming. Opponents of sociobiology argue that cultural and historical factors play a significant part in the social and psychological developments of females and males. These cause males and females to be treated differently in every culture, but not necessarily in the same specific ways.

According to Bem (1993), and a position that I support in the development of the arguments presented in this book, sociobiologists severely underestimate the importance of history and culture "not only because they pay too little attention to culture and history but because they also pay too little attention to what is arguably the most distinctively human feature of human biology: the ability of humans to transform their environment through cultural intervention and thereby to transform themselves" (Bem, 1993, p. 22).

Biological essentialism did not only function to create and maintain sexual discrimination, but also racial and class discrimination. Often coupled with sexist positions, racist and classist perspectives paralleled those of sexism in the application of scientific and medical "knowledge" and educational points of view. The cautions applied to girls and women in their educational and health-related pursuits, including sport and physical activity, were not universally applied, but were directed almost exclusively to the daughters and wives of white, middle- and upper-class men of some social status. These were the girls and women whose reproductive health was seen to need protecting.

There were no such cautions directed to women from the lower socio-economic groupings, including many immigrants and all women of colour. The demanding and often dangerously strenuous physical labour that was undertaken by these women for countless hours every day did not raise cautions regarding their reproductive health or femininity. "Threats to the standards of femininity and womanhood, which were often the basis for the underlying concerns regarding women and sports, were directed toward only those women who were seen to have a greater value within the social structures of the day" (Daniels, 2005a, p. 928). Sports participation may be one of the best indicators that biology is not destiny, and that many of the biological essentialist positions cannot be supported.

The interests of men of power were central to the organization and stratification of North American society as it began a significant shift caused primarily by the Industrial Revolution. Scientific inquiry, supposedly above common bias, was carried out by men who had been raised and educated in an androcentric, gender-polarized, and biologically essentialist environment. It is more than likely that an analysis of the history of science will reveal an unintentional (we hope) bias in the questions explored, the interpretation of the data obtained, and the application of the results. "Scientific" concerns regarding issues of sex and gender are as likely to be based on these biases as any other area of investigation.

Roszak (1999) cautioned us not to forget that it was men who were the founders of modern science. He states that "Henry Oldenberg, the first secretary of the Royal Society, the seventeenth-century prototype of all later professional associations in science, made it the highest priority of the new organization to establish a 'Masculine Philosophy'" (p. 56). One of the underlying meanings of this was the rooting out of anything woman-like or feminine within the men of the scientific community. "Seeking an ever more fundamental understanding of nature, might not men, biased so strongly against the feminine, intuitively subscribe to a paradigm that reflected their own personality?" (Roszak, 1999, p. 56). Coupled with the desire to eliminate anything deemed feminine in the scientists themselves were the sexual metaphors that identified nature as female and "science as an effort to control and conquer her. Are feminist psychologists so far from the truth in seeing a powerful masculine bias not only in science as a profession, but in science as a worldview?" (Roszak, 1999, p. 56). The inequality of the gender binary can be seen to be embedded in the patriarchal science that has defined it.

CONCLUSIONS

Androcentrism, gender polarization, and biological essentialism have worked together to create and sustain what has come to be known and accepted as gender. Gender, further defined as the natural femininity of females or the natural masculinity of males, functions in the same ways as androcentrism, gender polarization, and biological essentialism to keep females and males in different social strata with different social values and access to differing aspects of culture. Challenges to the very existence of gender have been made by numerous researchers. The need to eliminate gender has been proposed as one way to remove some of the power imbalance between women and men. The notion of gender is so entrenched in our mindset about women and men that most people would struggle with an attempt to remove gender from their understanding of people. In this book, I propose that accepting the polygendered nature of people—a fluid mixing of the components of femininity and masculinity—will go far in reducing differences and increasing the potential of all people.

Chapter 2

KNOCK KNOCK ... WHO'S THERE? THE SCIENCE BEHIND THE MYTH OF GENDER

> Perhaps, then, it takes a historian to observe the obvious. Namely, that the theories, methods and sensibilities of Western science have, for four centuries, been under the control of an exclusively male guild. For the greater part of that period, the society that shaped every scientist great and minor was male-dominated through and through. That society took all that was male to be "normal" whether in politics, art, the economy, scholarship, social ethics, or philosophy. As Londa Schiebinger has argued, "At the core of modern science lies a self-reinforcing system whereby the findings of science (crafted by institutions from which women were excluded) have been used to justify their continued absence." (Roszak, 1999, p. 14)

In the previous chapter, I provided a position from which the differences between people, primarily females and males, can be viewed from a gender perspective. There is much historical and medical support for this standpoint, as sex differences and sex roles have directed much thought and action in Western civilization since before the days of the Greek empire, from which we get many of our basic philosophical, medical, and social foundations. Centuries of scientific and social practice and the cultural developments that have arisen from them have become a foundation for the stratification of human beings and the power/privilege imbalances among them. It is not difficult to understand how many contemporary beliefs about female/male differences have come to be so strongly endorsed and seen as natural. Some have existed for millennia. Many have been enforced and reinforced by scientific and medical positions. The first organized challenges to the power imbalances embedded in the gender binary began only about 150 years ago, just a blip of time in the course of human events.

What needs to be included in our understanding of female/male differences, but is conveniently missing from a 21st-century analysis of the essentialist positions of the past, is a better understanding of history, particularly a bio-historical perspective of "science" and technology and their impact, or lack thereof, on human relationships. We need to find out when, where, and how the socially constructed gender binary became legitimized as a way of separating people into the two rigid boxes of femininity and masculinity.

That there are biological differences between females and males cannot be disputed. The amount of actual difference or, to put it in a more appropriate perspective, overlap is not really known, but certainly the overlap is significantly greater than the difference. This knowledge is inherently recognized yet often misused. Until very recently, almost all medical studies were conducted on male subjects. This was partially motivated from an androcentric and scientific position that what is male is normal, and the results of such research must therefore apply to all humans. The results were often extrapolated to females based on an understanding of the overlap among all humans. Any testing or knowledge or even questioning of potential effects or side effects to women were rarely considered until the use of a product or treatment caused different or dangerous results in female users. Although this practice is changing and more attention is being paid to female-specific conditions, there remains a huge gap in knowledge about the actual differences between females and males from a biological perspective.

FEMALE/MALE SIMILARITIES AND DIFFERENCES

Strength

One example of an area of difference/overlap that pertains specifically to female athletes is that of strength development.[1] Many people know something about testosterone, a naturally occurring hormone in all human beings. Common sense (and some stubborn scientific opinions) causes us to think that we know the importance of testosterone in the development of strength in all humans. At the very least there are many assumptions about this androcentric position. It is true that males have as much as 20 times more testosterone than females. The conclusion is that it is completely natural for males to be stronger than females.

But does the ratio of testosterone levels in males compared to testosterone levels in females translate into a direct ratio between male strength and female strength? No! There are very few males who can claim to be 20-times stronger than females of similar age and health, especially athletes. If a woman can, for example, bench press 40 pounds, then a man of similar age and health ought to be able to bench press 800 pounds. The number of men in the world who can bench press 800 pounds can probably be counted on one hand, less a few fingers. Even those who can press 10 times or even five times the amount of weight would be small.

Something other than testosterone must then be considered, as many females are as strong if not stronger than many males. The overlap in total body strength between females and males is about 75%. This means that the strongest woman is stronger than approximately 75% of all males (McArdle, Katch & Katch, 2007). Muscle strength is a measure of the cross-section of muscle fibre size, regardless of the sex of the person in which that muscle resides. How and why muscle responds to training has traditionally been studied in males and extrapolated to females. One study on female and male swimmers who were trained in identical programs determined that less than 2% of the strength differences between these athletes could be attributed to sex difference (Bishop, Cureton & Collins, 1987). It is only very recently that exercise physiologists have begun to study strength development in females and have learned that other natural hormones and chemicals, along with testosterone, are most likely recruited and utilized by the female body in the development of strength.

Box 2.1

Female/male differences in physical fitness components have a great deal to do with the way children are raised, the activities they are taught and encouraged to participate in, the level of anticipated excellence that can be achieved, and—yes—to some extent, biology. The differences among women or among men are actually greater than the average differences between women and men. When ratios of the cross-section of muscle are compared or when relative, rather than absolute, strength differences are examined, there is actually little significant difference between women and men in either upper- or lower-body strength.

For example, we can compare the bench press amounts of a 95-kg male who presses 114 kg and a 60-kg woman who presses 70 kg. In absolute terms the male is clearly stronger. However, in relative terms (if the bench-press weight is divided by the lifter's body mass) the result is very different. "For the man, strength divided by body mass equals 1:20; the ratio for the woman is 1:17. In the first comparison, the male was 'stronger' by 63%. Using the ratio score reduced the percentage difference in bench-press strength to only 2.5%" (McArdle, Katch & Katch, 2007, p. 516). How strength is measured and reported can go a long way in reducing misconceptions about male/female differences and the incorrect arguments that are often used to justify women's restricted participation in many activities.

Reproduction

A point that must be considered is that even our knowledge of the reproductive functions of females and males, probably the most obvious and essential sex difference, is not complete. For a large amount of human history, the female contribution to reproduction was seen to be little more than a vessel for gestation and a food source for infants. One early belief about reproduction was that the fully formed offspring was inserted into the female by the male. This creature was known as a "homunculus." Even when the functions of egg and sperm were more fully understood, the accepted gender differences between females and males were applied to reproductive function from an androcentric understanding.

As recently as the end of the 19th century, sex researchers Geddes and Thompson (1890) equated the "active, energetic, eager, passionate, and variable" metabolism of the sperm and the "passive, conservative, sluggish, and stable" condition of the egg to the ultimate personality developed by the resulting offspring (Bem, 1993, p. 13). That male and female children will develop personalities similar to the behaviours of the respective sperm and egg is quite a stretch considering that all human offspring, regardless of sex, are a combination of both egg and sperm.

What is indisputable is that females and males do have differing roles in the reproductive process. The female can become pregnant, carry a fetus to term, and breastfeed the infant. The male is needed only to get this process started. However, what is also indisputable is that until very recently in human history, and continuing today in many places, the technology did not exist to alter this process. The survival of human infants required the presence of the mother (or a mother substitute such as a wet nurse) to provide nourishment and care. Below a certain age, any significant separation of the infant from its mother meant certain death for the child.

Labour

Another indisputable fact of human history is that, until the recent invention of labour-saving machines, human strength was required to carry out most of the labour necessary to sustain human life. The Industrial Revolution showed that a great deal of female/male difference was historically and technologically based, rather than an absolute biological necessity. In a great deal of the world today, the need for physical strength remains only where modern technology has not appeared. Even in these places, the level of strength required by women to carry water for miles, till the land with ancient hand tools, skin animals and tan hides, and hand-grind grain into flour, all the while caring for children, would undoubtedly challenge the strength of many males who live in Western countries.

It appears that much human social organization has developed around the primary role of females in reproduction and child care and of males in the physical strength needed for some of the work undertaken away from the living site. These sex roles and the sexual division of labour are obviously not that clear-cut. Although females may have been constrained through their child-care responsibilities, the physical labour needed to maintain the "home" was not terribly less than that needed by males in their tasks. One reality of the differences in sex roles and the sexual division of labour developed with the Industrial Revolution, when a public sphere involving the development of cities and workplaces away from the home became the standard workplace for many men who were not exclusively involved with an agricultural life. Women were primarily confined to the private sphere of the home/farm. The public/private separation of male and female domains has contributed more to the power imbalance and gender polarization that we see today than any biological differences, or the essentialist interpretation of them, between the sexes.

Medical and technological advances in reproduction and child care, socio-economic changes affecting family participation in the workplace, and feminist sensibilities that reject the biological essentialism that supports androcentrism and gender polarization all act to provide evidence against and challenge contemporary definitions and the constraints of today's definition or interpretation of gender.

Technology has developed safer and more effective birth control, which allows women (those who have access to such technology) more control over their bodies and their personal choices about the number and timing of children or not to reproduce at all. The development of viable substitutes to a mother's milk has allowed mothers to control whether or for how long they breastfeed. Regardless of some faith-based and/or health-related objections to the uses of these technologies (such as the introduction of milk substitutes to healthy mothers in developing nations), they have had a significant impact in shifting sex roles with regard to family, child rearing, and women's and men's greater freedom of choice regarding family and workplace (Rich, 1976).

The sexual division of labour in the West has irrevocably shifted in a matter of a few decades, in contrast to the millennia preceding them. Physical strength is no longer a requirement for the majority of careers and child care is no longer the exclusive domain of mothers. These facts underlie the challenges to the existence of female/male differences that function to keep men in positions of power/privilege and women as second-class or *other* beings. They also help to confront the notion that gender is essentially linked to the sex of the body or that it underlies some natural female/male polarization.

Bem (1993) proposed that male power over females is produced or reproduced through the lenses of gender that she laid out. Through androcentrism, gender polarization, and biological essentialism, she said, females and males are channelled into different and unequal life situations. Although differences exist in most cultures, the way they are played out differs from group to group. This supports the socially constructed nature of gender. However, she questioned, in the light of the feminist analysis and activism that has taken place over the past 40 years, why, in the light of social and technological advances, do we still cling to gender differences and the inequitable outcomes that they produce? Her explanation for this was that "during enculturation, the individual gradually internalizes the cultural lenses and thereby becomes motivated to construct an identity that is consistent with them" (Bem, 1993, p. 3). Thus, gender becomes a framework through which we are socialized into being appropriate members of our communities. The question still remains as to how the specifics of femininity and masculinity have become exclusively attached to females and males, respectively.

THE LANGUAGE OF GENDER

An investigation of what gender actually is and how it has become entrenched in our thinking may help us to undo the effects of androcentrism, gender polarization, and biological essentialism that keep females and males from achieving their full human potential. Breaking through the gender binary that keeps femininity and masculinity as exclusive domains is one step toward achieving a polygendered acceptance of all individuals.

How did the word "gender" come to be entwined with our understanding of sex and result in femininity or masculinity being rigidly assigned? According to the *Oxford English Dictionary*, the word gender came from a similar derivation as the French word *genre*, meaning a "kind, sort, class ... genus as opposed to species" (Simpson & Weiner, 1989, p. 427). Its first apparent usage in this context was by Chaucer in the 14th century.

The *Oxford English Dictionary* presents the second definition of gender as a word used in a number of languages to connote the femininity, masculinity, and (in certain languages) the neutral for grammatical classification. "In the Indo-European [languages], there were originally three genders, the masculine and feminine, to which respectively belonged the majority of nouns denoting male and female persons or animals; and the neuter, including chiefly nouns denoting things without sex" (Simpson & Weiner, 1989, p. 427). This makes some degree of sense. "But a great number of words denoting inanimate objects were of the masculine or feminine gender, without even any figurative attribution of sex; and in some cases the names of objects possessing sex were of the neuter gender" (Simpson & Weiner, 1989, p. 427).

In modern English, the gender of a noun has no other purpose than to determine the proper pronoun related to it. Many of us who studied a second language in school (e.g., Spanish or French) will likely recall the often strange and confusing nature of attaching *f.*, *m.*, *or n.* to the vocabulary that we were attempting to learn and bemoaning the examination marks that we lost when we forgot to include them!

49

According to Funk (1950), *gen* is a root from a Greek word meaning to bear or to beget. The *gen* family is prolific and is contained in such words as *gentlemen*, *congenital*, *degenerate*, and *gender*. From Latin, *genero* is a word that means to produce or to give birth to (Funk, 1950). The notion of giving birth or begetting further entrenches, at least *gen*, into a somewhat sex-based interpretation of gender.

The use of the word "gender" continued to refer to *a sort or kind of a thing* until 1963, when Comfort first used the term in *Sex in Society* to relate to the learned aspects of being female or male that a child displays at as early as two years of age (Simpson & Weiner, 1989, p. 428). It is therefore an extremely modern grammatical usage that has linked the gender of a person to his/her biological sex. "A euphemism for the sex of a human being, often intended to emphasize the social and cultural, as opposed to the biological, distinctions between the sexes" (Simpson & Weiner, 1989, p. 428).

Much feminist writing uses this link between sex and femininity or masculinity (now referred to as gender) to explain the social, political, and economic power imbalances that continue to exist between females and males and which cannot be explained by biology, except through an essentialist viewpoint. One of the earliest 20th-century analyses of this feminist position was introduced in *The Second Sex* (de Beauvoir, 1952). In this work, Simone de Beauvoir puts forth the position that a female is not born a woman, but *becomes* a woman through the cultural pressures and expectations that maintain the androcentric structures and belief systems that support different sex roles and expectations for women and men (de Beauvoir, 1952). Although this designation was not used to refer specifically to the word gender at that time, today this relationship is identified as gender or even, as conceived by Peper (1994) and explained in the previous chapter, "gendex."

According to Butler and following on from de Beauvoir, feminist position recognizes "that the universal person and the masculine gender are conflated, thereby defining women in terms of their sex and extolling men as the bearers of a body-transcendent universal personhood" (Butler, 1990, p. 9). Thus, *woman* is defined in relation to man and not exclusively from her sexed body. If a female must learn how to become and to be a woman then the feminine gender must derive from cultural expectations that define her, as well as from her position as different to and created from the desires of the masculine = male (Wayne, 2005).

Gender, therefore, is a hierarchical designation with masculine in the superior position and restrictions of masculinity and femininity constructed to maintain this patriarchal hierarchy in North American culture and in any other culture based on an androcentric belief system. This, rather than biology, is likely the foundation of the nearly universal existence of gender polarization in the world's cultures.

If what is feminine is defined as not masculine then women must always be viewed in relation to men. Because of this, heterosexuality claims the same hierarchical position in most cultures as gender (Butler, 1990). The relationship between femininity and sexuality and how it impacts on the female athlete has been briefly discussed already and will be explored in greater detail in later chapters.

I have presented an argument that strongly supports how the gender polarization that exists in our culture came to be entrenched. I have also indicated that, for centuries, aspects of certain languages became designated as feminine, masculine, or neuter (without gender). None of this explains how the restrictive boundaries of femininity and masculinity as we understand and generally accept them today came to be—or how the requirement that females be exclusively feminine and males be exclusively masculine came to be. Aspects of androcentrism and biological essentialism, such as the notion of sex roles, the traditional mind/body or culture/nature philosophical position, and the emerging public/private domain dichotomies that occurred primarily with the Industrial Revolution, have all contributed to the cementing of not only a common-sense understanding of definite (and possibly understood to be essential) roles and responsibilities for women and men, but also to attributes that *seemed* to be exclusive to either women or men. These, therefore, became sex-dependent aspects of personality and sex-based normalities.

THE SCIENCE OF GENDER—THE EARLY YEARS

The "scientific" (presumably rational) link between gender and the femininity/masculinity designations of females and males, both respectively and specifically, has an interesting history. Some of the earliest (if not *the* earliest) "scientific" investigations into femininity and masculinity were conducted in the areas of personality and sexuality. In 1936, Lewis Terman and Catherine Cox Miles published the results of some of their research, begun in 1922, in a tome called *Sex and Personality: Studies in Masculinity and Femininity.*[2] Terman and Miles' work is frequently cited in studies of gender or in research that attempts to either knit together the concepts of gender and sex or to sever them completely. This is particularly interesting as the word "gender" never appears in their work.

Terman and Miles' research into femininity and masculinity was designed to investigate deviance in personality and/or sexuality, not to determine the characteristics that apply either naturally or through socio-cultural conditioning to females and males. As a matter of their own reporting, Terman and Miles did not support an essentialist position that female persons are or must be feminine and that male persons are or must be masculine. They supported feminine and masculine as *personality types* that *tend* to be displayed by females and males, but that vary according to culture, level of education, and historical time frame.

The idea that birth sex and gender, from the original meaning of a sort or kind, are not related through cause and effect is supported in Terman and Miles' research. Their studies offer "considerable evidence of the influence of nurture on the masculinity and femininity of human personality" (Terman & Miles, 1936, p. 8). They also proposed that it would be especially interesting to compare masculine/feminine differences in different cultures and in the same culture at intervals of one or more generations. In short, the measurement of masculine/feminine "differences will make it possible to greatly expand our knowledge of *the causes which produce them*" (Terman & Miles, 1936, p. 10; emphasis added). Thus, Terman and Miles based much of their research on the premise that masculine/feminine differences vary from culture to culture and within a culture over time, and do not have a strict biological foundation.

We can see that Terman and Miles' research did not set out to define the types of personalities that women and men should have. They even strongly supported the concept that there is a large, unmeasured overlap in the feminine and masculine personality types (Terman & Miles, 1936). This would translate into a large overlap in the characteristics, interests, and behaviours of women and men, because they found that feminine and masculine personality types are not exclusive to either sex. Although they hypothesized that there is a tendency for females to display a feminine personality type and for males to display a masculine personality type, Terman and Miles recognized that cultural and historical factors impact on their developments and definitions.

Terman and Miles even admitted that "investigations of masculinity and femininity have been retarded by lack of definiteness with respect to what these terms *should* connote" (Terman & Miles, 1936, p. vi; emphasis added). The use of the word *should* in this quote is an indicator of the desired outcome of their research. Their study design was planned in such a way as to establish definiteness to the feminine and masculine personality types. As we will see, their work also functioned to link the feminine personality to females and the masculine personality to males. Although Terman and Miles wrote that they did not assume this relationship, all of the research instruments that they used or created were based on this essentialist position. This may have accomplished the elimination of the global humanness of women and men by intentionally disregarding the significant overlap in feminine and masculine personality traits that exists in almost all people within their specific socio-cultural and historical milieu.

It is likely that most readers of this book were not alive when Terman and Miles conducted their research, but have hopefully learned enough history to be aware of the different privileges and constraints that existed between males and females, whites and non-whites, upper classes and working classes, and North American born whites and immigrants during the time of this research. The Victorian era, which was known for its rigidity with regard to socio-cultural factors and behaviours, was ending and a more open society (especially for white women of middle- and upper-class socio-economic positions) grew in the first two decades of the 20th century before the Depression, World War II, and the post-war 1950s brought opportunities for change. Tensions regarding these changes influenced many social and cultural factors, including educational institutions, the workplace, the media, and the growing women's and civil rights movements.

The post-World War I years of the 1920s were still more tied to *fin de siècle* sex roles, racial positionings, and traditional life experiences than not. The masculine and feminine experiences, interests, behaviours, and attitudes that Terman and Miles selected to determine personality differences could not have been easier to select or to predict. "Have you ever sewn a dress?" and "Have you ever played football?" would have elicited very few positive responses from males or females, respectively![3] Terman and Miles selected their test items to discriminate between the masculine and the feminine personality types. Given the historical time frame of this research, the tie-in between the sex of the subject and the masculine/feminine personality was all but assured for the majority of North Americans.

LANGUAGE, BIAS, AND THE BISECTING OF THE GENDER CONTINUUM

Terman and Miles developed and administered numerous versions of their test instruments to hundreds of female and male subjects over a decade and a half in the 1920s and 1930s. Their test instruments were constructed to use language as the medium of analysis. The process of creating the test began with searching an English-language dictionary "for words which looked as though *they might bring sex differences in responses* ... The selection was based in part on investigational data in the field of sex differences, but to a greater extent on subjective 'hunches'!" (Terman & Miles, 1936, p. 22; emphasis added). So although Terman and Miles stated that a feminine or masculine personality could be possessed by either a female or a male, their test instrument was constructed to determine sex differences in responses, thus suggesting that females would choose feminine-oriented words and males would select masculine-oriented words, as these were perceived by Terman, who constructed the word list.

Although Terman was searching for words that were intended to elicit differences in responses, his own bias was clearly injected into his selection of the words chosen for the test instrument. As a highly educated, white, male scientist, his selection of terms reflected those aspects of his background and understanding of socio-cultural factors, and were highly prejudicial in the establishment of female/feminine and male/masculine associations for other white, upper- or middle-class, educated persons of his day. The same biases existed in the creation of the Stanford-Binet IQ test, which decades later was seen to be highly prejudicial against children from differing socio-cultural and ethnic backgrounds (Bem, 1993).

With regard to analyzing their results, Terman and Miles eliminated from their test instruments all neutral terms or choices that would be as likely to be selected by both females and males, such as eating chocolate, looking at the stars, or the colour green. Because the overlap or similarities were discarded, the overlap in masculine/feminine personality types was also eliminated. This functioned in the desired way—to indicate deviance in certain extremes of personality—but it also began a process that not only exclusively fixed the feminine to the female and the masculine to the male, but in addition created a narrow understanding of how the characteristics of femininity and masculinity are defined and applied.

Although Terman and Miles did not affix an exclusively feminine or masculine personality type to females and males, and they recognized the huge overlap between women and men in various traits, their study design had the effect of creating and cementing a huge and non-traversable divide that would come to be applied to females and males as exclusive possessors of femininity and masculinity, respectively—in other words, the restrictive and compulsory gender assignments that are so well accepted today.

The purpose of the sex and personality research carried out by Terman and Miles was to identify extremes: deviance in the masculine or feminine personality types that would lead to behavioural or sexual abnormalities. They were hopeful that the results of their work would help to identify individuals who were at risk for deviance or to help medical and psychology workers to more successfully "treat" the deviant personality.

The Testing Process

Terman and Miles' original test, which was created from a list of about 500 words, was later thrown out, but this method of item selection was retained through the development of later instruments. Thousands of words were chosen to elicit a feminine or a masculine response, as defined by Terman and Miles. Any words that did not differentiate between these personality types were discarded. In the instrument described above, 260 of the 500 items were discarded because they revealed no female/male differences. Thus, this first test showed a greater than 50% commonality among females and males that was totally disregarded.

It must be remembered that Terman and Miles were attempting to discern deviant—not culturally normative—personality types. However, the effect of their instrumentation was to obliterate the obvious and extensive overlap in human personalities (including interests and behaviours). This had a devastating impact on how female and male persons came to be defined and how they were expected to conform to a compulsory feminine or masculine performative.[4]

All test items that indicated how females and males were likely to have the same experiences, interests, and behaviours, and therefore did not indicate deviance from either each other or normative feminine and masculine personality types, were discarded. In every version of the test instrument in which this process was used, the female/male and feminine/masculine separation was manufactured and highlighted. Female/male distinctions arose with the types of words that were chosen to elicit extremes in feminine and masculine personality types, which would, in reality, in the 1920s and early 1930s, translate into female/male sex differences based on the socio-cultural and economic realities of the day.

The final test instrument was extensive and was used to establish a masculine or feminine score. "The range of scores in the general population of adults is roughly as follows: for males: from +200 to –100, with a mean of +52 and S.D. [standard deviation] of 50; for females, from +100 to –200, with a mean of –70 and S.D. of 47" (Terman & Miles, 1936, p. 5).[5] It is interesting to note here that Terman and Miles refer to a general population of adults, yet they further indicate that "the score ... is influenced by age, intelligence, education, interests, and social background, and to such an extent that groups differing in these respects often show markedly contrasting score distributions" (Terman & Miles, 1936, p. 5). This shows that Terman and Miles recognized the vast sex and personality differences that exist in individuals from differing socio-cultural backgrounds. However, they proceeded with their research as if females and males were primarily different from one another, but homogeneous within their sex groupings.

One strong caution made by Terman and Miles to their readers regarded an incorrect interpretation of females who scored high in the masculine range and males who scored well below the masculine average. These scores were in no way to be seen as indicators of sexual inversion or homosexuality (which many might consider deviant according to these research results).[6] This type of interpretation of such a result will be discussed in later chapters, where the supposed masculinity of many female athletes is assumed to be an indicator of lesbianism.

Terman and Miles were aware of the bias they introduced into their research design, but they chose to negate it in the analysis of their collected data. "That sex differences in information are perhaps almost wholly due to environmental causes (granting sex equality in general intelligence) does not seem to us a valid criticism of the test as we have used it" (Terman & Miles, 1936, p. 34). They recognized that age, educational level, socio-economic background, and other life circumstances cause women and men to acquire large amounts of different information and experience, but were unwilling to use this information as they constructed conclusions from the data they had collected. The results of many of their studies found no statistically significant differences between males and females, yet Terman and Miles chose to ignore the fact that the basic premise of their research question and of their test instruments was flawed.

Data Results: No Significant Differences

The research instrument was used to collect information on such topics as interests, emotions, likes and dislikes, and educational aspirations. In the area of emotions, "the question [of] whether women are in fact so much more emotional than men cannot be answered by the data at hand" (Terman & Miles, 1936, p. 45). In the tests that explored areas of interest "it is obvious ... that even if both tests had a reliability of 1.00 they would still be measuring traits that have too little in common to warrant the use of either measure as an equivalent to the other" (Terman & Miles, 1936, p. 34). With respect to beliefs or opinions, "the frequency with which seemingly good hunches were belied by the response statistics inclines us to believe that men and women do not differ from each other very greatly in the opinions they hold about commonly discussed issues" (Terman & Miles, 1936, p. 45). It can be seen from these examples that the differences between women and men that Terman and Miles were seeking often did not appear.

For the general population, at least those populations tested by Terman and Miles, which were broad reaching, the results of their test, when compared with other variables, are also enlightening with respect to my (and others') basic premise that female/femininity and male/masculinity are social constructs that restrict the overall range of desirable and desired interests, behaviours, and (in contemporary constraints) appearance factors of everyone. Other results that Terman and Miles reported include that nearly all of the relationships between variables were low. This means that their test instrument was unsuccessful in locating masculine/feminine differences. They reported that: "Correlations of total masculine/feminine score with age... are so low as to be merely suggestive of a slight positive relationship," (though we shall see later that over wide age ranges the correlation is significantly negative for males) (Terman & Miles, 1936, p. 61).[7]

The relationship between the total masculine/feminine score and intelligence was approximately zero for males and somewhat positive for females. Males had a significantly positive correlation with mechanical ability tests, but females did not. This is not surprising given the gendered nature of such activities during the time frame of the data collection. What is most interesting relative to the concerns of this book regarding the femininity of female athletes is that the results of Terman and Miles' testing showed that "college women who engage in many extracurricular activities do not tend to test especially masculine" (Terman & Miles, 1936, p. 61).

It is interesting that so much research that ties gender to femininity/masculinity references Terman and Miles when their results do not support that female/feminine and male/masculine are given personality types for females or males at all. A more correct reading of their research would show that, except in cases of extreme deviance, females and males show considerable overlap in their masculine/feminine personality scores, as determined by Terman and Miles' test. In fact, they reported that masculine/feminine scores obtained through their test instrument in several experiments provided ratings that "seem to be less reliable than ratings of almost any other personality trait.... Certainly if all possible items of the general type found in a given exercise had been included, the overlap would have been much greater than has been found" (Terman & Miles, 1936, p. 64).

They further reported that "it is not to be supposed that the sexes really differ from one another in their interests, attitudes, and thought trends as much as the small overlap on the M-F test and its exercises might at first suggest; the fact that the test is composed entirely of items selected on the basis of their M-F discrimination necessarily exaggerates the true differences" (Terman & Miles, 1936, p. 65).[8] The findings of these studies showed females and males to be far more alike than different across most of the factors tested.

Searching for Difference

In the 1920s and 1930s, people showed increasing variability in how they defined a feminine or a masculine personality (in other words, how women and men should be or should act). To determine how individuals would rate the femininity or masculinity of individual subjects or potential "patients," a number of follow-up experiments were conducted by Terman and Miles. In one experiment, teachers of eighth- and 10th-grade students who had taken the masculine/feminine test were asked to rate the femininity or masculinity of specific female and male students from their classes. This evaluation was entirely subjective on the part of the teachers. The correlations between the rating of the teachers and the masculine/feminine score of each student were "so low as to preclude any considerable correlation with the test scores" (Terman & Miles, 1936, p. 69).

In a second follow-up experiment, 82 male Stanford University students who had taken the masculine/feminine test were asked to rate their own masculinity in a number of areas. "The five ratings correlated as follows with total masculine/feminine score: childhood interests, 0.08; vocational interests, 0.06; use of leisure, 0.22; emotionality, 0.21; general make-up, 0.13; average of the five ratings, 0.19 ± 0.07" (Terman & Miles, 1936, p. 69). For this group, there was basically no relationship between how they judged themselves as masculine persons and the masculine/feminine score that they received from Terman and Miles' test.

Due to the failure of these two experiments to show any connection between the masculine/feminine scores of the subjects and how the subjects themselves and individuals who knew them well rated their femininity and masculinity, it became obvious that the usefulness of the masculine/feminine score would be greatly limited in a clinical setting for working with persons who rated highly deviant from the norm of their sex.

Terman and Miles developed a further experiment in which judges rated subjects on their possession of certain traits that were deemed to be, in general, feminine or masculine, rather than on an overall perception of the femininity or masculinity of the subject. Most of the results of this trial showed trends in the expected direction, but none of the results showed correlations any higher or more significant that the previous two experiments.

Terman and Miles were still convinced of the validity of their masculine/feminine test. However, they did concede that "this kind of validity becomes a rather empty merit unless the scores yielded by the test can be shown to have demonstrable correlates in behaviour" (Terman & Miles, 1936, p. 70). Even after repeated failures to show masculine/feminine differences between males and females, Terman and Miles continued to dismiss their own results and refused to accept that their experiments did not support their hypotheses.

Terman and Miles' masculine/feminine test explored myriad characteristics, traits, and behaviours. Some of the results in certain areas are interesting when a contemporary understanding of femininity as it is applied to female athletes is looked at more closely. One of the most important results of their research, but which they continually ignored, was that their results supported that socially embedded notions regarding the femininity or masculinity of people cannot be linked directly to their sex or to confining notions of compulsory gender designation.

Falsely Cementing the Masculine/Feminine Divide

Just as Terman and Miles rejected results that were in conflict with their consistent belief in male/female differences, we can see where contemporary notions of the exclusive assignment of certain characteristics to women or men might have originated or been solidified. For example, "if masculinity and femininity are thought of in relation to health, robust would be *popularly* regarded as the masculine and frail as the feminine adjective. Furthermore, a correlation between M-F score and physical build should be expected if masculinity-femininity is an expression of personality type grounded in innate constitution" (Terman & Miles, 1936, p, 80; emphasis added). Physical activity can be participated in by all, although the degree of participation might be affected by one's health, with higher levels of competitive and leisure participation requiring a more "robust" state of health. It can be seen how the association of robust health to the *masculine*, rather than to a more global *healthy* person, could have been and continues to be an underlying factor in many female athletes being labelled as mannish or masculine.

This supports my argument that femininity and masculinity (gender) are not biologically determined. Even in the case of physical size and stature, Terman and Miles' data showed that "one cannot infer that there is any dependable relationship between M-F score and the physical measurements in the case of women" (Terman & Miles, 1936, p. 84).

Their investigations did reveal that both female and male college athletes scored a high masculine rating. This was an obvious outcome, as the test instrument classified most sports as highly masculine indicators. Sports and activities were put on a scale from two to 24, with a rating of 13 or higher indicating greater preference by boys and therefore given a masculine (+) rating. Terman and Miles rated wrestling, football, and boxing at 20. This is not surprising, and even today women who participate in these activities are considered to be highly masculine. What was prejudicial to female athletes, even in the era of Terman and Miles' research, was that they rated bicycling (20), baseball (19), and basketball (16) as highly masculine activities, even though large numbers of women of numerous socio-economic statuses were enthusiastically participating in all of these activities (Terman & Miles, 1936, p. 12). It could be that the populations that Terman and Miles tested did support their gendered selection of activities, but a broader population of test subjects may have resulted in far more neutral ratings of these activities than the results supported.

Box 2.2

Thirteen proved to be a very unlucky number for females in the research of Terman and Miles where sports and games were concerned. They constructed a masculinity index of 90 games and activities rated by girls and boys. The constructed scale ranged from two to 24, where a score below 13 showed that the activities and games were preferred by girls and a score or 13 of higher indicated a preference by boys (see Table 2.1). (These ratings were determined in 1922, when opportunities for girls and boys to engage in large group play away from the home would have been very different.) The numbers would later be incorporated into the masculine/feminine scale that Terman and Miles created. Higher numbers contributed to a higher masculinity rating. Girls who preferred to play the activities with higher numbers would find themselves with more a masculine rating than other girls.

Table 2.1. The scores (in parentheses) of selected activities.

Charades (9)	Bicycle (20)
Jump Rope (9)	Kites (20)
Tennis (12)	Baseball (19)
Skating (10)	Soccer (17)
Dance (8)	Basketball (16)
Hopscotch (4)	Swimming (15)

It is interesting to note that volleyball got a rating of 13 and was the only team sport in this study to be equally enjoyed by both girls and boys. It is also somewhat remarkable that volleyball is the only team sport on the Olympic roster to be added for women and men at the same Olympic Summer Games (1964 Tokyo). The majority of activities that were initially anticipated to be preferred by girls were simple games or activities played by very young children, and rarely would fit into a more generalized category of sport. Activities that were rated as the "most feminine" (as opposed to of little interest to older children) included cat and mouse, farmer in the dell, London Bridge, and ring-around-the-rosy. It can easily be seen that girls and women who engaged in more active sports would have higher masculine scores on the masculine/feminine test than those who did not engage in these activities. It is possible that this was the genesis of the notion of the masculine female athlete.

Traits such as leadership, interests of the same and opposite sex, social interaction with the same and opposite sex, aggressiveness, objective-mindedness, effectiveness, and originality were all included in the assessment of femininity and masculinity on the Terman and Miles' test. "It was shown that the extremely low correlations found could be accounted for in large part by the unreliability of the ratings, but that that coefficients would still be low even if the M-F scores were correlated with the composite of the rating of several judges" (Terman & Miles, 1936, p. 89). Once again, the results of the testing showed a great overlap in trait associations among females and males, thus negating a biological connection with femininity and masculinity.

THE DANGER OF REJECTING DATA CONCLUSIONS

With respect to what is understood more generally to mean feminine or masculine, Terman and Miles conceded that these terms were likely to be understood differently by various raters (Terman & Miles, 1936). These aspects of personality were so poorly understood that many of the correlations (although too small to be statistically significant) were actually negative. "Would the conclusion be warranted that M-F scores are almost totally uncorrelated with any of the various aspects of behaviour which go to make up what is known as personality?" (Terman & Miles, 1936, p. 95). Terman and Miles were unwilling to accept this, even though their data repeatedly supported such a conclusion!

This deduction showed a bias that may exist in science itself. As Roszak stated in his critique of the objectivity of science, "the great pitfall for scientists is to believe they have a method that uniquely and automatically guarantees they will transcend prejudice and preconception. That is not methodology, but ideology, and in the grip of ideology even great scientists may blind themselves to truths that simple honesty and a modicum of humility would make obvious" (1999, p. 20). This statement is certainly reflective of the reaction of Terman and Miles to their research results. The rejection of their results and their continued insistence on the correctness of their hypotheses and method undoubtedly made a contribution to incorrect contemporary ideas regarding the essential natures of femininity and masculinity.

Many of the outcomes revealed through Terman and Miles' research with respect to masculine females and feminine males further supported their assumption that masculinity and femininity can be used to explain personality differences and environmental influences, but not biological necessity. For example, university males showed significant differences in the area of extroversion (deemed to be masculine) and introversion (deemed to be feminine). Terman and Miles reported that males who rated as extroverted "showed less vocational aptitude ... than the ... introvert men for the occupations of their choice" (1936, p. 100). These occupations included mechanical engineering, personal psychology, law, advertising, and architecture. The males who rated as introverts "chose journalism, law, authorship, medicine, advertising, executive administration, and insurance" (p. 100). If the introverts were rated as more feminine in the masculine/feminine score, this has interesting implications if one continues to desire to link femininity and masculinity to the sex of the individual—according to Terman and Miles, those men who rated as more feminine were also more successful in their professions and more self-directed than males who scored high (masculine) on the masculine/feminine test.

More Similar than Different

It is interesting to note other areas in which masculine/feminine scores revealed surprising results. "Intelligence, which is more closely related to scholarship than any other single factor, is positively correlated with mental masculinity in the case of college women but not to any appreciable extent in the case of men" (Terman & Miles, 1936, p. 106). In other words, the higher the level of scholarship attained by men, the lower their masculinity rating would be, even though higher intelligence was rated as a more masculine characteristic in both females and males! They also reported that "whatever the level of intelligence there is a considerable negative correlation between scholarship and mental masculinity in the case of men" (Terman & Miles, 1936, p. 108). This aspect of their research showed that as both women and men achieve higher levels of education, their personalities all converge onto a mean or a level of a more neutral personality according to Terman and Miles' masculine/feminine test.

As men became more educated, their appreciation for art, music, other cultures, food, and social interaction grew in a more feminine direction. As women received more education, their appreciation for general science, mathematics, engineering, mechanics, architecture, and other professionally based career choices increased their masculine/feminine scores toward the masculine. In other words, as people become more educated, regardless of their level of scholarship, their personalities broaden—not narrow—into balanced and well-adjusted characters, rather than ones that are one-sided or, as Terman and Miles might deduce, show increased deviance. Even though the balanced personality (containing what had been defined by masculine and feminine indicators) might be the desirable human condition, Terman and Miles and later researchers held fast to the constructed (and obviously incorrect in many aspects) notion of femininity as the female norm and masculinity as the male norm.

Terman and Miles constructed their research to attain this outcome. Even though their results showed that their basic premise was flawed, if not biased, they eschewed their results and tied gender (masculine/feminine) to the sex of the individual. Except in cases of extreme deviant personality types, the norms of femininity and masculinity as the standard personality type for females and males, respectively, was shown to be a false association through Terman and Miles' research. The link between sex and gender came to be "scientifically" linked through this work, even though no data supported this conclusion.

The relationship between a higher masculinity score and athletic participation in women is just one of the damaging outcomes of this research. It is true that at least one group of university female athletes tested by Terman and Miles had a masculine/feminine score that was at least one full standard deviation above the mean for that of university women in general (Terman & Miles, 1936). It must be remembered, however, that the test instrument defined sports as masculine. This has become much more than a catch-22 for all girls and women who today desire to be athletes, but who also see a need to define themselves and to be defined by others as feminine.

It can be seen that the earliest research on femininity and masculinity was not only flawed, but also biased in its basic construction and conclusions. The realities of the lives of most women and men during the years of Terman and Miles' research might support their basic research design. But the fact that Terman and Miles, even though they recognized that conditions of time and place would change the factors they defined as feminine and masculine, would not accept the results of their own research further shows that scientific bias has had a tremendous impact on how femininity and masculinity are defined, understood, and, most clearly, misunderstood. Terman and Miles cannot be blamed entirely for these attitudes, but had they accepted the results of their research and consequently rejected their initial hypothesis that males and females were more likely to have masculine and feminine personalities, respectively, then ideas regarding gender at the time might have changed. This may have had a very different impact on how gender is understood and applied today.

The application of a male-defined, male-relational construct of a concept called "femininity" to all females is one example of the patriarchal realities under which we all live. There are many problems for men in being defined by the rigid constructs of masculinity. However, the assumed superiority of masculinity in our culture privileges men above women within the confines in which they are forced to live.

The embodiment of femininity must be analyzed from a broader perspective than that of patriarchal power over women. Bordo (1989) argued that "the network of practices, institutions, and technologies that sustain positions of dominance and subordination within a particular domain" (p. 15) must be considered. Turner (1984) proposed that "patrism" is a word that more closely represents the current social reality than "patriarchy." Patrism is the systemic exclusion of women based on "prejudicial beliefs and practices of men toward women without the systematic backing of laws and politics" (Turner, 1984, p. 155). Patrism, then, would be the force that holds femininity in its rigid state for any particular time.

Chapter 3

THE SEXING OF FEMININITY

That was the prophetic warning Mary Shelley placed
at the heart of her tale. Science, though it champions
reason, can degenerate into mad rationality. For all its
idealism, it does not dependably elevate us above sin;
into the wrong hands, it may only enhance our power
to do evil. (Roszak, 1999, p. 3)

In the previous chapter I provided some evidence on how a failure to be
objective regarding one's scientific inquiry can lead to a rejection of the
results. In the case of Terman and Miles' work on feminine and masculine
personality types, this contributed to a reinforcement of beliefs that were
in fact objectively or "scientifically" questionable. Their published results
tied together the masculine/feminine personality with the male and
female person, respectively, even though the results of their data strongly
refuted this association. By actively rejecting many of the results of more
than a decade of research in favour of supporting their original position,
Terman and Miles may have helped to create a relationship between sex
and masculinity/femininity that they hoped their research would reveal,
but actually did not.

Even today there is spirited disagreement among various experts in
myriad disciplines regarding the nature versus nurture aspect of sex-based
behaviours (Hester, 2004). One danger of science, or of any research, is
to base the underlying question on a biased belief and not be willing to
change that position no matter what the data reveal. "Only when we
admit to this will we realize the extent to which we may unintentionally bias the interpretations of our observations, or the very nature of the
questions we ask" (Roszak, 1999, p. ix). I believe that this is the case for
our contemporary understandings of gender.

In reality, women present themselves in almost as many ways as there are women. Their interests, abilities, dreams, and aspirations are varied and cannot be contained within fashionable notions of a range of characteristics defined as feminine. Yet most people can readily identify what is acceptable, or at the very least accepted, as femininity according to today's North American standards. Many women aspire to present themselves according to these beliefs. Most men expect women to do exactly that. Most women expect this as well, regardless of whatever "masculine" characteristics they also present, but disregard as masculine.

The first four decades of femininity/masculinity research following the work of Terman and Miles was primarily concerned with the variety of interests of female and male persons. This work continued to habitually link socially constructed aspects of personality to a particular sex (Helgeson, 1994). Items that indicated interest that apparently revealed differences between the genders were labelled feminine and masculine, regardless of the socio-cultural context or construct. This followed directly from the work of Terman and Miles, which focused on interests, knowledge, and abilities and created measures that were strictly one-dimensional—either feminine or masculine—after having eliminated all of the factors that showed no sex preferences or differences.

The persistent belief that females and males are in every sense opposite sexes, and are inextricably tied to femininity and masculinity, is one of the biases created and maintained through science that has been based more on socio-historical beliefs than on biological reality. In my opinion, the attempt to measure or define femininity and masculinity over the past 80 years may be one of the more misguided research quests. The need to measure and define socially constructed and continually changing factors of human beings may have done more to restrict personal and social growth than any other injudicious pursuit regarding female and male differences.

I propose that the hunt for female/male similarities, or the obviously polygendered state of being, may be a far more beneficial social project. Understanding the ways in which most of us share those qualities defined as feminine and those defined as masculine may help us to overcome the power struggles and systemic discriminatory practices that, in essence, restrict the lives of all women and men. The polygendered nature of people might be seen as an obvious and desirable condition. This might have been one of the greatest benefits of Terman and Miles' research if they had not discarded the countless similarities that they found in people in their particular time and culture. Nearly a century of research that has followed this early work might have been directed to bringing people closer together, rather than creating a dichotomous wedge and driving them apart through definitions that seem to have been created by the research in the first place. It is also possible, however, that the androcentric and patriarchal structures upon which our socio-cultural forms are based would have prevented this advancement. It is difficult enough today to achieve gender equity. A century ago it would have been a nearly impossible quest to propose, even by the early feminists who were attempting to take very small steps toward women's equality.

One of the most confounding results of Terman and Miles' failure to ignore their personal biases in the interpretation of their research results was the "scientific" wedding of one's sex to a gendered personality type. Even though Terman and Miles found many males with a strong association to feminine personality types and many females with a strong association to masculine personality types, they continued to separate personality type (feminine or masculine) along a rigid, two-sex-only divide. The notion of deviance, rather than personality type, apparently became frequently sidetracked in the interpretation of their research and the re-telling of their results.

Over time, as can be ascertained from more contemporary gender research that utilizes and oft-times incorrectly applies the research of Terman and Miles, the masculine/feminine personality type has morphed into what is today a code of gender behaviour called feminine or masculine and is inextricably linked to the sex of the female or male person. Terman and Miles did not invent gender, but as pioneers in research that attempted to tie masculinity and femininity to male and female persons, respectively, they laid a foundation (however false, as revealed by their data) for future social and natural scientists upon which to build.

"THE TIMES THEY ARE A-CHANGIN'" ... GENDER IS NOT

The rigidity of Victorian-era sex roles and differences in female/male knowledge, skills, experiences, and expectations led to differences in interests and behaviours not only between women and men, but also between women and men of differing ethnic, racial, and socio-economic classes. These differences would have been common during the decade of Terman and Miles' data collection. They were taken as natural/biological, despite the researchers' acknowledgement that these factors change over time and place. Still, Terman and Miles built upon them for their studies of sex and personality.

The establishment of fundamental female femininity and male masculinity became indisputable through the less than objective authority of science as it was applied here. The boundaries that grew up around the constructs of femininity and masculinity contributed to the androcentric, gender-polarized, and biologically essentialist lenses that were and continue to be used to view and interpret gender as we understand it today. Had Terman and Miles been somewhat more objective and accepting of the results they obtained, the average person might simply be accepted as possessing both feminine and masculine traits or being polygendered. The fault in today's understanding of gender does not lie with Terman and Miles, who simply wanted to find a method for identifying the deviant personality, but rather with a need to have our most basic beliefs and interpretations of the world validated by science, even if that science is somehow flawed. The need for a book such as this one, which explores the conflicts of gender as lived by many female athletes, would be unnecessary.

Gender Hegemony

The construction of gender and an increasingly strong common-sense belief in its naturalness is one site of conflict within a culture. It has become a defining and restrictive factor in the lives of many people. Inflexible interpretations of what women and men are and can be has contributed to a power imbalance among individuals and groups. This is particularly true for many individuals who question their basic sex assignment or who reject the structured confines of compulsory femininity or masculinity and the performative requirements of living such a gender assignment.

The struggle for meaning, not only of femininity and masculinity, but also of personhood, is central to this conflict (Miller & Penz, 1991). Through constructs of femininity and masculinity, social convention and expectation constrains and dictates how the body is seen and valued. Culture acts to construct the looks and uses of the body, regardless of genetics and physiology. One outcome of these restrictions is that although women are as biologically capable of sport participation as men, the cultural meaning of "woman" removes athletic competence from the narrow range of characteristics that are approved of as feminine. This lays the foundation for a struggle between the physical appearance and behaviour requirements for the feminine = woman and the appearance/ performance nature of those physical activities and sports for women that are traditionally defined as masculine.

The greater acceptance of sports participation by girls and women in the 21st century challenges this basic designation. But there is a narrow limit to the extent that athletic competence and the physical appearance of an athletic body fits into the constraints of femininity. The fact that these are now indicated as acceptable traits within the construction of femininity at all shows the constructed nature of gender and the reality of a polygendered nature for most individuals. The acceptance of the polygendered person is required for the emancipation of all people from the confines of compulsory gender performance. In either case, the elimination of gender altogether or the acceptance of being polygendered will permit us to take a step down this path and more fully recognize and accept our complete selves.

Feminist analyses of gender and power relations between the sexes contend that discourses of the female body, the requisite display of femininity, are primarily expressions of male interests and male concerns (de Beauvoir, 1952). "The hegemonic success of these discourses means that phallocentric and patriarchal meanings threaten to pre-empt all other, more positive readings of women's bodies" (Miller & Penz, 1991, p. 148). The physical appearance of women's bodies is one of the most visible and recognizable factors of compliance with the rules of femininity.

A Contemporary Problem: Masculinizing Sport

The expression of physical competence in most sports remains a quick indicator of non-compliance with the rules of femininity. Thus, positive readings of women's bodies, and therefore of women, are not likely to be found within the contextual medium of sport. "Historical analyses have shown how the exclusion of women from sport was an instance of male control over female bodies that enables the social as well as the physical domination by men of women" (Theberge, 1991, p. 128). This is further demonstrated through the inferior valuing of even culturally normative activities for girls and women below the sports and games of males or women's participation in more contemporary "non-gendered" sports.

As a consequence of the research on gender that took place over much of the last century (which was very likely also biased in terms of race and class), the concepts of femininity and masculinity have come to be understood as mutually exclusive. Masculinity is established and defined as the positive, active, and instrumental characteristics of men, while femininity is defined as the normative opposite: passive, receptive, and emotional. Whatever masculinity is, femininity is not. Masculinity is valued more highly than femininity because masculinity is translated as the normative state of men. In a patriarchal structure, this would always be considered the more valued and valuable condition.

Challenging the Gendering of Sport

The embedded meaning of what it is to be feminine is immediately challenged by women who wish to participate in activities or professions that are defined as masculine, including sports. These are activities that are measured, and most highly valued, in terms of physical competence, strength, power, and aggression. Not only do these factors not fall within the narrow construction of femininity, they are celebrated as masculine. The notion of female frailty and the natural inclination of all women to maternity as a woman's highest function are myths that kept most post-pubertal women from participation in any kind of sporting or skill-based physical activity until late in the 20th century (Daniels & Winter, 1989).

The early organization of sporting activities for women, where they existed, was predicated upon the myth that sport is a masculine domain and is therefore appropriate only for males. The modification of rules that limited exertion or physical contact among players was a common tactic instituted to "feminize" games and make them more acceptable for female participants. Although it could be argued that contemporary sporting organization is no longer founded on such gender bias, some sports still maintain different rules for females. For example, females are prohibited from competing in some sports at the World and Olympic levels, and sex testing of female athletes (also known as gender verification) still exists in the regulations and practices of certain international sports' governing bodies. The uncertain or reluctant acceptance of certain sports for women, such as bodybuilding, rugby, boxing, and certain extreme sports, begs the question of the femininity of the participants.

Through the construction of femininity and adherence to its changes over time, women are directed and compelled to display themselves and

72

to behave in ways that become a compulsory foundation for acceptance in a patriarchal society. Thus, the primary factors of femininity in any age are those that produce a female body that is sexually desirable to the dominant masculine structure of the culture. These factors do change depending on the various social and economic realities of the time.

In pre-industrial times, a white woman who was heavier represented someone whose father or husband could provide food. Therefore, her weight was a signifier of his success. In the Victorian era, the prototypical white woman was thin and pale, which indicated that she was a woman of leisure who did not need to labour in the sun. This was also a signifier of the status of her husband. Today, the trophy wife is a woman who is fit, tanned, and young-looking regardless of her age. These are signifiers of power—not of the woman herself, but of the man on whose arm she is seen to reside. The power of this woman lies in her mastery of compulsory gender performativity.

Obviously the majority of women, regardless of race, do not fit into these constructions, but the willingness of many to attempt to "perform" such a feminine presentation is an indicator of the power of gender conformity in the lives of women who desire a male-stream normality in their lives. In all of these cases, the racial and ethnic variability among women demonstrates the constructed nature of gender and how femininity is defined and valued differently among different women. Therefore, this "production of bodies is a means to constitution of social beings and social relations" (Theberge, 1991, p. 126).

The Power of Gender

Socio-cultural relations between the sexes are not based on biological (sex) differences, but on the power imbalance imposed through the construction of women and men through femininity and masculinity (gender). Analyses of this power imbalance, which is supported through androcentrism, gender polarization, and biological essentialism, underlie a great deal of feminist and cultural critique that has taken place over the past half-century. Foucault, a French philosopher, wrote a great deal about power and sexuality. His writings strongly influence contemporary sociological inquiry. However, in a critique of Foucault and his analysis of power and the body, Bartky (1988) wrote that "Foucault ... is blind to those disciplines that produce a modality of embodiment that is particularly feminine. To overlook the forms of subjection that engender the feminine body is to perpetuate the silence and powerlessness of those upon whom the disciplines have been imposed" (p. 64).

This "power over" women is clearly displayed through the body and its demonstrated uses. The physical compliance to femininity is a visual clue to the control and domination of women under patriarchal structures. The construction of femininity, the construction of women's bodies, is a stronger socializing agent than, for example, race or class, because all women must conform to a standardized ideal that is homogenizing and normalizing (Bordo, 1989). What a woman should look like and how a woman looks are among the strongest indicators of femininity and the success of the patriarchal hegemonic control of women. There are variations on this code among individuals of differing races and ethnicities, but within these differences there is still an understanding that compliance to a specific physical presentation is demanded.

Beginning around the turn of the current millennium, some specific muscularity and sporting competence was added to the range of acceptable feminine appearance standards. As bias and acceptance change so do the requirements of femininity, but many of the performative constraints have remained the same or increased. There are strict limits to the extent of these factors. Their application is applied more toward how the female body looks than to what can be done with that body. However, how the female body is to look impacts directly on its possessor's ability to participate and be successful in many sports and physical activities.

STEREOTYPES OF GENDER

Beginning in the 1970s, the *desirability* of characteristics ascribed to women and men was added to the research work around gender (Bem, 1993). Feminine/masculine characteristics, which were still viewed as sex-linked, were placed on opposite ends of a continuum. The effect of eliminating overlap in human interests and experiences (which was the basis of creating the masculine/feminine test instruments of Terman and Miles) was not questioned or corrected, but perpetuated through androcentric bias. Now the addition of the desirability of these interests for females or males was bonded to the bias. The research continued to be problematic because sex and gender were invariably linked by the test subjects and often not controlled for by the researchers.

The conflation of gender and sex continues to be a barrier to the study of femininity and masculinity and the application of gender to various human activities, including sport. Gendex, the perceived conflation of gender and sex, becomes strengthened as the conventional divide between femininity and masculinity is widened. This is one reason why it is important to keep sex and gender separate. As was reported earlier, biology defines many more than two sexes. If one's sex and gender are essentially linked, more than two genders would be required to characterize them all.

BOX 3.1

When gender and sex become linked as either different words for the same construct or as a cause and effect or essentialist relationship, the ramifications go beyond the characteristic gender- or sex-role expectations. Particular difficulties arise for female athletes when constructed gender roles/expectations (girl-appropriate dress and activities) and hetero-normative sex roles/expectations (all females aspire to be mothers) become conflated. Victorian notions of vitalism required females to temper their physical activities so as not to interfere with any potential childbirth concerns. It may seem that this reference is horribly out of date. However, young girls today frequently use the excuse of menstruation to avoid physical activity and pregnant women are often fearful of any exercise during their pregnancy. These ideas are often the result of a lack of education regarding the normal functioning of a woman's body, but they have their roots in an overly cautious bio-history related to particular white women. The word "gendex" reinforces an outdated, two-only gender designation with a two-only sex hetero-normativity. The mythologies perpetrated through gendex are restrictive. Keeping gender and sex as separate entities will make it easier to bring about changes in either or both constructs to the advantage of all individuals.

Because gender is socially constructed, as can be determined by its changes over time and place, then as the circumstances of time and place change there must be a means for greater acceptance of the complexity of each individual to be expressed. Regardless of the sex designation of a person, their personality must be appropriate to whomever they choose to be. Contemporary restrictions based on a rigid gender binary no longer serve individuals or social structures.

However, research continues to be undertaken on femininity and masculinity. It is apparent that arguments suggesting the total elimination of these constructs are not likely to be successful (Butler, 2004). We are increasingly bombarded with images and messages that not only further "naturalize" gender, but which attempt to inextricably link gender to sex. Therefore, knowing as much as we can about how individuals define femininity and masculinity, how they attribute these factors to actual persons and themselves, and how these perceptions constrain our lives is important in understanding gender power relations and how women and men do and can live in North American society. It is also important if a change to a polygendered acceptance of women and men is to be used to broaden the scope of personal diversity. This may result in a reduction in the power of gender and gender-performative requirements for all individuals.

Helgeson's (1994) work on femininity and masculinity, which attempted to discover lay perceptions of the prototypical dimensions of femininity and masculinity, provides a useful basis from which to look at the issues of femininity, women, and sport. Helgeson was interested in discovering whether her subjects could identify feminine and masculine females, feminine and masculine males, and the androgynous person. Attempting to control for perceptions of sex, subjects were asked to identify factors or characteristics of feminine females, feminine males, masculine females, masculine males, and both feminine and masculine persons. Due to the inability of the subjects to separate feminine and masculine persons from females and males, Helgeson dropped these categories from further analysis. It is interesting that the subjects in this study were able to classify individuals into feminine males and masculine females as well as the more traditional feminine females and masculine males, but were unable to self-define the "generic" nongendered or androgynous person.

Table 3.1 contains the prototypical features of femininity as Helgeson's subjects, university-aged students and their parents, defined them. The subjects were asked to construct their own lists of words (as opposed to the techniques used earlier by Terman and Miles of providing subjects with the word choices). Analysis of the resulting word lists showed that the responses could be separated into three general categories: interests, appearance, and behaviours (personality).

Table 3.1. Prototypical features of femininity.

1.	P	CARING	37.5	P	Homosexual	48.3
2.	P	Good manners	35.9	A	Thin	46.6
3.	A	Wears a dress	34.4	P	Insecure	31.0
4.	A	Long hair	29.7	P	Emotional	31.0
5.	A	WELL-DRESSED	28.1	I	LIKES ART	29.3
6.	P	Self-confident	26.6	P	CARING	27.6
7.	I	CONCERN W/ APPEARANCE	26.6	I	Women friends	27.6
8.	A	Attractive	23.4	A	WELL-DRESSED	25.9
9.	P	SOFT-SPOKEN	23.4	I	Dislikes sports	24.1
10.	I	Family-oriented	21.9	I	Interest in fashion	22.4
11.	I	Likes music	21.9	A	Gesticulates	22.4
12.	P	SOCIAL	21.9	I	CONCERN W/ APPEARANCE	22.4
13.	A	Make-up well done	20.3	A	High-pitched voice	20.7
14.	P	DELICATE	20.3	P	SOCIAL	19.0
15.	A	Small	20.3	P	SHY	19.0
16.	P	SHY	18.8	P	DELICATE	17.2
17.	I	LIKES ART	18.8	P	Weak	17.2
18.	I	Books	17.2	P	Sensitive	17.2
19.	P	Friendly	17.2	P	Creative	15.5
20.	P	Intelligent	15.6	P	Talkative	15.5
21.	P	Traditional	15.6	P	SOFT-SPOKEN	15.5
22.	A	Smiles	15.6			
23.	A	Manicured nails	15.6			

A = appearance; I = interest; P = personality. In Helgeson's tables, characteristics in capital letters were found on both feminine and masculine lists. The number following the feature is a weighting of commonality, not a percentage of subjects' inclusion, as some features represent a selected term that is representative of multiple responses by subjects.

One factor that will be discussed in more detail in Chapter 5, but is of note here, is that of appearance. Although both the prototypical feminine female and feminine male were somewhat defined by appearance, the difference in the number of appearance features is interesting. Eight of the 23 factors (35%) identified for the feminine female, but only four of the 21 factors (19%) identified for the feminine male relate to appearance. From this, we can question whether it is actually the femininity or the sex of the individual that is more of concern when appearance is in question. The embodiment of the feminine female plays a major role in her construction.

Sport and/or physical activity do not appear as an interest of the feminine female. The dislike of sport by the feminine male is the only characteristic that is stated in such strongly negative terms for any category of females or males in Helgeson's data. This will be an important factor to recall when issues of hetero-sexism are introduced into the analysis of women, sport, and femininity.

It is interesting to note that except for the two strongest indicators of the feminine male as defined by Helgeson's subjects (homosexual and thin), there is not a great range among the weightings of any of the characteristics on either feminine list. When compared to the weightings of the masculine male and masculine female (see Table 3.2), it can be seen that there is not an outstanding factor or groups of factors that heavily stereotypes the feminine female or feminine male.

The prototypical features of the masculine male and masculine female are found in Table 3.2. From these data, it can be easily seen that the female athlete faces a terrific and terrible challenge in the femininity game, even though sport has become a most consuming passion for myriad girls and women in North America today. The major identifying factor of the masculine female was "likes sports" (Helgeson, 1994, p. 664). The weightings of "likes sports" (64.7) and "muscular" (50.6), the top two stereotypical indicators of the masculine female, show considerably more importance to the test subjects than any factors given for the feminine female or feminine male.

Analysis of the results for appearance factors for the masculine female and masculine male is more problematic than for the feminine female and feminine male. Seven appearance factors (32%) for the masculine male are identified. Interestingly, this equates to the amount for the feminine female. Although it may be assumed that the gendered appearance of females is more important than the gendered appearance of males, in this study at least there is a more equal application in the importance of appearance for both the feminine females and the masculine males. This may be a consequence of the growing media attention and product development targeted to men, but these still come nowhere near the attention to appearance that is targeted toward women.

A considerable problem for the female athlete lies in the perception of the appearance or look of the prototypical masculine female. The masculine

Table 3.2. Prototypical features of masculinity.

1.	A	MUSCULAR	71.4	I	LIKES SPORTS	64.7
2.	I	LIKES SPORTS	52.9	A	MUSCULAR	50.6
3.	A	TALL	51.4	A	Short hair	37.1
4.	P	SELF-CONFIDENT	50.0	A	Dress casually	38.8
5.	A	Dark	30.0	A	Deep voice	30.6
6.	P	Arrogant	28.6	P	SELF-CONFIDENT	30.6
7.	I	Dates women	28.6	P	Aggressive	30.6
8.	I	FITNESS	27.1	A	No make-up	30.6
9.	P	Caring	25.7	A	Big	24.7
10.	A	Attractive	21.4	I	FITNESS	23.5
11.	P	Strong convictions	21.4	P	Homosexual	20.0
12.	I	CONCERN W/WORK	20.0	P	DOMINANT	16.5
13.	P	Intelligent	18.6	A	TALL	14.1
14.	P	DOMINANT	15.7	I	CONCERN W/WORK	14.1
15.	P	Emotionally strong	14.3	I	CARS	14.1
16.	A	HAIRY FACE	14.3	I	Drinks alcohol	14.1
17.	I	CARS	14.3	I	Men friends	14.1
18.	P	Honest/fair	14.3	A	Ugly	14.1
19.	P	Intense/persistent	14.3	A	HAIRY FACE	12.9
20.	P	Good manners	14.3	P	Not caring	11.8
21.	A	Rugged	14.3	A	Fat	11.8
22.	A	Well-dressed	14.3			

A = appearance; I = interest; P = personality. See notes for Table 3.1.

female has 10 defining factors that relate to appearance (48%)—the most for any group. Except possibly for a few emancipated women, most females would see almost all of these appearance factors as negative. A toned body is something that has become accepted for the prototypical female over the past few years, but the word "muscular" implies something beyond acceptable femininity, even though "fitness" might be more likely to appear today on the feminine female list. It is the whole package of the stereotype presented for the masculine female that becomes problematic for many of today's women—not just female athletes.

ARE YOU A BOY OR A GIRL?

"Physical appearance is that component of masculinity and femininity that is accrued earliest in life" (Helgeson, 1994, p. 658). Because of this, the actual physical appearance of a person is likely to implicate other components. This establishes a very shaky foundation for female athletes who, by the definition set here and reported in numerous books and research articles, are often labelled as masculine females—whose overall evaluation is based more on appearance than any other factor.

Having located Helgeson's article on the prototypes and dimensions of masculinity and femininity shortly after it was published, I began a casual experiment to determine if my university-aged students held similar perceptions of the feminine female, male, and person and the masculine female, male, and person. I asked my students to construct lists of words that described or defined for themselves the categories of individuals indicated above. As with the original experiment, my students were not very successful in identifying the feminine or masculine androgynous person, so after a couple of semesters I dropped these categories from my inquiry. For over 15 years I have undertaken this process in every one of my courses. This adds up to thousands of students. There have been very few overall differences in any of the lists.

One significant aspect that has emerged from this casual experiment lies with the (dis)comfort level of the female students in pinpointing which of the lists they would most like to be identified with. The men almost all want to be seen as masculine males, regardless of their sexual orientation. This continues to be true even as this list has been modified over the years to include terms as "bully," "drunk," and "steroid user"! My students are aware that the prototypical lists they create are stereotypes, so the men are willing to associate themselves with the potential negativities to acquire the positive masculine male (read: heterosexual) label.

My female students have had a much more difficult time identifying which list they would place themselves on. The highly negatively perceived masculine female list, which has become more derogatory in its terminology over the years (including "butch," "dyke," "ball breaker," and "man hater") does not attract them. But neither does the feminine female list. It is important to note here that most of my teaching takes place in a department of kinesiology and physical education, and the majority of my students, female and male, are athletes or are very involved with physical activity. Even though "likes sports," "fitness," muscular," "assertive," and "self-confident" almost always appear on their classmates' constructions of the masculine female prototype, these women reject this label due to the implied lesbian association for not only masculine women, but also for female athletes. Interestingly, the female students often refuse to choose any of the four lists as representative of themselves due to the perceived meaning of the label regardless of the list's contents. Although I applaud this as feminist resistance, I strongly doubt that many of the students would accept this label for themselves either.

The continuing responses of my students to this activity indicate that gendered stereotypes of women and men are alive and well, and that they continue to have the same dichotomous and hierarchical positioning as any traditional interpretation even as the characteristics change. Although the male students often reject a number of the factors that they themselves include in the masculine male prototype, they are quite unified in labelling themselves as masculine males. Any other choice for the men is seen as admitting to having or to liking some femininity in their personalities and to most, at least publicly, this is unacceptable. Many men will admit to preferring some of the characteristics on the feminine male list over some of those on the masculine male list, but rarely admit to preferring characteristics on either of the female lists. The most flexibility shown by some of the men in rejecting a masculine male label is to side with the females in not accepting any of the stereotypes for themselves. This has been a rare occurrence.

The strong position of the women in rejecting all of the categories that they and their peers have created shows that they reject the rigid confines of socially embedded notions of femininity. It also shows that any construction listed as masculine is not for them either, even though a number of the masculine characteristics are needed for successful athletic participation. The refusal of these women to identify with a prototypical feminine or masculine label is a more recent phenomenon, occurring in only the past four or five years. They want to be seen as feminine in whatever construction they have made of that for themselves. But they are not willing to give up those parts of themselves that are traditionally seen to be masculine in order to "qualify" for their preferred label.

The dilemma of femininity and the strength of the concept of gendex are obvious with these university-aged female students/athletes. "... Individuals have a preference for the groups to which they belong ... and they perceive this group at a higher social level than and possibly superior to other groups" (Angelini, 2008, p. 134). Thus, my students were giving preference to their perception of their in-group, even at the expense of rejecting femininity, which, consciously, they were unwilling to do at least in the classroom environment.

We might hope that how we feel about ourselves as women will have the greatest positive effect on our self-esteem and our choices. However, and unfortunately, the desire to belong, to be accepted, is likely to be a stronger determinant. The wish to be viewed as a feminine female, and therefore more "normal," might ultimately be a stronger agent in guiding women's choices than their desire to be physically active/successful in sport and, ultimately, physically fit and healthy over their lifetime. According to gender schema theory, sex-typed people are motivated to choose behaviours that conform to and avoid behaviours that violate the cultural norms of femininity and masculinity (Matteo, 1988, p. 42). Cross-sex-typed people, however, may be equally aware of gender and conform to gender norms, not because they believe that is how the world should be, but because they have learned that to do otherwise is to risk being labelled as "gender deviant" (Matteo, 1988, p. 56). Female athletes, by traditional definition, are cross-sex-typed in at least their interest in participating in sports. This is particularly true if the sports they choose are culturally normative activities for males. The gender deviancy of women in sport, or those who want to be physically active, is particularly problematic.

Over the last four decades, the public perception of the importance of sports for girls and women has grown dramatically; right along with the exponential rise in their level of participation. However, the confines of compulsory heterosexual femininity have also grown. The explosion of articles in women's magazines that suggest exercise and work-out routines is staggering. But these same magazines contain parallel articles on weight loss, diets, plastic surgery, make-up, dress, and behaviour. A narrow form of the physically fit female has been inserted into the popular perception of "today's woman," but the female athlete still must continue to conform to an ever-narrowing image of the media-genic glamazon.[2]

BOX 3.2

Mediation is a process that intervenes or interposes between two or more positions. The cultural form we know as "media" derives from this term. Rarely are we exposed to neutrality through the media. Left/centre/right political affiliations inform the spin used in the creation and delivery of news stories. Magazines and internet sites are created to attract specific target demographic groups who are then enticed to consume stories, images, advertisements, and ideas put forth by the creators/editors (= mediators) of the products. Sports are among the most mediated of all forms. The sports we can view on television or streaming video (for "free" or for an additional costs for access) or read about in newspapers or sports magazines, the athletes who are highlighted during and after the games, and the camera angles that are shown to viewers are all carefully planned and packaged for the consumer of sports.

Another mediated aspect of sport is the images that we see of athletes in various forms of advertisements. Compared to male athletes, there is limited visual access to female athletes through televised commercials or magazine advertisements. There is an even greater limit to the variety of female athletes who are selected for these productions. The term "media-genic" refers to a woman whose looks are representative of hetero-sexy feminine ideals and, very importantly, which translate well into the medium of production. If a woman does not look good on film, she has less chance of being seen in commercials or advertisements.

"Glamazon" is a mixture of "glamorous" and "Amazon." The Amazons, from Greek mythology, were supposedly a nation of female warriors. Certain types of female athletes have frequently been referred to as Amazons, but not in a complimentary way. Generally, the term is meant to indicate the large size and unusual strength (masculinity) of the female athlete. The word "glamazon" celebrates a particularly attractive female athlete who is likely to have all of the media-genic qualities needed to entice a viewer to buy whatever product her image is endorsing. Rarely can the female athlete be distinguished from the other hegemonically beautiful women who pose in these advertisements. Even though she may have been selected because she is an athlete, her athleticism is often negated through the mediated construction of her image.

DEALING WITH GENDER VIOLATIONS

For children and adolescents, the need for peer approval might be the strongest factor in their choices of activities and presentation of self. Gender-based expectations develop very early in life. Children as young as five years of age can interpret deviations in gender stereotypes—including behaviours, traits, and roles—as wrong (Cann, 1993). Children are also very aware of culturally normative stereotypical girl/boy differences in activities and gendered abilities. The rise in bullying activity in schools is partly due to children's rigid acceptance of gender norms and an increasing intolerance for any imagined or perceived gender deviance.

Children are often wise beyond their years, however, and although children learn very early on the desirable characteristics of femininity and masculinity and the importance of adherence to them, children's ratings of personality traits reflect strong biases in favour of their own sex. When children of eight to 10 years of age were asked to define traditional feminine and masculine personality traits as positive or negative, they assigned more positive and fewer negative traits to their own sex (Powlishta, 1995), regardless of the standard acceptability of the traits as either feminine or masculine. The notion of "opposite" sex refers to more than just biology. The gendering of interests, abilities, and other characteristics is inherently understood as inequitable, at least for oneself. However, to reject the dichotomy is to place oneself in a position of great discomfort and ostracism, or of a potential physical, psychological, and/or sexually violent response.

In-group biases also apply to individuality. Individuals are more likely to see and accept variability in their own behaviours than in those of others. This is one strategy that assists the female athlete in valuing her athleticism as positive, even while negotiating the rocky terrain of femininity. What becomes problematic, especially for the female athlete, is that "both men and women focused on physical attributes when describing others and focused on current roles and characteristics demanded by roles when describing themselves" (Helgeson, 1994, p. 656). Once again, the female athlete is placed in a position where she is judged by others on her physical appearance, which in many circumstances will be interpreted as masculine.

Thus we come full circle. We learn early that deviations from expected gender roles are perceived not just as different but as wrong. We see that both women and men judge others more on appearance than on other gender factors. And it is perceived that women who like sports are considered to be masculine, and their identifying physical attributes as unattractive or negative.

Traditional and contemporary acceptance of femininity is problematic for all women, regardless of their level of understanding of the impact of gender in their lives. To be feminine is to be female. To be feminine is to be not masculine. To be feminine is to be defined in relation to contemporary notions of what it means to be male in a patriarchal society. This constrains males as well as females, but females and femininity are situated in a secondary position of impor- tance to anything identified as male or masculine.

Chapter 4

THE EMBODIMENT OF FEMININITY

It takes little effort these days to recognize the dis-
tortions wrought by gender bias in our society. Even
scientists blush to realize no more than a few generations ago, when talents as bright as Marie Curie were
being denied an education, their male chauvinist
predecessors regarded women as frail, small brained,
hysterical, squeamish little things unsuited to the
laboratory or the classroom. (Roszak, 1999, p. 13)

The previous chapters present some ontological assumptions and
theoretical underpinnings for our contemporary understandings
and acceptance of gender stereotypes. The next three chapters will
further explore femininity, its components, and its performative
requirements for today's female athletes. In particular, I will base my
analysis of contemporary understandings of femininity and feminine
performativity on a proposed analytical structure put forward by Sandra
Bartky (1988). I find her breakdown of contemporary understandings
of femininity, particularly the embodiment of femininity, into
three specific categories to be especially useful in the analysis of the
dilemma of femininity/gender and the female athlete. These categories
encompass: 1) a body of particular size and configuration; 2) specific
gestures, postures, and movements appropriate to a feminine woman;
and 3) outward decoration of the body (Bartky, 1988).

In essence, the next three chapters explore the female body and how
femininity can be inscribed upon that body. "Our everyday life is dominated by the details of our corporeal existence" (Turner, 1984, p. 1). This
analysis of the body goes beyond concerns for basic survival needs such as
food and shelter. Women are often defined by and frequently judged on

their bodies. How a woman performs her femininity in this context can be a measure of her success as a human being, regardless of the skills and talents she possesses. As Turner (1984) further stated: "The body is at once the most solid, the most elusive, illusory, concrete, metaphorical, ever present, and ever distant thing—a site, an instrument, an environment, a singularity and a multiplicity" (p. 8). Here, Turner is expressing how the body is perceived beyond the biological. An understanding of femininity must include an understanding of how the actual embodiment of females lies far beyond the physical body. The cultures and various sub-cultures that we all inhabit have definitions and expectations of women's roles and presentations that are expected to be followed.[1] Ignoring or intentionally or unintentionally rebelling against these cultural expectations can bring censure in a variety of forms.

As women, we can never leave our female bodies behind.[2] In many ways, we are our bodies. We cannot go anywhere without them. We must carefully attend to what they look like, how we dress them, how we move them, what we feed them—especially in public—and how our compliance to contemporary standards of femininity confirm or betray our status as women in these communities. This is not easy. It is especially difficult as many of us move through a variety of communities every day. We must learn the rules of each setting and perform them to an acceptable level in order to continue to be seen as a welcome member of that community.[3] Many of us consciously reject the rules of gender and femininity set out by the various communities through which we live our lives. A tremendous amount of energy can be expended through this choice, as our rejection often has self-imposed limits that must be constantly evaluated, negotiated, and changed in accordance with some imposed standard that we choose to resist.

THE FEMALE ATHLETE AS FEMININE

An additional burden on the female athlete within this negotiating process is the fact that she may be engaged in activities that have a traditional designation as masculine, even though women have been active participants throughout the history of many of these activities (e.g., basketball, baseball, ice hockey). One factor for any level of successful execution of the required motor skills and performance objectives of her sport is that she will most likely have physical attributes that are also traditionally designated as masculine.[4] Although contemporary Western definitions of femininity include a body that has good muscle tone and general fitness, the female athlete often develops a body that crosses an invisible line that separates the feminine body from the masculine one.

Muscular development, which is a requirement for the successful performance of sport-specific skills, and is therefore necessary for participation in sporting activities, places the female athlete in a problematic position. She will have some of the attributes required for meeting contemporary hegemonic feminine presentation. At the same time, she will demonstrate a strong and muscular physique that not only equates with masculinity, but is one of the most obvious and accepted signifiers of masculinity. This paradox is not lost on females of almost any age, and can become an insurmountable barrier to the entry of some girls and women into physical activity of any kind, let alone competitive sports. The "tensions between the sporting body and the social body" (Krane et al., 2004, p. 317) are ever present in many female athletes, even as they desire to continue their participation and improvement in their chosen sports.

The invisible line that separates feminine muscle from masculine muscle is not based in physiology but in the socio-cultural meanings given to muscles (Choi, 2000). This is more obvious when one realizes that this line moves according to which female athletes are being judged on their level of muscularity, and therefore masculinity. For example, gymnasts and figure skaters are, pound for pound, among the strongest of all athletes, male or female. The muscular development and power of these athletes is obvious. Yet at the same time, it also seems to be invisible. The gymnast and the figure skater participate in culturally normative activities for females. The mediated focus of these sports is directed toward the grace and aesthetics of the movements rather than the strength and power they require.

Although these activities are recognized as sports (masculine), they are placed into a special category of activities that are labelled feminine and are, therefore, made acceptable for females.[5] Because these activities are labelled "feminine," the athletes who participate in them are also seen to be feminine. This does not remove the gymnast or figure skater from the critical evaluation of her as an embodied and sexualized female, but her participation in feminine sports filters the lens through which she is seen and hides the obviously masculinized body she possesses beneath her sparkles and flesh-coloured uniform inserts. Labelling certain activities as feminine, regardless of the strength and power required to engage in them, automatically feminizes the participant on a number of levels.

This de facto feminization of the participants in these feminine sports functions to feminize males who wish to engage in these sports. The reality of these "feminine" sports is that they are truly polygendered, as are the female and male athletes who participate in them. They require physical attributes and movement forms that are both highly feminine and highly masculine in their constructed designations. The cultural lens through which gender-appropriate activities for girls are filtered is what separates the activity from the realm of "real" sport (i.e., masculine sport).

The level of feminization (if not infantilization) of their bodies does not necessarily remove gymnasts or figure skaters from the perpetual self-surveillance for feminine signifiers in which most women engage. These athletes have a significant portion of their bodies on display through the tight-fitting and scant uniforms that they wear. They often feel especially sexualized by this required aspect of their sport (Krane et al., 2004). Because of the minimal body coverage afforded by their uniforms, these athletes are forced to pay particular attention to the size, shape, and presentation of their bodies. Eating disorders are frequently reported in the research on athletes in feminine-designated sports, which often also tend to be judged sports. How the athlete looks can directly impact her final score, although the rules for judging these sports do not specifically include deductions for this (Ryan, 1995).

BODYBUILDING: MASCULINE + FEMININE = POLYGENDERED

If there can be an opposite side to the invisible line separating feminine muscles and masculine muscles, this is where bodybuilding would have to be located. Whereas gymnastics and figure skating are seen to be feminine sports due to their performance focus on the aesthetics of both the movements and the athlete, bodybuilding is easily socially identified as a masculine sport because of the prototypically masculine body size and shape that is the training goal of the athletes. The judges' interpretation of the body displayed by the bodybuilder is a masculine one, regardless of the sex or gender of its bearer (Heywood, 1998). The closer a woman's body gets to achieving what would be considered the embodiment of the quintessential athlete in this sport, the more maligned and denigrated the woman will be. There is probably not a greater example that contradicts hegemonic femininity than the female bodybuilder who attempts to achieve the highest level of success in her sport.

Most people would not have a great deal of difficulty accepting that not only is such a body not a feminine one, but that any woman who would chose to build and sculpt her body in such a way is actively rejecting any self-acceptance of her own femininity. However, even a very cursory analysis of the sport of bodybuilding can challenge this conclusion. The sport of bodybuilding is entirely about attention to the body and how it looks. What the body can do with the muscles that are developed through training is never considered within the competitive arena. This attention to the look, rather than the function, of the body has been considered a role of women all the way back to Plato.

A bodybuilder, by necessity, must be consumed by attention to all aspects of the body. The training undertaken to develop the size, shape, and balance of the muscles must be accompanied by excessive attention to every morsel of food that is consumed. Readying oneself for competitive events requires tanning and oiling of the skin, attention to hair cut and styling, the appropriate style and colour of the posing uniform, and an excessively unhealthy eating regime to dehydrate the body and eliminate all fat. These activities, if viewed away from any sporting arena, would be understood to be feminine. This excessive attention to the display of the body by men, except possibly for male models, would be suspect. Yet the sport of bodybuilding, which epitomizes feminine bodywork, is labelled as masculine, and it is the women who now engage in these feminizing practices who are seen to be suspect. The polygendered nature of bodybuilding ought to be as obvious as it is in gymnastics or figure skating.

ANYTHING YOU CAN DO, I CAN DO BETTER

The assimilation or embodiment of one's gender is not as easily acquired nor even accepted as might be presumed through common-sense understandings and definitions of gender. Although very young children have fairly concrete understandings of gender, as it has been taught to them through the various socializing agents in their lives, they also recognize stereotyping and are quick to reject the positive attribution of characteristics to the other sex that they see as valuable for their own. "Children who associated positive characteristics with girls tended to associate negative characteristics with boys. Although results were generally consistent across measures [academic and social domains], children were more likely to show same-sex preferences when they were asked to compare boys and girls explicitly" (Heyman & Legare, 2004, p. 227). It was presented earlier that children perceive cross-gender behaviours as wrong, although they are likely to ignore this when they themselves are engaged in the cross-gender activities.

"Children's beliefs about gender differences can influence how they interpret socially relevant information." These beliefs can be so strong that "children often fail to encode or recall information that is inconsistent with their beliefs" (Heyman & Legare, 2004, p. 227). It becomes more apparent from this that cross-gender behaviours or appearances may make the actual sex of the observed person invisible to a child. They will see a socially constructed, gendered individual rather than the actual person who is being viewed. Thus, all doctors, police officers, soldiers, and athletes may be interpreted to be males, even though children will have seen many women in these roles. The appropriateness of these activities may be seen to apply only to boys and negatively impact the interests or aspirations of girls.

In children and adolescents, the need for peer approval might be the strongest factor in a child's choice of activities and presentation of self. Therefore, if girls and women see sport as an important and desirable activity in their lives, they may be likely to see sport as completely appropriate for themselves and other females. However, for both women and men who see sport as a masculine (or at least masculinizing) activity, the physical signifiers of femininity will be critiqued and likely found wanting.

Writings and other (re)presentations of the body are not new. How these writings and (re)presentations of the body have changed over time is an indicator that certain factors related to the body are constructed, as are the changing gender requirements underlying them. The meanings of feminine embodiment are confounded by the female athlete who is often sexualized by her attention to and display of traditional femininity within her sport, and by the female athlete who participates in culturally normative masculine activities. Although the participation (and success) of girls and women in a full range of sporting activities is widely accepted today, sport itself is still one of our culture's strongest masculinizing practices.[6] This contradiction is felt by many female athletes and by many girls and women who reject or avoid any involvement in sport or physical activity in their lives. It translates into a time-consuming and often destructive self-surveillance in the pursuit of an elusive, but required, attribute called femininity.

AN ANCIENT IMPACT

The ancient Greeks, once again, can be "thanked" for the place of the body in a hierarchical and androcentric philosophical position. The ancient philosophers set out arguments related to the relationship between the mind or soul and the body, and the belief that these aspects of the person are separate and can be viewed as independent parts.

These positions view the mind/body split and the culture/nature dichotomy in essentialist frameworks. These divides have traditionally placed the body in an inferior position to the mind and nature in an inferior position to culture. "Plato's dialogues are filled with lessons about knowledge, reality, and goodness, and most of the lessons carry with them strong praise for the soul and strong indictments against the body" (Spelman, 1999, p. 34). Because Plato and others associated women more with the body and with nature, the importance of these feminine-related positions has been further diminished within patriarchal structures that celebrate anything seen to be masculine above anything seen to be feminine. Although other philosophical and religion-based positions on the unity of the mind/soul and body have been put forward, enduring support for the philosophical foundations of Western thought proposed by the Greeks seems to undermine any more holistic analyses.

The inferiority of the body to the mind and the association of the body with the feminine have contributed to a number of lasting beliefs that underlie Western patriarchal viewpoints. Further to this, Plato equated the mind/soul to the rational and transcendent self, and the body to the irrational or immanent (Young, 1980). This distinction carries with it enormously charged value, particularly as Plato frequently equated the nature of the body to "woman." It is interesting to note that in Book 5 of the *Republic*, Plato wrote of the basic equality between women and men in the ideal state. He proposed that "there is no pursuit of the administrators of a state that belongs to a woman because she is a woman or to a man because he is a man. But the natural capacities are distributed alike among both creatures, and women naturally share in all pursuits and men in all" (quoted in Spelman, 1999, p. 39). He acknowledged that the only significant difference between women's and men's bodies is that of strength, but that this does not make any difference in their souls.

However, as Plato further supports his position on the inferiority of the body his misogyny becomes clear. To support his position that the soul is the most important aspect of the person, Plato was forced to establish the body as inferior. He wrote in the *Republic* that "because he cannot *point* to an unadulterated soul, he points instead to those embodied beings whose lives are in such bad shape that we can be sure that their souls are adulterated. And whose lives exemplify the proper soul/body relationship gone haywire? The lives of women (or sometimes the lives of children, slaves, and brutes)" (quoted in Spelman, 1999, p. 39). Plato wrote in the *Republic*, *Timaeus*, and other works that it is woman-like to attend to the body over the soul. He cautioned men that if they live their lives without due attention to the soul then in the next life they are sure to incarnate as women!

This is an obvious foundation of the concept of misogyny—the hatred of women—or at least the hatred of anything feminine within men themselves. The lesson carried down through the centuries from the work of Plato is that attention to the body is the most highly undesirable of all pursuits and that women live their lives in this activity. The association of women with bodies and the inferiority of women to men are not only innately tied through Plato's philosophy, but they take on an essentialist nature that is supported through the continuing androcentric lens of Western culture. As all people have bodies that must be attended to, the concern is the degree to which the body is attended to over other pursuits. The role of women in ancient Greek society likely had a great deal to do with why they paid so much attention to the body or were compelled to do so.[7]

Partly due to this traditional view of the mind/body duality, with the greater significance seen to be lying with the mind (and therefore culture), until very recently less attention has been paid to the study of the body and the embodied state of existence in the physical world. In 1984, Turner focused on this relative invisibility of bodies in sociological theory as an "analytical gap" (p. 30). In the last 25 years, however, this has completely turned around and it is "apparent that bodies are now an integral concept in social theory" (Miller, 2001, p. 29). This is a very short time frame in which to change millennia of ideas about women and bodies.

BOX 4.1

There is a widely held belief that women's involvement in sport is a relatively new endeavour. While it is probably true that various men's sporting contests and festivals of ancient civilizations are the foundation for contemporary sporting structures, it is also true that girls and women were involved in sports and their own ceremonial sporting festivals. Many of these events were probably tied to fertility rites rather than purely competitive endeavours.

Archaeological evidence indicates that Greek women engaged in running activities as far back at the sixth century BCE. The girls of Sparta were given the same physical training as the boys as early at the fourth century BCE. The beginnings of the Heran Games are unknown, but this festival for girls was a local event in Olympia that was held following the men's Olympic Games and was celebrated in a quadrennial manner, as were the better-known Olympic Games.

Although not likely to be classified as women's "sport," "the earliest evidence we possess of physical activities, the 4,000 year-old tomb drawings at Beni Hassan in Upper Egypt, already depict women dancing, performing acrobatics and playing ball. The same would go for the bull-fighting and bull-vaulting of women in the Minoan culture on the island of Crete around 1,500 BC" (Simri, 1983, p. 11). Whether classified as "sport" or something else, women have been engaged in competitive physical activities for millennia!

As humans, we are embodied. We cannot go anywhere or do anything without attending to the concerns of our corporeal self. Particularly in the study of physical activity, the embodiment of the subject is central to any analysis. To overlook the body and any social construction of its values and restrictions is to lose the meaning at the core of one's analysis (Theberge, 1991). When sport is labelled a male domain, it is not necessarily the male body, but the construction of masculinity and culture, that is fundamental to any analysis. When women are the subject, however, the body becomes not only an object, but central to the most basic analysis of the topic at hand. "The presence of vigorous and robust female athletes demonstrates that sporting prowess is not 'naturally' masculine" (Miller, 2001, p. 23). Therefore, what describes a feminine body becomes problematic.

BODIES AND CULTURE

In expressing a post-structuralist view, Bordo (1989) described the body as a medium or text of culture. The body, quite literally, embodies the rules and constraints of culture and the construction of gender. The representation of these rules and constraints is based on the otherness/difference

95

of women to men, and although these rules have changed somewhat over time, their earliest constructions also remain (Hall, 1997). This construction of woman-gender is most clearly represented in hegemonic rules of femininity. From both historical and contemporary philosophical positions, "body-morphology has provided a blueprint for diagnosis and/or vision of social and political life" (Bordo, 1989, p. 13). Women's involvement in sport has been built from this blueprint, especially in the late 20th century and with increasing pressure as we move more deeply into the 21st.

Feminist analyses of gender and power relations between the sexes contend that discourses of the female body are primarily expressions of male interests and male concerns. These become the primary readings of women's bodies. The physical appearance of women's bodies is the most visible and recognizable expression of compliance with the rules of femininity. The expression of physical competence through most sports participation is a quick indicator of non-compliance with the rules of femininity. Thus, positive readings of women's bodies (and therefore of women) are unlikely to be found within the contextual medium of sport. "Historical analyses have shown how the exclusion of women from sport was an instance of male control over female bodies that enabled the social as well as the physical domination by men of women" (Theberge, 1991, p. 128). Some might argue that the muscular "masculine" female is a current cultural icon (Heywood & Dworkin, 2003) or that her body shape is "a prize rather than a curse" (Miller, 2001, p. 11). I would hope that this might be true, but these sentiments may be a bit optimistic yet. Hopefully, they are on the horizon.

Femininity and masculinity are by definition mutually exclusive constructs. The embedded meaning of what it is to be feminine is immediately challenged by women who wish to participate in sports—activities that are measured, and most highly valued, in terms of physical competence, strength, power, and aggression. These factors do not fall within the narrow construction of femininity. In 16th-century Europe there was a fear that exercise "could transform women into men" (Miller, 2001, p. 22). It can be surmised that we may not have moved as far forward in our thinking about women as we might like to believe.

The embodiment of femininity must be analyzed from a broader perspective than simply that of patriarchal power over women. Bordo (1989) argued that "the network of practices, institutions, and technologies that sustain positions of dominance and subordination within a particular domain" (p. 15) must be considered. According to Bem (1993), "hidden assumptions about sex and gender remain embedded in cultural discourses, social institutions, and individual psyches that inevitably and systematically reproduce male power in generation after generation" (p. 2). The inertia of these assumptions is assisted by a social gaze that is both internal and external to the female athlete.

One explanation of this self-gaze can be ascertained from the work of Foucault (1978) in his discussion of the concept of "panopticism." This is a process of surveillance in which the subject is never certain that he/she is being observed. The "panopticon" is essentially a prison with unique architectural characteristics. It consists of an outer building that is divided into cells with a high tower at its centre. Guards or supervisors can see into the cells, but the prisoners can see neither the supervisors nor the occupants of the other cells (Foucault, 1978). "The awareness that one may be watched leads to an internalization of the gaze and a policing of one's own behaviour" (Shogan, 1999, p. 37).

Although it may be somewhat obvious to the female athlete that she is being observed in practise and competition situations, she wishes to avoid any negative values or assumptions of deviance made about her from these observations of her as an embodied and sexual individual. Compliance with the dominant confines of feminine and heterosexual normativity provides one less way for the panoptic gaze to find fault. Fusco (1998) discussed how some lesbian athletes present themselves in ways that allow them to "pass" as heterosexual and with appropriate levels of feminine compliance.

As many female athletes are at risk of a lesbian label, the practices utilized for "passing" may be the same for heterosexual athletes who want to be seen as appropriately feminine as they are for (stereotypically imaged) lesbian athletes who want to be seen as straight. "When athletes 'retreat into sameness,' they actively suppress expression of their sexual identity because 'they feel pressure to conform' and 'want to appear like one of the crowd.' At some stage the participants have or still actively attempt to cover-up their lesbianism and pass as heterosexuals" (Fusco, 1993, p. 101). The most obvious way to attain this sameness and avoid any negative consequences of questionable identity is to adopt outward signifiers of femininity that define the hetero-sexy woman, enforced by the panoptic gaze.

Obviously the body will play a central role in any analysis of the female athlete, but unfortunately the analysis rarely stops there. Our perceptions of female athletes are often built from those at the highest level of sporting achievement. These are the athletes who are most visible in the media. They possess bodies that are different in many ways to those of other women, including those of girls and women who participate in sport and physical activities at all levels below the top. It is these mediated images and the impressions that are built from these representations that often inform cultural understandings and interpretations of the body, and therefore the femininity of the female athlete. Sport "should emphasize the body, which is the instrument of athletic skill and achievement. It is difficult, however, to have images of bodies in action, at the peak of their physical perfection, without those images also, in some way, carrying 'messages' about *gender* and about *sexuality*" (Hall, 1997, p. 231; emphasis in original). This is an ongoing aspect of the dilemma of femininity and the female athlete.

There are many aspects to femininity. To attempt to analyze it as a monolithic or completely unified concept would probably result in an incomplete critique and one that misses important points relative to understanding femininity and its impact on the female athlete.

BOX 4.2

Bartky (1988) identified three categories that represent and are recognizable as feminine. They all relate to the body as opposed to any other factor of a woman that might be identifiable as feminine, such as interests and behaviours. The three categories are broken down into practices: "those that aim to produce a body of certain size and general configuration; those that bring forth from this body a specific repertoire of gestures, postures, and movements; and those that are directed toward the display of the body as an ornamental surface" (p. 64).

Bartky's categories present a particular predicament to the female athlete, and indicate how the organization of sport can function as an agent to perpetuate the rigid range of compulsory femininity as it impacts the female athlete. Female athletes of certain body types and who participate in certain activities can be slotted into Bartky's categories quite easily. It is those who cannot or choose not to have such a body type who often face challenges to their femininity, their womanness, their sexuality, and their value as persons.

Chapter 5

THE SHAPE OF HER SKIN

... the most important thing about a female body is
not what it does, but how it looks. The power lies not
within us, but in the gaze of the observer. In retro-
spect, I feel sorry for the protofeminist gym teachers
who tried so hard to interest us in half-court basketball and other team sports thought suitable for
girls in my high school, while we worried about the
hairdo we'd slept on rollers all night to achieve. Gym
was just a stupid requirement you tried to get out of,
with ugly gym suits whose very freedom felt odd on
bodies accustomed to being constricted for viewing.
(Steinham, 1994, p. 93)

Focus on the body as a primary site for the assessment of feminine signifiers
is one of the easiest ways to appraise the attention paid by a woman to this
aspect of her socially or culturally assigned gender. A woman's beliefs, attitudes, and behaviours must be demonstrated or voiced before any judgment
related to feminine adherence can be made on these aspects of her obedi-
ence or disobedience to her gender assignment. The body, however, exists
in a very public realm. The gaze of the other, whether engaged in a passing
glance or obvious scrutiny, cannot be avoided. We cannot even always
be aware of when or by whom we are being subjected to a gaze. Conclusions
reached through the gaze of the other may never be known to us, but fear
of the results of the appraisal may be enough to cause a girl or woman to
engage in self-surveillance, often constant and almost always critical, of her
faithful attention to her presentation of self (Wolf, 1991).[1]

There is an assumption that viewers of women's bodies or the creators
of media representations of women's bodies understand contemporary

gender roles and differences (Ellison, 2006). Viewers base their critique of what they see on a singular ideal of femininity that, although constructed and changing, is understood to be a complete picture. "The hegemonic values and expectations of gender-role appropriate behaviours are so deeply ingrained in our culture that they rarely are questioned" (Krane, 2001, p. 117). This applies not only to what a woman does in a generalized behavioural sense, such as choosing to be a mother or an athlete, but also to appropriate behaviours related to the presentation of herself as a prototypical hetero-feminine female.

According to Wolf (1991), the rules of femininity are contained within a beauty myth that "*is always actually prescribing behavior and not appearance*" (p. 14; emphasis in original). The correct behaviours are often directed toward creating an appropriately feminine appearance for all women, at all times. It can easily be seen how many female athletes are not able to comply with this demand, especially when they are engaged in athletic activities. It will be seen, however, that this supposedly hegemonic feminine presentation is "violated" all the time and is not necessarily seen to be problematic for certain groups of women, generally non-white, non-able-bodied, or non-young women.

Although women are aware that there are numerous gaps in the visual representations of women in the media and that casual analysis of any group of women will reveal multiple femininities, the self-surveillance and critique that women apply to their own bodies seem to take precedence over their attention to this breadth of female bodies and presentations. This narrow view of acceptable feminine gender presentation is supported by objectification theorists.

Objectification theory supports the concept that "a culture that objectifies the female body and sexualizes women" (Muscat & Long, 2008, p. 2) may cause women to objectify themselves. The effects of this process can manifest in many ways. If women buy into the media images of women's bodies as the only suitable constructions then they may see themselves more as a body than a whole person. Female athletes may be more at risk for self-objectification than non-athletic women, and may use a feminine presentation of self as a survival strategy in negotiating what is perceived as a masculine domain (Brown, 2006; Krane, 2001). "The sport environment poses a particular threat ... because athletes are frequently exposed to body shape and weight pressures" (Muscat & Long, 2008, p. 3). It is the unique shape and weight of the individual woman that can contribute to her success in her chosen sport. These shapes and sizes are rarely celebrated even though they directly contribute to an athlete's level of excellence. Rather, they are often fated to be criticized because they do not meet some imaginary feminine ideal.

THE IMPOSSIBILITY OF BEAUTY?

A woman's self-surveillance may determine how she fixes her hair, whether she wears make-up, and what clothes she chooses to wear for any particular occasion. But it also includes how she attends to her body to guarantee that it meets the standards for femininity as laid out by community expectations. What and how she eats, whether to engage in exercise, sports, or other physical activities (and which kinds), and whether she undergoes more extreme measures of body modification such as plastic surgery to attain a more acceptable body must be thought out and negotiated by each woman. The degree to which this attention to self and the presentation of self is attended to will be influenced by a number of factors, including the demands of parents, peers, partners, employers, or other socializing agents in a woman's life circumstances. In the world of sport, this includes coaches, trainers, and officials (Caldwell, 1993). In certain sports or in sports at particular levels, even team mates may pressure one another to emphasize their feminine presentation and behaviour in order to balance "the perceptions of masculine athleticism with feminine appearance" (Krane, 2001, p. 116).[2] Regardless of the gendered classification of the sport, the presumed need to manage one's attention to femininity is all-pervading.

Various races, religions, and/or ethnicities will often require or simply accept variations on contemporary hegemonic feminine presentation and performativity, but these variations are not necessarily accepted in a mainstream critique of feminine presentation, especially in sport. A recent furor over a Muslim girl wearing her hijab during a soccer game might be considered a racist reaction to this non-traditional addition to the soccer uniform, but it could also be a critique of how women are supposed to wear their hair,[3] which cannot be seen because of the hijab.[4] Some still believe that women do not belong in sport in the first place, and therefore any changes to the game, uniform, or rules are also not acceptable.

In the case of any woman, the amount of time and money that might be directed to body attention and bodywork will vary by choice or external pressures. Bodywork is central to the performance and evaluation of gender conformity for females. "'Beauty knows no pain' is the motto millions of women adhere to as they starve themselves to the point of anorexia or develop bulimia, have noses broken and sawed, teeth pulled, lips surgically thinned or pumped by injections, ribs removed, thighs and stomachs suctioned, breasts reduced or added to, faces lifted and tucked, eyes reshaped, and buy contact lenses not to improve their vision but to have the eye color of their dreams—perhaps in a perfect shade of emerald green" (Weitz, 1998, p. 186). These extreme body modifications may not be practiced by a lot of female athletes because they recognize the importance of their natural physical gifts in the performance of their sports. Anorexia, bulimia, and disorder eating patterns, however, are endemic in women's sports. Eating is one activity that can be controlled by female athletes in an attempt to present a more acceptable feminine shape.

Hegemonic stereotypes of femininity are created and based on the dominant race and culture of the country and the times. Contemporary understandings of femininity are founded on the economic and sexual desires of white, upper- and middle-class males, although they are applied to women of all races, ethnicities, and classes (Caldwell, 1993; Caudwell, 2006). Women of certain age groups and/or who possess various obvious physical or cognitive disabilities may not be the intended targets of the male gaze or social critique because there may be an unconscious de-sexualizing of these women due to their lack of desirability to males (Hamilton, 2005). However, females in these groups are not free from self-surveillance and compliance with gender performance, even though its observance would not be seen to be mandatory for women who are not seen to fulfill a sexual or child-bearing desirability.

NOT ONE THING OR THE OTHER

As gender assignment only comes in two designated forms, femininity and masculinity, all women learn only one set of rules and are expected to abide by them (Lorber, 2008). This applies most specifically to the feminine presentation of the body (as opposed to compliance to other aspects of the gender-role expectations) because the body is the most obvious signifier and can be assessed with no interaction with the female other than a gaze.

When critically analyzing the impact of gender performativity specifically regarding female athletes, the racialized constructions of femininity become particularly problematic for women of colour. Social and sexual expectations of women of African descent in the United States and of various First Nations, Métis, and Inuit women in both Canada and the United States are constructed from the perspectives of the white colonizers of these groups within the historical frameworks of these nations. Racist practices have placed these women, and all other women of colour, in a position of "less than" relative to white women. Impressions of the role of women of colour within their communities and/or the forced labours of women of non-white groups have led to an assumption that members of these groups have greater physicality and less intelligence.

"Race intersects with gender and sexuality in complex ways in ... cultural venues" (Carty, 2005, p. 133). How athletes are sexualized and which female athletes are more likely to be criticized for non-compliance to femininity constraints changes with the sport and the race of the athlete in important, but biased, ways. "The fact that the sexuality of black females is often marginalized in mainstream media portrayals reflects the different historical experiences of white and black women. Thus the characteristics that are deemed 'appropriately feminine' are different for white and non-white athletes" (Carty, 2005, p. 133). The application of different standards of femininity for certain groups of women again shows the constructed nature of femininity and the reality of the performative, rather than the essential, nature of gender.

The general acceptance of a race-based physicality of non-white athletes actually provides the athlete of colour with a greater flexibility in her choice of sports that may not be seen to negatively effect an assessment of her femininity, feminine performativity, or sexuality. Events or positions that require maximal power output (e.g., the throwing events in track and field) or head-to-head combat (e.g., boxing or certain martial arts) are seen to be more acceptable activities for girls and women of colour within their communities, and are less criticized in the mainstream for being less feminine because the athletes themselves are seen to be less worthy in a more global and racist context where their physical beauty and desirability are less than those of white athletes. This is explored in greater detail in the next chapter, where an analysis of Bartky's category regarding gestures, postures, and movements is undertaken.

The performance of the gender- and self-surveillance required to evaluate one's "success" as a feminine female are as much a part of the life of a female athlete as any other woman. Even though female athletes understand that the media-genic "ideal" body is unrealistic, studies have shown that they express narrowly constructed femininity demands that reflect a mainstream, "white, heterosexual perspective" (Krane et al., 2004, p. 319). Although images and representations of the female athlete have changed over the past century, as have standards of femininity, sport itself is still closely aligned with the masculine. An "optical consistency" between the female athlete and her feminine presentation/performativity is assumed to be necessary by the female athlete and the viewer of many sports (Ellison, 2006).

It is possible that attention to femininity and its corporeal signifiers might be located even more centrally in the bodywork of a female athlete than in that of other women—including fashion models and actors. Athletes understand that there is a conflict between "feminine," in this respect, and being an athlete, which even many female athletes acknowledge is generally accepted as masculine by definition. University-aged female athletes are more able to self-define what is not feminine than what is: "'not sweaty,' 'opposite of being a tomboy,' 'not wearing baggy jeans,' and 'like hitting the weight room' [are] not feminine" (Krane et al., 2004, p. 319). Yet, except for how one wears her jeans, all of these non-feminine identifiers are essential, to some degree, for athletic training and participation.

Every athlete is required to pay extensive attention to the training of her body. This fits the feminine requirement of bodywork, but it is also a very specific and possibly feminine-contrary type of bodywork. Carefully thought out and carried out training regimes must be attended to in order to attain, maintain, or improve the physical components needed to engage in sport. Many of these factors, such as flexibility and agility, might be seen to improve a woman's feminine appearance and performativity. Many other factors, however, such as strength and power (especially as obviously demonstrated by large or well-defined muscles) are deemed "masculine" and may be seen to detract from a woman's gender adherence. Female athletes walk an invisible, undefined, and yet undeniable line that separates a feminine athletic body from a masculine = athletic body.

An athlete will be concerned with the development of physical attributes that are integral to the successful acquisition of the skills and performance variables needed in her sport. A serious athlete is unlikely to consciously apply gendered labels to these attributes, but she will be acutely aware of the limit of some physical qualities beyond which she may not trespass without criticism, either real or anticipated. Many female athletes are familiar with the scrutiny and judgment directed toward them—not always for their athletic performances, but often instead of them. The need to display a feminine and heterosexually attractive self, even when that athletic body is by necessity composed of masculine signifiers, has been a central aspect of the lives of many female athletes for over a century. Attention to this need may be imposed by the athlete herself as well as by others. In this regard, the rest of this chapter will focus on Bartky's (1988) first category of femininity: production of a body of a certain size and general configuration.

ONE SIZE FITS NONE

All one needs to do to educate oneself on the contemporary require-ments for the size and shape of the prototypical feminine woman is to walk by any newsstand and look at the covers of magazines targeting the female buyer, watch television for an evening, or go to almost any North American-made movie with at least one token female character. There is an eerie similarity among all of the women seen in these locales that is non-existent in the actual diverse population of women. Women come in all sizes, shapes, skin colours, ages, levels of (dis)ability, hairdos, styles of dress, and occupations. This reality is rarely reflected the forms and presentations of females in today's media, whether their intended consumption is for females or males. That many girls and women strive to emulate the fantasy of the media-genic glamazon staring out at them from the glossy pages of magazines is not surprising. There are no other models to emulate that promise the fulfillment that will only be found through this singular presentation of self.

Female athletes who receive media attention or endorsements that put their image into the public realm outside of the athletic arena are an exceptionally good fit with the ideal contemporary representation of the feminine. These athletes are privileged over other female athletes based on a hetero-desirability in their looks (Krane, 2001) and not necessarily their athletic ability. Some of the most recognized female athletes are not the best or most successful representative of their sport, but they are the most beau-tiful or heterosexually alluring. Images of tennis player Anna Kournikova are among the most searched for on the internet. Very few of these images actually show her playing tennis or even dressed for the game.

The assumed contradiction of athleticism and femininity may mean that many other female athletes who have received product endorsements targeted at women and seen on television or in magazines are not even recognized as athletes, but merely as attractive women. Girls and women who follow a particular sport may not even recognize an athlete out of her uniform (which in some sports covers the entire body and face) or in air-brushed glamour mode.

The genesis of women's perceptions of the need for ideal women's bodies is historical, but has dangerous contemporary effects. The pandemic of dieting and disordered eating practices among women and girls as young as seven or eight years old is one outcome of the pervasiveness of these "ideal" images and the need to acquire them (Bordo, 1993). The increase in plastic surgery is another. The message is clear: look like the media image or *fix* yourself. The implication is that what is naturally female is abnormal. This obsession with attempting to achieve a particular look is so entrenched in North American culture that television shows such as *Extreme Makeover* and *The Swan* have been created to feed this desire, not to mention myriad "infomercials" selling diet products and panacea fitness machines.

A historical path can be traced that labels conditions of females as not only abnormal, but socially problematic. This further sets women apart from men, and qualifies that difference as inferior. Anorexia, bulimia, "hysteria," and agoraphobia are more frequently identified or diagnosed in women. Because of this, these differences are often labelled as "disorders of women." The implications from this are more serious than a mislabelling or misapplication of a condition. In reality, all of these conditions are disorders of society. "The thrust of this claim is that any sociology of the body involves a discussion of social control and any discussion of social control must consider the control of women's bodies by men under a system of patriarchy" (Turner, 1984, p. 2). That men also present with these "disorders of society" is minimized or overlooked entirely. Even when these conditions are identified in men they may be named and treated differently, which further separates the sexes and medicalizes the socially negative conditions of females over those of males. This also acts to further connect women to their bodies à la Plato. One focus of medicine is to cure or fix problems of the body. *Fixing* the way the body looks is just the latest incarnation of the relationship of women to their bodies and the inferiority of this position relative to men.

The desire of many women to meet the compulsory requirements of femininity is one way in which women have to attempt to "normalize" their bodies and themselves. This is a nearly impossible mission under a patriarchal structure that provides for a constantly changing ideal through targeting the desirability or acceptability of a particular type of a woman's body (and generally overlooking the particular age or race of that body). Over time, the changing definitions of beauty have been applied to the whole of a woman's body. During the early Victorian era a larger, more rounded, pale-skinned woman indicated a woman of leisure or class, and was an outward signifier of the ability of her husband to feed her and not require her to do physical labour. During the 1920s, the small, animated flapper was an indicator of a woman who represented a more open and accessible sexuality. During World War II, Rosie the Riveter exhibited strength and competence in order to demonstrate her physical ability to contribute in a patriotic role.

Contemporary standards of feminine beauty tend to require changes to specific pieces of a woman's body rather than to the overall size and look of the total body. Large breasts versus small breasts, pouty lips versus full lips, straight lines versus toned (but not too large) muscles are just some of the factors to which women must attend. Attempting to meet these contemporary physical attributes is far more costly to well-being than to the wallet or the clock. It forces women to see themselves more as pieces than as a whole and, through almost any assessment, as lacking.

Women are forced to work harder and harder to achieve what is genetically unattainable for most of us. Even if some women are able to morph pieces of their bodies into some of the fashionable contours, other aspects of beauty *de jour*, such as large eyes or long legs, cannot be achieved through any amount of working out or cosmetic surgery. Thus, except for the cover model of the day (who is professionally coiffed, made-up, Photoshopped, and airbrushed), very few women can meet the demands of compulsory femininity in its constantly changing design. Although the quest to achieve this may be a futile one, the social rewards that are alluded to for the woman who adheres to the pursuit of a contemporary hegemonic feminine presentation are compelling.[5]

This is seen, by some, as a backlash to the feminist movement that functioned to promote more equality between women and men. One idea of the feminist movement was that the more independent women became, the less dependent they would be on men to provide them with the necessities of life. They might choose to select a life path that appears to reject the traditional gender roles of wife, helpmate, and mother. Some women might choose to become single mothers. However, except for some lesbians and other women who simply choose to not share their lives with men, most women who reject traditional gender roles still want to share their lives, to various degrees, with men. These changes may have contributed to the changing demands and requirements of feminine presentation in order to attract a male partner.

Even young girls are not excused from the pressure of conforming to standards that will attract the rewards of womanhood. "As girls enter adolescence, not only do the rewards for looking attractive increase, but the rewards available from other sources diminish. Girls whose parents used to take pride in their tomboy ways now start viewing those same traits as sources of concern, and begin encouraging them to adopt a more feminine appearance and demeanor" (Weitz, 2004, p. 72). The bar has been raised for all women regarding compliance to femininity.

There are other alluded-to rewards for the female athlete who embodies feminine beauty. Product endorsements are profitable lures that can hook female athletes who are generally less well paid (if paid at all) than male athletes at a similar point in their career. Attention to the attractiveness of the female athlete has been a concern for over a century. As is particularly true today, the media has often been the venue through which a critique of the femininity of the female athlete is presented, rather than a celebration of her accomplishments. In 1912, an article entitled "Are Athletics Making Girls Masculine?" appeared in the *Ladies Home Journal*. In this article, girls were encouraged to exercise to maintain beauty and reproductive health, but were cautioned regarding rough-and-tumble activities. A feared outcome of participation in sports of the wrong kinds was that those sports might masculinize women's bodies and characters.

FEMALE ATHLETES ARE "INDECENT, UGLY, AND IMPROPER"[6]

This masculinity referred to females' bodies as well as their characters, and a large number of journal and newspaper articles in the early part of the 20th century presented scathing critiques of the way female athletes looked both on and off the playing field. Many of the male journalists who wrote these articles indicated that the female athletes were unattractive to them, thus placing the athletes into the realm of a sexual being rather than that of athlete, even within the context of athletic participation. This practice, while possibly not quite so overt, continues today and has a strong negative impact on the self-perception of girls and women who are or may strive to be athletes. A focus on the femininity of female athletes over their performances as athletes functions to keep them in the realm of "culturally acceptable women" (Krane, 2001, p. 116), while simultaneously sending a message to the athletes that moving too far from the ideal will draw criticism and further guarantee self-surveillance and critique of their bodies.

The persistent attention of many women to bodywork makes Plato's pronouncements of women's attachment to the body prophetic as his ideas have endured in Western beliefs about women and their bodies. Although the desired outcome of women's bodywork has changed according to the fashion of the time, there has been little change in the means to the end. And although the value and outright necessity of the alluded-to rewards (protection for a woman and her children through marriage to a man) has changed with women's changing status in society, the acceptability of a woman is still based on her attention to bodywork and her success in being appropriately feminine, regardless of her other accomplishments (Wolf, 1991). Women's self-surveillance and attention to their bodies is still their greatest measure of success as feminine in a number of ways.

The particular dilemma that lies at the centre of any historical and negative association of women's bodies and women to their bodies is that, for female athletes, much of their self-identity is tied to how well they use their bodies as instruments of achievement in their sports. The physical training that is required for any sporting endeavour focuses on the body. What an athlete's body actually looks like may not necessarily be central to her assessment of her body, even in sports where the physical presentation of the body is important.[7] The specific kinds of bodywork in which female athletes engage provide a sense of challenge, accomplishment, and worth. It is desirable that women perceive their bodies to be strong and powerful (Theberge, 1985/1994), and sport is one of the best ways to experience these attributes. "The female sporting body can generate material embodied change and body-for-self experiences" (Brown, 2006, p. 164). This is true for male athletes, but it is not so clearly accepted for female athletes.

Female athletes' attention to bodywork, which is often much more time consuming and focused than for many other women, is not celebrated through their acquisition of the motor skills and physical attributes needed to participate in their sports unless the resulting body also meets contemporary standards of femininity. The basic problem with this is that a hegemonically "ideal" body may be one that is unproductive, or even counterproductive, to success in sports. In a study that Krane et al. (2004) conducted on university-aged female athletes, the researchers reported that "the athletes considered their muscular bodies as the primary hindrance to being perceived as heterosexually feminine in social settings" (p. 326). These athletes reported that they felt different when compared to "normal" girls. They perceived their bodies as more muscular, and because of their larger size they were unable to fit comfortably into stylish clothes. "Even though they embraced the function of their bodies, being too muscular was disconcerting. It was an unwanted source of social attention, a constant reminder that they were different from other women" (Krane et al., 2004, p. 326).

One of the interesting things about the bodies of athletes, especially female athletes, is that they are representative of much of the range of sizes and shapes of women in any population. If we were to ask "what does a female athlete look like?" we would undoubtedly get a vast range of answers depending on the sport or event that was being envisioned. Out of uniform and out of an athletic venue it would be impossible to look at a group of women and determine which were athletes based only on their size, looks, or demeanour. "Female athletes come in myriad shapes and sizes due to the needs of their sports and their own interests as physically active individuals. Yet, what a female athlete looks like has been, and continues to be, a very important aspect of the social construction of not only female athletes, but of women in general" (Daniels, 2004, p. 51). Female athletes range in size and shape from tiny gymnasts to very tall basketball and volleyball players to powerfully built shot putters and rugby players. Women of a range of heights and weights play golf and field hockey, run track and cross-country ski, ride horses and mountain bikes, sail and row, and dive and engage in swimming events, including synchronized swimming and deep-water diving.

Whereas a sport or physical activity to learn and participate in should be chosen only on the interests of the girl or woman, success in sport at a high performance level generally requires a good fit between the body of the athlete and the fitness components that she needs to acquire and execute the motor-skill requirements of the position or event in which she is engaged. Fortunately, there are enough sports, with numerous positions and events, to fit the physical construction of all girls and women.[8]

Women of all shapes and sizes are successfully participating in all of these sports. They are also engaged in numerous physical activities that are as yet not defined as "sports," or which have not yet caught the attention of the profit-driven media.

However, even in the 21st century when women have more than proven their worth in athletic endeavours across the entire realm of sport, the very notion of the "female athlete" continues to be an oxymoron. To many, athletes are still by definition masculine males and regardless of women's successes, many of the sports they excel in are also masculine. The incongruous juxtaposition of "woman" and "athlete" continues to conjure images of masculine-looking, non-feminine females. In addition, these images are frequently translated to mean lesbian (Cahn, 1994). The images of female athletes in the mainstream media parallel the ideal-woman icon. They focus most frequently on the feminine presentation and hetero-sexy appeal of the women rather than on their skill, physicality, and success as athletes. The polygendered nature of all athletes is obliterated by this attachment to a feminine-only designation for women.

It would be uplifting to be able to report that female athletes rise above the requisite media images and the consequent perpetual self-surveillance of their bodies and their attention to signifiers of compulsory femininity.[9] Given the unique relationships that female athletes have to their bodies and the centrality of the trained body as a necessary instrument for participation in sport, it might be possible to build a foundation upon which female athletes construct a radical shift in what it means to be a woman and an athlete, and to expand what is understood to be feminine into a broad expanse of "multiple femininities" (Connell, 1995) or a polygendered state. However, female athletes may not have an advantage over non-athletes in seeing their bodies in a distinctive way, even though their bodies play a unique role in their self-identity. In North American culture, sport "acts a technology of domination that anchors women into a discursive web of normalizing practices" (Markula, 2003, p. 88), such as careful attention to feminine presentation.

BOX 5.1

Normative images of the hetero-sexy, feminine woman eliminate the myriad sizes and shapes of most women's bodies. This applies to athletes as well. While the necessity of good body fit to sport is less of a requirement for entry-level competitors and recreational participants in sports, the importance of having the right body size and shape cannot be denied for the highest level of competitive athlete. What is interesting to discover, however, is the range of body heights and weights within particular sports even at the highest levels. An examination of the heights and weights of some of the female athletes from the Beijing Olympic Games reveals tremendous variability among the athletes both within and among the sports. The following information is a brief (and more than likely incomplete) overview of some of the largest and smallest of the 4,746 female athletes (42% of all athletes) who competed in these Games and their sports. This information does not include any of the 1,380 female Paralympic athletes from Beijing, for who statistics are less readily available.

The women ranged in height from 136 cm/4'6" (diving) to 200 cm/6'7" (volleyball) and from 30 kg/66 pounds (diving) to 125 kg/275 pounds (judo). Athletes under 153 cm/5'0" (136 cm /4'6"–151 cm /4'11") weighed between 30 kg/66 pounds and 58 kg/128 pounds. These women competed in the marathon, diving, gymnastics, judo, and weight lifting. Athletes between 153 cm/5'0" and 168 cm/5'6" were reported to weigh between 40 kg/88 pounds and 85 kg/187 pounds. They competed in archery, athletics (10,000 m, 100 m, marathon, hurdles, triathlon), badminton, basketball, BMX cycling, mountain biking, road cycling, diving, gymnastics, equestrian show-jumping and three-day eventing, fencing, soccer, trampoline, team handball, field hockey, judo, rowing, shooting, softball, swimming, synchronized swimming, tennis, tae kwan do, table tennis, volleyball, weight lifting, water polo, and wrestling!

Athletes between 169 cm/5'7" and 184 cm/6'0" weighed between 47 kg/103 pounds and 125 kg/275 pounds and competed in archery, athletics (10,000 m, 100 m, 800 m, marathon, hurdles, shot, discus, pole vault, long jump, high jump, triathlon), badminton, beach volleyball, BMX cycling, mountain biking, road cycling, diving, gymnastics, equestrian show-jumping, dressage, three-day eventing, fencing, kayaking, soccer, team handball, field hockey, judo, rowing, shooting, swimming, synchronized swimming, tennis, tae kwan do, table tennis, volleyball, weight lifting, water polo, and wrestling.

Female athletes between 184 cm/6'0" and 200 cm/6'7" weighed between 62 kg/136 pounds and 123 kg/272 pounds and competed in athletics (shot, discus, long jump, high jump), basketball, beach volleyball, team handball, rowing, swimming, tennis, volleyball, and water polo. It cannot be ascertained from simply reading this information which weights go with which heights or from which sports these statistics have arisen. Some are surprising, and I would encourage the reader to visit the Beijing results sites to dig deeper into the specifics of the vast ranges of sizes and shapes that the best female athletes in the world embody.

Many female athletes are significantly challenged when it comes to meeting contemporary standards of femininity as they relate to a body of a certain size and configuration. The bodies of female athletes fill the same myriad sizes and shapes as most of the female population. However, their understanding of their place within the masculine domain of sport may put female athletes at greater risk for harmful consequences from critiques of their bodies than non-athletic women. In a study by Muscat and Long (2008), it was discovered that female athletes were more likely than non-athletes to recall critical comments about their bodies and that women at higher levels of sporting success were more likely to recall critical comments made about their bodies than athletes at lower levels. Almost half of the athletes interviewed could remember a critical comment made about their body. They "indicated that it had *quite a bit or a lot* of impact on their behaviour and attitudes toward their body, 48% felt *quite upset or very upset* by the person's comment about their body, 50% indicated that they felt *quite a bit or very conscious* about their body shape, diet, and weight as a result of the comment" (Muscat & Long, 2008, p. 10; emphasis in original). What is most harmful about the attention put on these athletes' bodies is that "those who recall more threatening (i.e., severe) critical comments, also reported greater disordered eating" (Muscat & Long, 2008, p. 16). This study found no difference within or between athletes in myriad sports.

It might be assumed that athletes with more typically feminine body types, such as gymnasts or figure skaters, might be more protected from a critical gaze than female athletes with what might be considered more masculine bodies, such as rugby players or shot putters. Apparently this is not the case, although the reasons behind the critical gaze and negative commentary might differ for different sports (Crocker et al., 2000). The outcome, however, is the same: female athletes objectify their bodies and engage in unhealthy practices to control the way their bodies look.

This becomes problematic beyond the practice of disordered eating patterns and objectification of the body because the female athlete also uses her body to acquire motor skills and to train for participation in her chosen sport(s) and activities. Her choice of sport(s) is often based on the size and shape of her body as it will give her the greatest advantage in being biomechanically successful[10] in acquiring and executing the necessary motor skills and advancing as far as she can in her chosen sport. This body type, although perfectly suited to successful participation in the chosen sport, may be far from the requisite feminine body size and shape of contemporary cultural standards.[11] Even though this woman may never possess a body that reflects contemporary femininity standards, she is not excused from this standard when choosing to participate in a sport for which her body may be ideal.

WHICH BODIES COUNT THE MOST?

There are many female athletes who easily fall within the restrictions of Bartky's first category of femininity: production of a body of a certain size and general configuration. The sports and physical activities that they participate in are those that have generally been regarded as gender-appropriate for females. In order to be successful both biomechanically and in achievement, gymnasts, figure skaters, divers, dancers, synchronized swimmers, aerobics participants, and cheerleaders generally require a body type that is small, flexible, graceful, and "feminine" looking. As stated earlier, however, a female gymnast has one of the greatest strength-to-weight ratios of any athlete, male or female.

The strength of the female gymnast or individual figure skater is generally made invisible by a number of factors such as her age, often prepubescent-looking body, or outward feminine accoutrements such as make-up and sequined costumes. First, the most successful of these athletes today are usually very young. This was not always the case. Prior to the 1970s the most successful (in terms of accomplishment) gymnasts and figure skaters were women, not teenaged girls. They had obviously woman-like bodies, including womanly breasts and hips. This was true throughout the first six decades of the 20th century.

The Impact of Television

The growing availability of television and the increase in broadcast hours of the Olympic Summer and Winter Games, beginning in the late 1960s, made the changes to the age and physical maturity of these athletes more accessible to those who only followed these sports on television. In the early years of televised Olympic broadcasts the best female gymnasts and skaters primarily came from the Eastern Bloc countries of the USSR. At the 1972 Munich Games, Olga Korbut, the youngest member (and an alternate) of the USSR's women's gymnastics team, was showcased for her unusual and daring elements on the balance beam and uneven parallel bars. Contrary to popular myth, Korbut was not the greatest gymnast at those Games. She did not even win a medal in the all-around competition.[12] Korbut was not originally scheduled to compete in Munich, but was entered at the last minute in an ill-fitting leotard and pigtails (a calculated departure from the typically well-groomed and sophisticated-looking Soviet gymnast). This was a political move by the movers and shakers of Soviet gymnastics to foil the decisions of the International Federation of Gymnastics, which had prohibited the moves that Korbut would eventually perform[13] and that the world would see showcased again and again on television. The audience in Munich and the worldwide television-viewing audience were captivated by Korbut's unusual and risky moves. The greatest impact of the Korbut-strategy was a demand by viewers for more risky and exciting gymnastics routines, which could only be performed by youthful bodies. Following Munich, women's gymnastics rapidly became girls' gymnastics.

Although gymnastics has always been a popular sport for young girls in the West, no Olympic medals were won by any Canadian or U.S. gymnasts between the entrance of the USSR into the Olympic Games in 1952 and 1984.[14] As world success in gymnastics became the purview of young girls rather than more mature women, more and more pressure was placed on young gymnasts. By 1984, prepubescent-looking gymnasts from the United States were standing on top of Olympic and World Championship medal podiums.[15]

The Intentional Cover-up of Masculinity in Young Female Bodies

Most people would not associate such young, petite females with the exceptional strength, power, and endurance demanded by their sport. Even though these attributes are as important as flexibility, grace, and agility to the successful execution of gymnastic elements, these female athletes are generally not at risk for having their femininity, or their sexuality, questioned. The assumed masculinity of the physical attributes of strength, power, and endurance are masked by the feminine designation of the sport and the petite, often prepubescent-looking bodies that are required for participation. There is not only a general lack of understanding of the power required of these bodies, but there is also a "prevailing cultural discourse which equates femininity with a youthful appearance" (Dinnerstein & Weitz, 1998, p. 189). Both of these factors allow gymnasts and other female athletes in culturally gender-appropriate activities to meet the demands of Bartky's first category of femininity, regardless of their possession of myriad masculine athletic characteristics.[16]

Figure skaters easily fall into this category as well, but in a somewhat different way than gymnasts. The strength and power of the figure skater's body has the same invisibility as that of the female gymnast, but it is hidden behind a veneer of sexuality (of the stereotypically hetero kind) rather than of extreme youth. Female figure skaters are also getting younger, but one aspect of the "ladies" short and, especially, long programs is the hyper-sexualization of the costumes and movements that have come to be expected in the highest levels of women's figure skating. The expressive sexuality of these young competitors both on and off the ice reflects contemporary notions of femininity and sexual expression that would be disturbing to see in young girls in any other venue (and is disturbing to many viewers concerned with the hyper-sexualization of young girls in any context).

Constructed Rivalries

The media has fed, if not created, rivalries between top contending female figure skaters that could parallel the relationships of soap-opera characters or prime-time drama divas. These rivalries function to remove a lot of the focus off the ice, away from the competitive sport, and into the constructed realm of rivalry and femininity. The competition for medals is put on par with romance-novel-like rivalries between beautiful heroines. Through the "duel of the Carmens" between Katarina Witt and Debi Thomas in Calgary in 1988 and the media frenzy regarding Nancy Kerrigan and Tonya Harding leading up to the Lillehammer Games in 1994, these rivalries were portrayed as typical female "cat-fights," not previews to exciting athletic competitions with exhilarating and uncertain outcomes.[17] In more recent years, the youth and traditionally defined "wholesome beauty" of the top female figure skaters has been used to balance the increasingly obvious sexually suggestive costumes, which have more daringly exposed flesh rather than the more modest, but sexually suggestive, flesh-coloured insets that were popular in the 1980s and 1990s.

The larger the female athlete gets in height and/or weight and the more apparent the strength she displays through muscular development, the less feminine she is often considered to be, especially by sports broadcasters and reporters and often by fans. The acceptable limits of these dimensions have grown over the past three decades. However, critique of the too muscular/masculine female, as defined by contemporary standards, remains quite constant.[18]

For example, the 1980s tennis rivalry between Chris Evert and Martina Navratilova was characterized by the physical (and early-on implied sexual) differences between the players, because neither had a sufficiently better game than the other to establish dominance. Navratilova was portrayed as the less desirable player relative to her femininity. Her obvious strength and successful use of tennis strokes that were characteristic of the typical men's game, such as a backhand topspin, coupled with her alluded-to bisexuality/lesbianism, made her a target for criticism. She was portrayed as playing like a man and having muscles like a man. Evert, on the other hand, played a traditional women's game. She was pretty. Reports about her invariably mentioned the man she was dating, engaged to, or married to. She was the desirable female athlete. Her femininity was displayed through her body and her game, and her heterosexuality was paraded before the public. The media rivalry between Evert and Navratilova was presented as one of feminine versus mannish, straight versus lesbian, and normal versus deviant.

Today, neither Evert's nor Navratilova's game would hardly hold up against the majority of professional female players as all strokes, including the very "masculine" backhand topspin, are standard in most games. Navratilova's size and muscularity would look nearly petite when contrasted with the height and muscular development of the top women on today's tour, most particularly Venus and Serena Williams. Despite the criticism levelled toward her and her femininity, Navratilova successfully pushed the envelope of muscularity in women's tennis.

Moral panic for "playing like a man" has been a focus of the media reporting on women's tennis for decades. Players such as Billie Jean King, Martina Navratilova, and Amélie Mauresmo, who also all happen to be lesbians, have fanned the flames of this critique. "For their part, journalists used the controversies to construct and normalize gender, sex, and sexuality" (Miller, 2001, p. 107). Linking the strength and sexuality of these players "confirmed their masculinity" and was thus reported in many media outlets. This reporting also created a challenge to whether these "women" should be playing on the tour at all.

Fans of tennis today recognize the need for greater strength in the game, making the acceptable limits of muscular size for female players much greater than they used to be. Only history will reveal if the acceptance of the obvious muscularity flaunted by the Williams sisters through skimpy tennis dresses will also apply to white female tennis players. The acceptance of greater physicality for female athletes of African descent has been briefly discussed, and may be one reason why the muscularity of the Williams sisters is somewhat more acceptable and does not translate into a media-generated implied masculinity or homosexuality. Whether this privileged interpretation of muscle and sexuality will hold sway on any white or other raced tennis players who follow the Williams sisters is yet to be seen. Additionally, the images of these very popular female athletes are controlled and contributed to through easy access to information beyond their on-court performances. Off-court appearances and the exposure of other interests of the Williams sisters contribute to their positive images. What is unknown to most consumers of their images is just how much of what is seen is carefully calculated and scripted to produce a profile that is most appealing to their acceptance by the public, in general, and sponsors (actual or potential), specifically. This is just one more example of the "objectifying and sexualizing tendencies of the male gaze over the female athlete's body" (Brown, 2006, p. 164).

It needs to be noted that this practice is not restricted to Venus and Serena Williams. They have been used simply as an illustration of one the differences in the promotion of female athletes today as opposed to only a couple of decades ago. The existence of specialty sports channels, satellite television, the internet, and a plethora of sports magazines directed toward both women and men makes the transmission of information and images, and the interpretation thereof, a greater tool for the producers and consumers of women's sports and participants. Careful attention, requiring great amounts of time, must be directed to creating and controlling the information that is produced and distributed regarding any public figure, including female athletes.

BODY OUTLAWS VERSUS FREEDOM FIGHTERS

In some respects, the female bodybuilder, weightlifter, thrower, rugby player, or linebacker, for example, rejects the rigid requirements of a traditional female soma[19] as a signifier of her femininity, whether or not this is a conscious decision or rebellion. Although the size and shape of her body are part of her natural physiology or ergogenically enhanced body,[20] and they directly contribute to her choice of sport and/or level of success, these factors are rarely considered when her femininity is assessed. Regardless of body size, all girls and women must have the right to participate in any sport or physical activity that they choose.

It is a reality that the size of a body is likely to be a significant factor in the ease of acquisition and successful execution of certain sport-specific motor skills. Consequently, certain bodies will be better suited to achieving excellence in performance in specific sports, events, or positions. This point cannot be disregarded. Fortunately, there are many sports, events, and positions and myriad body types are needed to fill their rosters. It is important then to either refrain from criticizing bodies that are suited for this excellence based on constructed gendered norms of the bodies themselves or the physical activities, or to accept that all sports require a polygendered collection of attributes.

This reality has been negated within the androcentric and gender polarization lenses through which sport and female athletes have been viewed. Sex testing of female athletes and the formal prohibition of women from competing in certain sports at the highest levels[21] are ways of controlling the actions of women who want to participate in sport at all levels. "Advantages from the intentional development of physical strength in order to succeed in sport or specific forms of labour was not only seen to be the domain of males, but was characteristically used as 'proof' of male superiority and natural dominance over women" (Brown, 2006, p. 174). Female athletes challenge this position every day, regardless of the size and shape of their bodies.

The gendered designation of sports and physical activities themselves is one of the underlying causes of negative assessments of people who are seen to be making gender-inappropriate choices in their sporting involvement. It also functions to create a stratification of activities—thus designating "male" sports as having greater cultural value and preserving the domain of sport as a masculine one. This, in turn, requires the sporting body to be a masculine one. Females whose bodies are best suited to the performance of motor skills that have been artificially placed within this masculine domain become targets of negative labelling, such as non-feminine, mannish, masculine, and, often by extension, homosexual.

One effect of successful gender socialization of young girls is their understanding of the importance of physical appearance. Bodywork, the management of appearance (Miller & Penz, 1991), is a central skill to be learned and maintained throughout a girl's or a woman's life. Failure to learn the skills or rejection of the process of bodywork at any time in a female's life is met with responses ranging from a mother's lament to outright social rejection. "Physical appearance may be the most potent component in influencing judgements ... and misjudgements [about people]" (Miller & Penz, 1991, p. 287). Another concern for some female athletes is that the features of masculinity that appear to come most readily to mind when considering a gender-incongruent target compared to a gender-congruent target centre on physical appearance (Helgeson, 1994, p. 665).

GENDER AS EMBODIMENT

If "female athlete" is considered to be a gender-incongruent role and the female athlete is also considered to be masculine, then the physical appearance of the female athlete becomes central to the gaze to which she is subjected and the resulting evaluations made of her. Although the importance of physical appearance and presentation is increasing for males in our society, they have a long way to go before the restrictive nature of this evaluation will equal that imposed upon females. Male athletes are particularly favoured with a gender-congruent status. Their physical appearance—although not necessarily considered as strong a factor in their masculinity as a feminine (read: heterosexually attractive) body is to the female athlete—is positively highlighted.

Culturally normative activities for girls and women concentrate on femininity and appearance. Although females are encouraged to exercise and even participate in a growing number of sports and physical activities, the activities that are appropriate choices for girls and women are still primarily those that require grace, balance, poise, and, apparently, nothing else. There are exceptions to this rule. There are some physical activities that contain all of the speed, power, strength, aggression, and even body contact of male-appropriate designated sports, but in which men do not participate.[22] In North America, field hockey is one example of this in team sport. Field hockey was originally brought to North America from Great Britain so that young women could participate in a highly competitive team sport without negative criticism because they were not seen to be trespassing into male territory (Daniels, 2005b).

Even though the components of field hockey contain most of the masculine elements of many other team sports, they are invisible relative to the critiques aimed at women's sports because the sport is deemed gender-appropriate for females. Other examples of sports that receive mixed criticism relative to the acceptable femininity of the participants are those that are most commonly participated in by immigrant ethnic groups or lower- and working-class individuals of various races, such as athletics, basketball, or bowling.

The more socially acceptable a competitive sport is for females, the more petite the body morphology that is required for a greater potential of success. Gymnastics, figure skating, and other activities that have already been mentioned would fit this requirement. These are also sports in which the masculinity and sexuality of male participants and competitors are frequently questioned based on the feminine assignment of the activity. Thus, the cultural value of these "feminine" activities is also less in general, because even if males are participating in these activities they are considered gender-incongruent males and often labelled as homosexual, even though they are athletes.

There is a dangerous side to this aspect of compulsory adherence to a feminine body size. Disordered eating is nearly endemic in girls' and women's sporting activities. Many female athletes suffer from anorexia nervosa or bulimia or other more generic forms of disordered eating. Besides the media, parents and coaches are often to blame for the mixed messages that female athletes receive. On the one hand coaches are directly responsible for training female athletes to develop strength (which can only be obtained through muscular hypertrophy—increased size), while on the other they frequently tell athletes that they are "fat," or worse (Ryan, 1995). The conflict between having a strong body for successful athletic performance and having to look feminine is not lost on the competitor. The female bodybuilder often attempts to pump her body up to its largest possible proportions. Yet the dieting required to display the definition and the ripped look so desired by bodybuilders shows the directly conflicting sides of bodywork and, therefore, femininity.

The 1994 death from anorexia of Christy Heinrich, a world-class gymnast from the United States, became a red flag to all parents, coaches, officials, physical educators, and media workers that the focus on the size and shape of women's bodies is a threat to the health and lives of many very young girls and adolescents. It seems that even the sports participation of what ought to be considered very feminine females with very feminine bodies is challenged in insidious ways. The most successful participants in culturally normative feminine sports are young girls, teenagers, or young women who are under the strict control of coaches (Ryan, 1995). The dangerous focus on body size, image, and weight combined with (if not above) the excellence of performance places this aspect of femininity highest in the minds of females who have often not finished growing and are not mature enough to make appropriate decisions for themselves. The pressures to conform to a feminine body size are causing lifelong physical and psychological damage to girls who are in turn role models for other young girls.

Heinrich's death became a shocking wake-up call regarding pathological attention to the size and shape of girls' and women's bodies—including eating disorders—among female athletes. There have been no other high-profile, female athlete, eating disorder related deaths since 1994, but this does not mean that there have been none or that the problem has been solved. It merely means that, like the increasingly sophisticated means of hiding drug use in sports, disordered eating has become a more subversive practice that is still engaged in by countless female athletes of all ages in all sports. As recently as the 2006 Olympic Winter Games in Torino, U.S. figure skater Jamie Silverstein revealed her career-threatening (and life-threatening) anorexia. Numerous interviews with former U.S. Olympic figure-skating gold medallist Dorothy Hamill in relation to this story revealed the unrelenting weight-control practices, including penalties for weight gain, in the Ice Capades. What figure skaters look like is at least as important as how well they perform.

Activities that require more masculine characteristics, such as the height required for basketball, the musculature necessary for throwing or lifting events, or the body contact and roughness found in soccer or rugby, are primarily still seen to be inappropriate for girls and women because they are not defined as feminine by North American culture at large. They not only require masculine-defined actions, but they also necessitate a "masculine" body morphology for success. Even if that is the somatotype that the woman was born with, it is not considered to be a feminine one.

PERCEPTIONS OF GENDER COMPLIANCE/NON-COMPLIANCE

Perceptions of the appropriateness of certain sports and physical activities for women and men change with the level of perceived femininity or masculinity of the observer. "Sex-typed individuals differ from non-sex-typed individuals in their use of gender as a dimension to encode and organize information even when other, more relevant dimensions, are equally available" (Matteo, 1988, p. 42). Sex-typed individuals, specifically feminine females and masculine males, are more likely to value perceived sex-inappropriate behaviour as problematic. In a study conducted to determine the suitability of activities for females and males, both male and female sex-typed subjects expressly stated concerns about the gender-appropriateness of sports more often than either androgynous or undifferentiated subjects (Matteo, 1988). In other words, the gender, and therefore the femininity or masculinity of the body, is important to many individuals.

This assessment is not lost on young girls who are just learning the contemporary rules of compulsory gender performativity. It is interesting to ponder "how many little girls partake in deliberative physique-building activities from a young age and how many continue with these through the critical age of puberty, where their pursuit of a desirable heterosexual feminine image leads them instead to construct a physical manifestation of the very image they see and assign to their own somatic destiny?" (Brown, 2006, p. 172).

The sport ideal is most positively reflected in the masculinity of the masculine male: sport is what turns boys into men. As in-group favouritism refers to the tendency of people to treat and judge other members of their own group relatively more positively than members of the out-group, the masculine male and the feminine female are both going to view women's participation in non-sex-appropriate sports negatively (Carpenter, 1994). This assessment translates, consciously and unconsciously, into an assessment of that body within the inappropriate sport.

In a study by Cann (1993) that looked at the perceived appropriateness of a person's name and a social role, the "results indicated that when the person's name and the role were consistent with the gender stereotype, a positive evaluative connection made the statement easier to recall than a negative evaluative connection. However, an inconsistent name–role pairing was easier to recall when the evaluative connection was negative rather than positive (p. 667). Statements such as "Sally, the basketball player, is so big and muscular," a negative evaluation according to the data in Table 3.2, is more likely to be remembered than "Sally is a great basketball player." To sex-typed individuals, this reinforces the negative associations of women and sport.

Fortunately, androgynous and undifferentiated subjects are less likely to draw sex-consistent conclusions about sport choice (Matteo, 1988). The value of the opinions of these people may help to reduce the overall negative connotations and evaluative conclusions of sex-typed individuals toward women and culturally normative non-gender-appropriate sporting activities. The question to ask here is: how many parents, coaches, journalists, or broadcasters are androgynous or undifferentiated subjects who might be able to influence change in how people view and judge the female athlete's body of a certain size and general configuration? If all of these individuals were to embrace their natural polygendered state, it might be a lot easier!

Chapter 6

YOU THROW LIKE A GIRL:
GESTURES, MOVEMENTS, AND POSTURES

> The basic difference which Strauss observes between
> the way boys and girls throw is that girls do not bring
> their whole bodies into the motion as much as the
> boys. They do not reach back, twist, move backward,
> step, and lean forward. Rather, the girls tend to re-
> main relatively immobile except for their arms, and
> even the arm is not extended as far as it could be.
> Throwing is not the only movement in which there is
> a typical difference in the way that men and women
> use their bodies. Reflection on feminine comportment
> and body movement in other physical activities reveals
> that these also are frequently characterized, much as
> in the throwing case, by a failure to make full use of
> the body's spatial and lateral potentialities. (Young,
> 1980, p. 142)

The previous chapter provided an overview of femininity from the perspective of the size and shape of female bodies, the requisite attention
to a feminine presentation, the bodywork needed to achieve it, and the
limited (albeit temporally changing) range of acceptable feminine sizes,
shapes, and appearances. An initial analysis was also presented regarding
specific class and race differences in this aspect of gender performativity.
It was shown that female athletes, as a group, are both in compliance and
non-compliance with the gender/femininity requirements depending, to
some extent, on the best fit of body to sport. This can be both a conscious
and unconscious process, which may have a component of intentional resistance (Heywood & Dworkin, 2003) by some athletes in specific sports

and physical activities, or one of compliance necessity or encouragement in other more traditionally gender-appropriate activities.

As can be seen by the quote at the start of this chapter, differences between the movements of girls and boys are noticed and frequently used as evidence that girls' bodies move differently than boys' bodies. These observed differences always highlight the apparent deficiencies of girls' movements and, therefore, are used as further evidence that girls ought not to participate in most sports. The fact that there are certain movements that girls execute with greater efficiency and grace than boys is ignored, even though these movements are also necessary for successful performance in almost all sports.

Observed differences between the sexes are seen to be natural and universal. The fact that many young girls are never properly taught to throw using an overhand pattern, or many other essential sport-related patterns, is rarely seen to be an issue. A throwing pattern that evokes the phrase "you throw like a girl" is also demonstrated by boys who have an immature overhand throw, but this is also generally ignored or denied when, or if, analyses of girls' movements are undertaken.

Bartky's second signifier of femininity refers to the specific gestures, postures, and movements appropriate to a feminine woman. As the majority of sports are still designated as masculine activities,[1] all of the gestures, postures, and movements required to participate in these activities would not only be de facto masculine, but could also be seen to be masculinizing—part of the process by which males, presumably, would learn masculinity. This category of Bartky's classification of femininity would therefore place all female athletes in these masculine-designated activities into a masculine realm.

THE MASCULINITY BARRIER

As discussed earlier, the labelling of female athletes as mannish or masculine is a difficult obstacle for some girls and women to overcome. Participation in a sport in which the mere learning and execution of the requisite motor skills places the participant into a masculine/masculinizing realm might be enough to deter many females from acquiring the skills needed to participate in that activity.[2] This will contribute to the continuing stereotypes of these sports and activities as appropriate only for boys and men, and of female athletes who participate in them as masculine and, possibly, lesbian. This is one more example of the applications of social-role theory and objectification theory. It places restrictions on a feminine gender role and causes girls and women to question their involvement in many sporting activities, if they even consider physical activity an appropriate option for themselves at all.

If Bartky's classifications are correct, and posing and posturing to display the body are indicative of femininity, then not only do gymnastics activities, dance, figure skating, and synchronized swimming fit these criteria, but, ironically, so does bodybuilding. This is a sport that would seem to occupy a place at the extreme opposite end of the gender continuum from any feminine-designated sport. The classification of bodybuilding as a masculine/male sport would not be questioned by most North Americans. However, bodybuilding is a sport of appearance. Judging is based on the execution of poses and the successful outcome of the attempts at bodywork undertaken by the athletes. Therefore, it is more feminine in nature than masculine—at least within its competition mode (Daniels, 1992). Female bodybuilders are not vindicated by this analysis.

The contradiction of attempting to classify a sport such as bodybuilding as feminine comes from the notion that contemporary standards of beauty are an indicator of femininity. Even though a toned body is now more accepted (and frequently celebrated) as an appropriately feminine body, muscles remain an indicator of masculinity. Therefore, muscles do not equate with beauty or, consequently, femininity. The posing component of a bodybuilding competition is the medium through which the competitor displays the size and definition of large, "ripped," masculine muscles. The feminine component of posing is overshadowed by the masculine association with muscle and the masculine movements in the weight room needed to achieve those muscles. Bodybuilding could possibly be labelled a sport of "musculinity" (Hargreaves, 1994), where the existence of muscles makes the activity masculine. This is demonstrated by the reluctance of bodybuilding judges to evaluate female and male competitors by the same criteria. They often determine that women who are the most muscular are not necessarily the winners or the best representatives of the sport. This completely overlooks bodybuilding as the quintessential polygendered sport. Even when sports are contested according to traditional feminine comportment, if the sport is labelled as culturally normative for males, any association with femininity is discounted. This becomes a double bind for women who choose to participate in certain sports or activities.

One might be hard pressed to define many of the gestures and postures that are common to the successful participation in sports as feminine. The tremendous exertion seen on the body and in the face of the female shot putter would not be classified as feminine by many observers. Neither would elbowing opponents in the key in basketball, executing a sliding tackle in soccer, being covered with mud and sweat in a three-day event in equestrian competition, or hanging off the side of a cliff in rock climbing. If the actions performed by women are not identified as feminine then it follows, through everyday logic, that the women who execute those actions are not feminine either. The less feminine the actions, the less feminine and, consequently, more masculine the performer must be. This analysis relates more to the traditional outcomes of the gender binary than to the reality of the abilities of female and male bodies to execute movements for myriad purposes.[3]

Although there are no anatomical or physiological reasons for movements to be limited to either female or male bodies (or any other forms of intersex or trans bodies),[4] it is interesting to consider that, in reality, the natural and learned movements that *may* be accomplished by any human body are often limited by the sex of that body. These limitations actually have nothing to do with the biological sex of the body, but rather the cultural conditions of gender that are imposed on those sexed bodies.

TAKING UP SPACE

When postures, gestures, and movements are gendered and their appropriate use places them within particular social spaces, they then have the "generative potential that [is] facilitated and enhanced when combined with gendered physical *artifact* (language systems; clothes; dedicated social spaces; equipment, such as batons and pom-poms, rugby balls and gum shields; personal belongings, etc.) that are themselves designed for gendered bodies and have the effect of gendering bodies" (Brown, 2006, p. 171). The same cultural limitations that set out the acceptable look and display of the feminine and the masculine body dictate the appropriate postures, gestures, and bodily motions of female/feminine and male/masculine bodies. How females are taught to move and position their bodies in various spaces and situations has a strong impact on how girls learn to live and understand their lives and to prepare for becoming women—as if there is only one way of being a woman.

Chapter 1 discussed the definition of femininity in dualistic relation to masculinity. Females are positioned as *other* in relation to males. Therefore, what is feminine can only be defined in opposition to what is masculine. It was also discussed that these gender assignments are created rather than natural because they change from time to time and culture to culture. "This problem of shifting definitions is exacerbated by our inability to define either masculinity or femininity except in relation to each other and to men and women.... We end up attributing to 'masculinity' ways of being that are found in dominant male groups in particular social circumstances" (Paechter, 2006, p. 254).

There is an assumption embedded in this process: that we know what it is that boys and men do and that they all do the same things. This is certainly erroneous! However, we often proceed with our lives and allow our social structures and institutions to function as if there are universal truths about what boys and men do. Therefore, these are things that girls and women ought not to do if they are to be seen as feminine.

Most sports, games (including those that are officially designated as "national sports" such as lacrosse [summer] and ice hockey [winter] in Canada),[5] and other activities that require a strong and capably trained body are contained within the assignment of masculinity. Even though sport participation by young North American girls is approaching almost universal levels, there is still a stigma placed on many girls, teenagers, and women who choose to participate in those activities that have been traditionally defined as masculine. Much of this stigma comes not only from the supposedly non-/anti-feminine body displayed by these women, but also from the requirements of the sport participants to position or move their bodies in ways that are deemed to be masculine. Movements that are executed by the female body are constrained to fit contemporary ideals of femininity. Most movements required in sports and physical activities do not meet this standard. It is not only how a body looks that determines its femininity. Rather, how that body moves must also be recognized and interpreted as feminine (Lock, 2006).

The assignment of some sports as masculine or feminine could be the result of the early work in masculine and feminine personality, such as that undertaken by Terman and Miles in the 1920s and 1930s. It can be recalled from Chapter 2 that Terman and Miles (1936) created a personality test that resulted in a masculinity rating. The selection of items for their final test instrument was based on preliminary data collection using tests made up of items that were created by the researchers and based on *their* perceptions of what would elicit positive associations from either female or male subjects. It should be restated that Terman and Miles were looking to discover deviance/extremes in masculine and feminine personality types regardless of the sex of the subject. However, their data came to be used to set the parameters of gender that would define persons with male bodies as masculine and those with female bodies as feminine. There was very little flexibility in these designations because all similarities and shared characteristics were eliminated in Terman and Miles' research methodologies.

In the area of sports and games, Terman and Miles confirmed the preferences of boys and girls for a variety of activities. Results of their work showed that boys had a preference over girls for activities such as bicycling, archery, bowling, hiking, horseback riding, kite flying, swimming, and skiing (Terman & Miles, 1936, p. 12). These may seem odd today, as these activities are not generally designated as masculine or feminine and many girls and women participate in all of these activities. However, these activities require a freedom of movement that may not have been available to many females in the 1920s and 1930s, and may explain the preference for them indicated by boys.

The team and contact sports that seemed to be preferred by boys in the 1920s' studies have maintained their masculine designation to this day.[6] Football, wrestling, boxing, baseball, and basketball continue to carry stigmas for female participants, and the opportunity for girls and women to even learn the skills needed to participate in some of these activities is limited. Had Terman and Miles conducted their research in Canada or certain northern regions in the United States, then ice hockey and lacrosse might have generated similar results. If their work had been conducted in many countries of the world, the only team sport mentioned at all might have been soccer. The omission of these sports and other activities underlines the argument that time and place, race, class, and ethnicity can all contribute to the forever-vacillating components of gender as they relate to sports and physical activities themselves, as well as to the participants who choose or are permitted to engage in them.

One probable reason that these activities were seen to be preferred by boys over girls is that they were taught to boys in schools and were the foundation of interscholastic and intercollegiate competition in institutions that were often closed to girls. In addition, industrial leagues were open to male blue-collar workers and/or immigrant masses. That the postures and movements needed to play these sports are still designated as masculine is not difficult to understand.

The only activity that was significantly preferred by girls over boys in Terman and Miles' studies that would still be designated as a "sport" today was skating (Terman & Miles, 1936, p. 12). It cannot be overlooked that today's feminine designation for figure skating has the same negative impact on male figure skaters that masculine sporting activities have on female athletes. The male figure skater is vilified and often assumed to be gay because of his involvement in an activity that is seen to be feminine due to the grace and dance-like movements required, and is thus "reserved" for females (Adams, 1997). It is interesting to note that figure skating (feminine) and ice hockey (masculine) both have skating as their most basic skill. Speed skating, which obviously also has skating as its most basic skill, is not labelled as either masculine or feminine in a North American context. This could be because both females and males began to engage in organized competitive speed skating at the same time, and because both Canada and the United States have had many female and male world-class skaters arise together. It is desirable that sports not be gendered.

Other physical activities that were preferred by girls in the Terman and Miles (1936) study included dance,[7] hopscotch, and jumping rope.[8] Although these physical activities are not considered sports, they involve movements that require grace, balance, rhythm, and agility. These are all factors that are still indicative of gender-appropriate activities for girls. These attributes are also downplayed in their importance in masculine activities, even though without them success in all sports would be limited! Grace, balance, rhythm, and agility are overlooked in "masculine" activities in the same way that power and endurance are overlooked in "feminine" ones. The gestures and movements displayed in the execution of all of these activities represent some of the actions and postures about which Bartky might be concerned in this aspect of femininity designation.

A LADY DOES NOT GRUNT

Prior to the explosion of girls' and women's participation in sport in the latter third of the 20th century, the "rules" of appropriate movements, gestures, and postures were clearly laid out by various sports governing bodies and well understood by the female physical educators who were responsible for fostering feminine sporting comportment in their female students. But just as the accepted/acceptable size and shape of the body has changed over time, and can be applied differently to women of races and classes that are not the dominant race/class of the time, gestures and movements have also had a strict application. What was appropriate sport-related femininity for women of the dominant culture was different from that for women of other races and classes.

A somewhat humorous example of this comes from women's tennis and the Wimbledon tournament. During the 1990s, many of the powerful strokes of the female players were accompanied by loud grunts. Anyone who has ever attempted to lift or push something heavy has probably made similar sounds and found this actually helps to accomplish the task! However, with British royalty in their courtside box, the grunting was seen to be very un-ladylike and players were instructed to curtail, or at least tone down, the practice. For a while, women's tennis became a quieter, more ladylike game. Today, the grunts are back and the complaints are gone. The level of excellence and the high entertainment value of the women's game were seen to be more important than artificial restrictions placed on exertion that might have been more appropriate in the time of Queen Victoria.

BOX 6.1

Appropriate movements and behaviours for aristocratic women were well understood in the late 1800s. Class and race separations were accompanied by different expectations for the deportment of girls and women from various classes and races. What was considered appropriate behaviour was designated specifically for white, upper-class women and became the foundation for what would be considered to be feminine. At the same time, "moving" pictures became a reality through advances in photographic technologies. Eadweard Muybridge, a photographer and leader in creating "moving" pictures, was asked to establish a program in photographic research at the University of Pennsylvania.

His "moving" picture series included thousands of photographs of men and women apparently engaged in prototypically masculine and feminine poses and movements. The photographs of men showed dynamic actions involving a variety of sporting motions such as throwing, striking, and jumping, and strenuous physical labour activities such as heavy lifting and swinging an axe. Some of the photographs of women showed movements such as walking and throwing, and household chores such as ironing, carrying laundry, and picking things up. Most of the images capture what must have been considered to be useful and typical feminine movements of the day. Some of these series are titled "woman walking, throwing scarf over shoulders"; "woman with hand to mouth walking down incline"; "woman walking upstairs and waving handkerchief"; "woman turning, throwing kiss, and walking upstairs"; "woman pirouetting"; "woman turning while carrying fan and flowers"; and "woman sitting down in chair and drinking tea" (Muybridge, 1955).

If these were the appropriate actions and gestures of feminine women of the time (strange as they may seem), then the rough-and-tumble actions of sporting activities that required expansive extension of body parts and movements through large areas of space would never have been acceptable as appropriate for the feminine woman. These "feminine" gestures, postures, and movements are now captured on celluloid. Muybridge's pictures became the first media "motion" pictures. They were seen by enthusiastic audiences in nickelodeons, who got a glimpse of "proper feminine movements."

CAUTIONS ON THE FREEDOM OF MOVEMENT

When I was an undergraduate in the late 1960s and early 1970s, the rules of dress and deportment for the female physical education majors and other competitive female athletes were made very clear to us, repeatedly. Many of our teachers were second-generation female physical educators. They had been taught by those original female teachers who had worked so hard to protect the femininity and reputations of the women, primarily white and middle/upper class, who went to university and wanted to participate in competitive sports. Underlying the admonitions regarding how we were to dress and move both on and off the field was the ever-present, lightly veiled spectre of lesbianism and lesbian labelling. The cautions regarding avoiding inviting this interpretation of our comportment were not only to "protect" those of us who played the traditionally masculine sports, but, very likely, themselves as well. Many of our teachers and coaches were the subjects of gossip regarding their sexuality. I now know that among those who were the most curious about or critical of these women were those of us who hid deeply in our own closets, sometimes for decades, to avoid the bogey-woman terrors of fitting the stereotype of the lesbian athlete.

Much of this analysis came from the easy freedom of movement of our bodies and the actions we performed in our sports. How we walked, sat, and moved were repeatedly scrutinized. "For many women as they move in sport, a space surrounds them in the imagination which we are not free to move around; the space available to our movement is constricted space" (Young, 1990, p. 143). This reality, as stated by Young, was one to which many of the physical education majors and athletes did not ascribe, yet was obvious in many of the non-athlete women on campus. We had a freedom of movement that took up all of the space we felt we needed, that had a confidence and a flow, and that was seen as anything but ladylike to our professors. On some level, I believe that all the while they corrected us on our movement behaviours they envied our refusal to comply with the constrictions of feminine movement—unless they impacted negatively on a grade or recommendation! I make this last conclusion based on my own reactions to my current female students and athletes who play sports and move in ways that, in some cases, would have seemed too far out of bounds to me as an undergraduate student. I celebrate their freedom of movement and their comfort in their bodies when they are not engaged in their own feminine self-surveillance.

DE COUBERTIN'S INFLUENCE LIVES ON

During the 1960s and 1970s, one of the most influential and oft-quoted books regarding women, sports, and feminine performativity was by Eleanor Metheny, a professor of physical education at the University of Southern California. Her book was entitled *Connotations of movement in sport and dance: A collection of speeches about sport and dance as significant forms of human behavior* (Metheny, 1965). This collection contains one essay entitled "Symbolic forms of movement: The feminine image in sports." This essay explores interpretations of the forms of sport, and thus the movements they contain, that are appropriate for women as determined by the International Olympic Committee (IOC). This is particularly significant because every nation that wishes to join the Olympic movement and include female athletes (and to a much lesser extent female coaches and officials, who still comprise insignificant numbers at the world level in all sports from all nations) in their delegations were subject to these IOC rules. The IOC was, therefore, extremely influential in spreading and maintaining "acceptable" gender-based actions and behaviours of female athletes worldwide.

Metheny (1965) wrote: "I have interpreted the Olympic events as symbolic formulations of man's conception of himself as a consequential force within the universe of space, time, mass, and energy" (p. 43). In her essay, Metheny evaluated the appropriate roles for women in movement and sporting behaviour and outlined the sport forms that the IOC (a group made up at this time entirely of upper-class, primarily white males, many with royal titles appended to their names) determined were "proper" for women in the Olympic games, and most likely everywhere else:

> At the international level, some forms of competition appear to be *categorically unacceptable*, as indicated by the fact that women are excluded from Olympic competition in these events.
>
> These forms include: Wrestling, judo, boxing, weight-lifting, hammer throw, pole vault, the longer foot races, high hurdles, and all forms of team games—with the recent exception of volleyball. (p. 49; emphasis in original)[9]

Metheny described these forms as appearing to be characterized by one or more of the following principles:

> *An attempt to physically subdue the opponent by bodily contact*
> *Direct application of bodily force to some heavy object*
> *Attempt to project the body into or through space over long distances*
> *Cooperative face-to-face opposition in situations in which some body contact may occur.* (p. 49; emphasis in original)

Beyond the obvious classification and common-sense understanding of these sports and movement characteristics as masculine and therefore not proper for women, when further analysis regarding participation in team sports is given, this classification also implies racism and classism. Metheny explained modifications of the above sanctions as they applied to college women in the United States. She wrote that team games are generally acceptable for and enjoyed by these women at an "intramural level." Most college and university female athletes at this time were white women of middle- and upper-class standing. The specification of "intramural level" is indicative of the non-interscholastic/intercollegiate programs offered by many high schools and colleges. Intramural games generally do not attract spectators or involve training or coaching, and are generally not seen to be in any way equivalent to the competitive programs (supported by scholarships in certain sports) that are available to male college and university athletes. Removing public competition from women's involvement in team sports added to their acceptability to white, middle- and upper-class women because they were more private and removed from the masculine forms played by men. Metheny offered no further explanations regarding the involvement of non-white women or those from lower socio-economic classes in these team sports.

Race and/or class differences in the application of feminine movements and gestures are more obvious in Metheny's second classification of appropriate sports and activities. She wrote: "Some forms of competition are generally *not acceptable* to college women in the United States, although they *may be acceptable to a minority group* within the college population" (Metheny, 1965, p. 49; emphasis in original).

> It *may be appropriate* for women identified in the lower levels of socioeconomic status to engage in contests in which:
>> the resistance of an *object of moderate weight* is overcome by direct application of bodily force
>> the body is projected into or through space over moderate distances or for relatively short periods of time
>
> It is *wholly appropriate* for women identified with the more favored levels of socioeconomic status to engage in contests in which:
>> the resistance of a *light object* is overcome with a *light implement*
>> the body is projected into or through space in aesthetically pleasing patterns
>> the velocity and manoeuvrability of the body is increased by the use of some manufactured device
>> a spatial barrier prevents bodily contact with the opponent in face-to-face forms of competition (Metheny, 1965, pp. 51–52; emphasis in original)

The notion of appropriate activities and the acceptable deviations from white, middle- or upper-class, and heterosexual femininity when applied to women of colour or lower classes does not only exist in college and university populations but in all aspects of performance sport. Not only can the size and shape of the non-white body be bigger and more muscular, but there is a greater acceptability of non-white women executing gestures and movements that are larger or require more power and strength. As was presented in the last chapter, the assumed physicality of women of colour, making them "less than," is one benchmark of racist thinking. It was certainly true during the time that Metheny was writing the above "rules" as absolute truths, but many of these ideas continue to be accepted today. As Caudwell (2006) wrote based on a study conducted on women's soccer in England, "black femininity and white-working class femininity are often understood as tasteless and sexually deviant" (p. 153). It is apparent that masculine/feminine differences are as biased as any class and racial biases that continue to exist in sport.

One example of the outcome of such racist and classist attitudes can be seen in an overview of the throwing events in track and field at the Olympic and World levels over the years. This provides an illustration that might not prove race-based differences in this aspect of femininity, but which gives cause for speculation. Results of the shot-put event at the Olympic Games since track and field became a sport for women in 1928 reveal an interesting pattern. In general, women from Canada and the United States, countries with fairly similar cultures and attitudes toward women and sport, have not fared well in this event at the Olympic level. Even in 1984, when the then Soviet Union boycotted the Los Angeles Olympic Summer Games and kept the world's best throwers out of the competition, only one North American woman, who was African-American, reached the finals. The statistics available for the all-time top performers in shot put, discus, javelin, and hammer list almost no North American women. It can be said that the former Iron Curtain countries have dominated these events to the exclusion of women from all other countries. For the most part this is true, but we still might ask why the United States and Canada chased so vigorously after the Soviet Union in gymnastics and figure skating, but not in the more masculine-identified sports and events? The answer to this question ought to be obvious.

There could be many reasons for the absence of highly successful North American women in these events, but if Bartky (1988) is correct in her first two identifying conditions of femininity, then both the body size required for successful performance and the non-feminine nature of the gestures and movements of certain events might be considered too gender-deviant for the comfort level of North American women who want to be accepted within the dominant cultural expectations for femininity. It is possible, however, that the gold-medal-winning performance in the discus event at the 2008 Beijing Olympic Summer Games by Stephanie Brown Trafton, a white woman from the United States, will be a harbinger of an important change in attitude toward this event. Miller (2001) supported this when he wrote: "female masculinity can now be rearticulated as a prize rather than a curse" (p. 11). The movement toward the acceptance of female masculinity is an important one relative to achieving gender parity (Halberstam, 1998).

Metheny (1965) identified other activities that were generally acceptable for college women, including "swimming, diving, skiing, figure skating, and such non-Olympic events as golf, archery, and bowling"[10] (p. 50). She also listed "fencing [and] such non-Olympic sports as squash, badminton, and tennis"[11] (p. 50) as generally acceptable. Her reasons for indicating that these sports and activities were acceptable enough in movements, gestures, and postures to be deemed feminine were that "competence in these events does not appear to militate against social acceptance by males within the college population" and that there is "no implication of limited social acceptance for successful competitors" (p. 50).

It is also important to note that most of these sports and activities have a tradition of being associated with or restricted to participation by the upper classes. They have traditionally required time, money, and access to facilities that, up to this point, had generally been private and closed to non-white, lower-class members, and often to followers of specific religions such as Judaism and Catholicism. Metheny included bowling in her grouping of acceptable sports, but indicated that the lower cost of participation and the heavy ball made the activity popular with middle-class women. Bowling and volleyball were also acceptable for white, middle- and upper-class women because they were increasing in popularity as mixed social activities among women and men.

It can be seen that movements, postures, and gestures that are considered feminine within the sporting realm have less to do with being female than with being acceptable and attractive to white, upper-class males who are seeking appropriate marriage partners. Once more, designations of femininity and masculinity have more to do with power and privilege than with having a female body or a male body. Any biologically based arguments regarding the ability of girls and women to acquire and execute "masculine" movements, gestures, and postures in sport have been shattered in the short period of time since the belief system discussed by Metheny (and the restrictions of the IOC) had common-sense acceptability. Males also participate in sports and activities that contain the acceptable feminine-designated characteristics outlined by Metheny. The polygendered nature of all athletes becomes more obvious.

BACKLASH AT AN OLYMPIAN LEVEL

The push for greater sport involvement by and for girls and women was already beginning to occur in North America when Metheny's book was published in 1965. The pressure was obviously worldwide, because in 1968 the IOC implemented its practice of sex testing female athletes entered in the Olympic Summer and Winter Games. The powerful men of the IOC and the IOC Medical Commission were suspicious of the increasingly high performances of female athletes. In many cases, female Olympians were breaking Olympic and World records that had been set by male athletes (particularly in swimming and track events) only a few years earlier. The overall performances of female athletes were improving at a much faster rate than those of men. The only possible explanation there could be was that men were masquerading as women, because women could not possibly be such excellent athletes in so many sports and events. In reality, many of the female athletes, especially in the weight and throwing events, did not fit into an acceptably attractive package in either physical look or the performance of feminine movements.

The practice of sex testing was controversial from its inception and protests dogged its existence until it was finally stopped by the IOC for the 2000 Olympic Summer Games in Sydney. The fact that the IOC changed the name of the testing from "sex testing" to "femininity testing" to "gender verification" before eliminating the practice shows that there was greater concern for the attractiveness and sexual appeal of the female athletes than for their incredible sporting talents.

The initial passing of Title IX, the United States law that prohibits discrimination based on sex in all schools that receive federal funding, occurred in 1972—only seven years after the publication of Metheny's influential book and four years after the inception of sex testing. The most significant effect of Title IX was the staggering increase of girls' participation in school and university sports. Whereas opposition to the IOC's practice of sex testing came from women's groups, the subsequent opposition to Title IX, a law that helped to promote female sport participation and that continues to this day, remains primarily from men's groups.

Rejecting the Backlash

In the last 40 years, almost all restrictions on women's involvement in sports and in events at the Olympic Summer and Winter Games have disappeared, although attitudes have not always kept pace.[12] In the United States, female participation in school and university sports has increased by more than 500%. Girls and women have been involved since the beginning of many of the new risk-based sports such as snowboarding, aerial skiing, and white-water kayaking and canoeing. They are also active participants in most sports and activities that get little attention from television and magazines, such as water-skiing, rock climbing, rugby, BMX racing, and mountain biking.

If female bodies were not able to acquire and successfully execute the skills needed to participate in these activities; if females were not intrigued by the challenges, risks, and mental/physical/spiritual satisfaction of participation; and if females were not loving training and competing in all sports, then challenging the notion of gender would be moot. Muscles are strong—not male or female. Sport was a creation of people, not nature. The movements that muscles can make are essential for all sorts of human tasks both on and off the playing fields. The designation of movements, gestures, and postures as masculine or feminine has outlived the social and economic necessities that imposed the gender roles once required by our culture. It is time to put this aspect of Bartky's classifications of femininity to rest.

Chapter 7

PUTTING ON YOUR GAME FACE:
THE BODY AS AN ORNAMENTAL SURFACE

> What I noticed about the freshman was that she was
> the only player with auburn hair. For the most part,
> that's how I keep track of the players—their dos.
> Granted, it's not foolproof given all the faux-blond
> ponytails. (Vermillion, 2006, p. 3)

In Chapter 3, I reported on the research of Helgeson (1994) in which
subjects described their perceptions regarding some of the strongest indicators of the feminine female. These included wearing a dress, having
long hair, being concerned with appearance, and having manicured nails
and well-done make-up. None of these appearance factors would be listed
if one were to ask a group of people to list the characteristics of an athlete!
However, female athletes are assumed—and in some cases required—to be
"feminine" simply because they are women.

How does the outward presentation of the body and the bodywork
required to achieve it impact the female athlete who, we now realize, could
have a body size and shape and perform movements and postures that are
recognized as masculine and are located exclusively within that gender
assignment? The definition or perception of bodywork for females is also
problematic because the female athlete spends hours everyday on various
aspects of bodywork, including proper nutrition and physical training of
her body according to the specific needs of her sport. Does this not count
as feminine bodywork? Possibly not, because it is undertaken for the
purpose of caring for and shaping the body for what is often recognized
as masculine: sport!

Many female athletes, quite likely, spend greater amounts of time
attending to feminine-designated bodywork than many non-athletic

women. Athletes in traditionally gender-appropriate sports for females are required to present themselves as feminine and hetero-sexy for competitive situations, so feminine bodywork becomes part of their sport-specific training regimen. In this way, some female athletes are more like fashion models or movie stars, who also are required to have a feminine presentation of self as part of their work lives. On the other hand, female athletes in traditionally gender-appropriate sports for males may spend an inordinate amount of time in feminine bodywork practices to create an acceptably feminine presentation of self or to "disguise" a body size and shape that is ideally suited to their sporting practices, but which may not be otherwise identified as anything but masculine. Lesbian athletes, who might otherwise have a stereotypical lesbian presentation of self, may undertake a specific regimen of feminine bodywork in an attempt to "pass" as straight in order to be acceptable to coaches, team mates, sport organizations, or sponsors who might reject or overlook them because of their sexuality. Therefore, many women in these areas experience implicit or explicit pressure to present themselves in ways that are unequivocally hetero-feminine.

In these contexts, the word "feminine" has become a codeword for precisely this heterosexual image (Lenskyj, 1995, p. 48). Because of this, many female athletes will undertake personal bodywork in an attempt to present a body that is read as feminine regardless of its size, shape, or the movements it performs. The purpose of this is to present a body and perform a gender that is seen to fit with the contemporary ideal of "woman." "It is usual to assume that such feminine display either functions to appease [the] male gaze or is the corollary of hetero-patriarchal control and regulation" (Caudwell, 2006, p. 152). Regardless of the underlying reason for demonstrating a feminine = woman = heterosexual display of the body, this gender performance for female athletes has become almost compulsory in the North American context.

Female athletes are not very different from myriad non-athletic women who treat their bodies as a canvas to meet the needs of feminine presentation and a hetero-sexy image. They often decorate their bodies and create an illusion of femininity that goes beyond the general social expectation of gender-role conformity.[1] When women apply make-up they refer to it as "putting on" or "fixing" their face. This could be interpreted as a mask behind which the real woman resides in order to display her proper gender through gender-appropriate display. "Women's bodies have long been considered little more than malleable clay to be reshaped to meet whatever the standard of the day, no matter what the risk, discomfort or pain" (Weitz, 1998, p. 186). Female athletes are not excused from this need to meet a feminine standard. Many have to negotiate a fine, yet undefined line between creating the body that is necessary for their sport and not creating a body that is perceived by critics to be masculine, even with today's greater acceptance for women's bodies to be toned and somewhat muscular.

A GAME WITHIN A GAME

For the female athlete, whether in training, practise, or competition, to attempt to hide behind a mask of proper feminine performativity seems to be a practice that could be interpreted as anything from a waste of time to ridiculous if it impacts her athletic performance. However, this practice does seem to give an air of feminine legitimacy, and therefore greater acceptance as women, to many female athletes.[2] Off the field, some female athletes may be even more concerned with their presentation of self. How they dress, wear their hair, and use make-up, jewellery, and other accoutrements of femininity may be a strategy to deflect further critique or to intentionally invite a gaze that will evaluate and interpret them as heterosexually feminine. This may occur regardless of an athlete's personal interpretation of gender and sexuality.

The focus on sex and sexuality cannot be overlooked or minimized in the assessment of a woman's body and the presentation of her embodied self, whether she is an athlete or not. "Society's focus on female sexual characteristics—a glaring, virtually voyeuristic focus—has made girls excruciatingly self-conscious" (Dowling, 2000, p. 116). At a very young age, girls internalize the images of females created by and for a male-dominated culture. Girls "learn to overvalue their external selves. Generally speaking, when one body part is given importance above the others, the image of the body as a whole is distorted" (Dowling, 2000, p. 116). The attention female athletes pay to this aspect of self has, in the past, been referred to as an apologetic—an attempt to be valued as feminine females while consciously choosing to remain involved in a masculine-defined activity (Ellison, 2006). There would be no need for an apologetic position from the polygendered female athlete.

Although there are no feminine signifiers that are universally adopted by female athletes in their attempts to present themselves as hetero-sexy, feminine females, one comes close: the ponytail. Even athletes who are comfortable with their polygendered selves and do not engage in a conscious practice to feminize themselves often sport a ponytail! Often the only way to tell whether a group of participants engaged in a sporting competition is female or male is to see the ubiquitous ponytails on the female players. In North America, the ponytail is seen in great enough proportions to have become identified as a female gendex characteristic of athletes. The importance of the ponytail as a key signifier of not only young females, but also of female athletes, is clearly illustrated by the following quote from *Rapunzel's Daughters: What Women's Hair Tells Us about Women's Lives*: "When I asked ten-year-old Janet whether her hair is part of her identity, she says, 'Yes. When I have it in a ponytail, that's when I feel most like myself. I'm a sporty girl: always ready to play, energetic, running, and willing to do things. I can do all that if it's in a ponytail'" (Weitz, 2004, p. 63).

Prior to the Title IX era, a sex-role conflict between being female and being an athlete was great enough to keep many girls and women out of most sports altogether. Post-Title IX, being involved in sport is taken to be a right by most North American girls and their parents. However, girls' involvement in sports, especially traditionally gender-appropriate sports for males, coupled with the success of feminist movements in improving women's positions in all aspects of society, has come at a high price—a social backlash that has put even more pressure on women to present themselves as feminine. Underlying this backlash is a long-held social need for difference, which underlies all hierarchical and hegemonic structures.

The more equal women and men become, the less power the artificial social stratifications between them have. This also applies to race, class, age, ethnicity, sexuality, and any other socially constructed hierarchies that function to keep some people/groups in a position of privilege over other people/groups. "Without difference you cannot have hierarchy, or one up, one down. You cannot have better and worse, weak and strong, superior and inferior. Hierarchy is how social inequality is maintained, and 'masculinity' and 'femininity' are about hierarchy" (Dowling, 2000, p. 48).

If sport itself continues to be used to maintain masculine hegemony then the women who participate in sport will be forced to prove their femininity in order to be accepted and acceptable as athletes. The most obvious way to do this is through manipulation of the body. The feminine presentation of self (off the court, if not on it) is one of the surest ways for these women, who experience a social gaze and critique in a most public showground, to garner some social acceptance.

WHEN APPEARANCE COUNTS

To this end, Bartky's third category of feminine identification applies here: the outward appearance of the body. Women's bodies have always been a canvas upon which women paint their public face. The necessity of feminine bodywork in the realm of sport is an incongruity for which there can be no explanation, other than to maintain expected gender roles and keep girls and women as less-than participants in the domain of sport even as their performances begin to rival and sometimes surpass those of their male counterparts.

There are some sports in which the appearance of the athlete does have an impact on her final placing in a competition, or even her admittance to the sport/physical activity in the first place. These are the judged sports such as figure skating, gymnastics, and synchronized swimming. Too often a judgment is made regarding the appearance of the athlete at the expense of her performance score.[3] Because of this reality, many young girls (who are the primary participants in these sports) develop extremely distorted notions of their bodies and how they must be displayed. However, the importance of maintaining a feminine presentation of self extends to all female athletes in all sports, even if that presentation has nothing to do with performance factors or the end result of a competition.

In an attempt to overcome any question of femininity in the female athlete, numerous outward signifiers of what is considered feminine often adorn the athlete, even when such displays might be inconvenient or even dangerous to the competitor (Daniels, 2002). Florence Griffith-Joyner (Flo-Jo) might well be remembered more for her flamboyant uniforms, long and decorated fingernails, flowing hair, and jewellery than for her world-record-setting performances in track and field events at the Olympic Games. Her powerfully muscled body was in clashing contrast to the ornamentation with which she adorned herself. Brandi Chastain, a member of the World Cup championship U.S. women's soccer team is likely to be remembered more as "that female athlete who tore off her shirt at the end of a game" and turned herself, in the gaze of the spectator and much of the media, into a sexualized female with a sports bra rather than a world-class athlete. It is likely that most people, even soccer fans, could not pick Chastain out of a group of women, but that her name would be easily recalled by people shown the much-publicized picture of her at the end of that game on her knees, shirt held high overhead, and sports bra exposed. The muscle-revealing clothing of Serena Williams could almost be seen as a challenge to the white, upper-class sensibilities of tennis where the "model" of contemporary feminine display and deportment is expected to be adhered to by the female player. Female athletes whose bodies are covered with shape-distorting uniforms such as ice hockey players, or whose bodies are obviously female but are engaged in quintessentially masculine activities such as boxing, are often seen holding their small children following a competition. This not only represents a traditionally gender-appropriate role for them outside of sport, but it hints at heterosexuality for participants who more often than not are whispered to be lesbians.

Make-up, long and somewhat inconvenient hairdos or hair ribbons, jewellery, and long artificial fingernails are not usually mentioned when one lists the equipment necessary for participation in sport. Many female athletes, however, can be seen using such femininity markers in competitive situations. The contrast between the feminine trappings and the masculine somatotype of the female athlete reflects the need of some competitors to visually proclaim a feminine nature for their sport and for themselves.

Some female athletes obviously choose a feminine presentation of self because they are comfortable with the fit between their bodies and a social expectation of a feminine gender performativity. They may or may not be consciously aware that their choices of clothing, shoes, hairstyle, and make-up will often constrain the free-flowing movements of their sporting bodies into more "feminine" socially and spatially restricted ones when "off the court." Their choices may require them to take small steps when walking in high-heeled, pointy-toed shoes or to sit in a manner that forces their body to take up limited (and possibly uncomfortable) amounts of space due to cultural expectations as well as tight microskirts. They may move with less effort or speed in order to keep their hair in place or to avoid sweating (glowing?!). Whether or not they are comfortable with these restraints, their bodies are being controlled by a social expectation of sex- and gender-role display. Performing femininity, as engaged in by the female athlete, is akin to spectacle. The body is an object that is created, decorated, and displayed for the purpose of putting forward an image to signify compliance with one's gender, and therefore for female athletes, femininity (Caudwell, 2006; Theberge, 1985/1994).

BOX 7.1

It is often the case that rules apply only in specific ways or to specific groups. Although many Muslim female athletes display appropriate outward gender signifiers, many choose to wear the hijab during athletic participation as well as other times that they are in public. This head covering is worn to display feminine modesty. This is an obvious signifier of gender compliance. In sport, the hijab has not always been seen as a sign of feminine conformity, and has been problematic for some Muslim girls. After having played indoor soccer in a Calgary league for five years, a young Muslim girl was ejected from a game for refusing to remove her hijab. The official who made this ruling stated that it was for safety reasons only. Inquiries into why her hijab had been perfectly safe for the previous five years were not answered satisfactorily. The provinces of Ontario and British Columbia allow the wearing of the hijab in soccer games; Alberta and Quebec do not. Although an acceptable "soccer hijab" is now available in the marketplace, this Calgary player solved her problem by fashioning her hijab into a bandana— an acceptable solution to the official. Provincial and federal associations are still looking into the appropriateness and safety of this particular feminine signifier. It is interesting that an obvious feminine signifier and expression of modesty can cause such concern. The issue of an acceptable head covering for Muslim females wanting to engage in physical activity situations was dealt with in a 2009 episode of the Canadian comedy show *Little Mosque on the Prairie*, entitled "Baber is from Mars, Vegans are from Vegus." In this episode, Rayyan, a Muslim physician wanting to run in a charity event with her mother, finds a sports hijab which enables her to run in public with a head covering that is suitable to both sport participation and expected modesty.

Other female athletes may choose a feminine presentation of self out of fear of ostracism, lesbian labelling, or loss of their place on a team, or to encourage scholarship awards or lucrative sponsorship deals, which are often necessary for women to continue their training as amateur athletes or to survive as professional athletes, who generally make significantly less money than male athletes in the same sports.[4]

Some female athletes simply refuse to play the gender game at all!

Regardless into which of these groups (or others) female athletes fall, they all possess and display a polygendered existence simply because they are female athletes. The compartmentalization of the bodies and lives of female athletes[5] functions to maintain an internal (and possibly internalized) hierarchy that places the feminine = non-athlete aspect of their lives above the non-feminine = athlete (= masculine, = mannish, = lesbian?) aspect of their lives.

THE PRIVILEGE IN GENDER HIERARCHY

The hierarchically superior position of the feminine female over the perceived masculine female impacts the public exposure of all female athletes. It also places the physicality of female athletes in a hierarchy that renders and celebrates feminine bodies, gestures, movements, and hetero-sexy visages over all others. Female athletes who fulfill all three aspects of Bartky's categories of femininity have greater media appeal than those who are deemed to be lacking in one or more areas. Greater media exposure contributes to the maintenance of common-sense understandings of females who are also athletes. This mediated presentation of female athletes is carefully constructed and contributes to adherence to Bartky's third category: the outward appearance of the body.

Among the most popular televised women's sports, especially during coverage of the Olympic Summer and Winter Games, are gymnastics and figure skating. The athletes that participate in these sports are among the fittest and, pound for pound, strongest of any athletes—male or female. This aspect of these competitors is rarely mentioned, and any potential for it to be recognized by the viewer is veiled in skimpy, body-clinging uniforms (called "costumes" in figure skating and synchronized swimming to further move these sports closer to stage performance).

Outside of the Olympic Games, the most frequently televised women's sports are tennis and golf. These particular sports still carry with them a white, upper-class sensibility that informs viewers' notions of acceptable feminine demeanour and media (re)presentations of these activities, regardless of the race or ethnicity of the players. Women's beach volleyball has rapidly increased in popularity as a spectator sport and has consequently received increasing amounts of television coverage. The beautiful and scantily clad feminine-identified bodies of the athletes have most likely contributed to a large portion of this sport's popularity.

The clothing of female athletes in the most media-exposed sports often reflects a hyper-feminine or hyper-sexual image, which has escalated in the post-Title IX era. Figure-skating costumes have undergone a radical shift over the past few decades. The presentation of the female figure skater has always been one of femininity. Her costume, hair, and make-up leave no question that the athlete on the ice is female. Up until the 1970s, women's figure-skating outfits were feminine, but they were also demure. Arms and torsos were completely covered and skirts, although often short, were frequently long and generally flowing. Legs were always sheathed in tights or stockings. In the Title IX and post-Title IX eras there has been a progressive sexualization of the costumes and routines. Gradually, flesh-coloured inserts were strategically placed in the costumes to give the impression of a bare back or décolletage. More revealing and risqué costumes began to appear as successes in the feminist movement were met with a cultural backlash that required all women to display themselves as feminine, even as they built and/or climbed social and corporate ladders. Flesh-coloured inserts began to be seen at the midriff and the full length of the sleeve. Today, the inserts have disappeared and the skin that they were attempting to imitate is now clearly exposed. The female figure skater is not only required to display a highly feminine presentation, but also a dramatic and obviously heterosexual one. The frequently seen excessively sexualized routines performed by female figure skaters somewhat camouflage figure skating (and the masculine-identified physicality of the skater) as a sport behind a curtain of entertainment and spectacle.

Gymnastics uniforms are a second skin by necessity of the safety concerns of performance and the amplitude of body movements used in all the events. However, even the outward presentation of the female gymnast has changed. The standard long-sleeve, scoop-neck leotard of the mid-20th century initially began to be modified in the 1960s. The basic one-colour suit was adorned with lace piping at the neckline and sleeve hem and then with psychedelic-like, multi-coloured stripes and shapes, but it still retained the traditional form. Then, as with figure-skating costumes, gymnastics leotards became higher cut at the hip, lower cut at the back, and frequently sleeveless, and today are often decorated with flesh-coloured inserts. Sparkles frequently mirror the glitter worn on the cheeks and in the hair of the gymnasts. The often boyish, prepubescent bodies of the athletic young gymnasts somewhat remove them from the realm of "woman," but heterosexuality has taken a foothold in the requisite presentation of these (often) child athletes nonetheless. This is most particularly true of floor-exercise routines, which often contain sexually suggestive movements or facial expressions.

Gymnastics, figure skating, synchronized swimming, diving, tennis, and golf all fall among the most appropriate and acceptable sports for girls and women. These sports are also highly mediated as attention to the most attractive athletes may be broadcast instead of coverage of the best athletes' performances. However, even in these "feminine" sports the necessity for an outward display of the body to meet the requirements of contemporary hetero-sexy femininity is not diminished. It is obvious that for the majority of female athletes who have body shapes, sizes, movements, and postures that are understood to be masculine, how the body is decorated and displayed becomes even more problematic.

How female athletes dressed, styled their hair, walked, and behaved off the field was once as important a part of a coach's responsibility as the athletes' on-field training and performance. For the first three-quarters of the 20th century, coaches and promoters often attended to the dress and deportment of their female athletes.[6] How the women looked and behaved on and off the field was closely monitored because of the idea that female athletes were frequently seen by spectators, news reporters, and broadcasters as trespassers in the male territory of sport. Avoidance of the mannish and/or lesbian label was paramount to schools, organizations, and promoters (Hult, 1994). Compliance with contemporary rules of feminine presentation is generally no longer addressed within the structure and training regimens of sport, but it remains a central aspect of the bodywork that is seen to be a requirement for themselves by many female athletes, even as they continue to train their bodies and develop the necessary skills for competition. How athletes dress on planes and buses travelling to and from competitions, in restaurants while on the road, and in hotels on away trips is often closely monitored. This is equally true for male athletes because their comportment is seen as a reflection of their schools, sport organizations, or countries. However, bad behaviour by males off the court is often dismissed as "boys will be boys." Similar behaviour from female athletes is condemned with "girls will not be boys"!

CODIFYING FEMININITY IN WOMEN'S SPORTS

In the latter years of the 20th century and into the 21st, some sports governing bodies changed their required uniform specifications, apparently for little reason other than to sexualize the athletes in an attempt to attract more spectators and television coverage. The most obvious perpetrator is Fédération Internationale de Volleyball, the governing international volleyball association. Although many shirt and short styles would be functional for high-performance volleyball play, even the seaside attire that is appropriate for beach volleyball, the stipulations for women's volleyball uniforms state:

> The top must fit closely to the body and the design must be with deep cutaway armholes on the back, upper chest and stomach (2 piece) ... The briefs should ... be a close fit and be cut on an upward angle toward the top of the leg. The side width must be a maximum of 7 cm. The one piece uniform must closely fit and the design must be with open back and upper chest. (Fédération Internationale de Volleyball, 2004, p. 40)

There can be no mistaking an enforced sexualization of female volleyball players through this regulation of tight-fitting, high-cut at the leg, and low-cut at the chest uniforms. Volleyball has always been considered to be an appropriate team sport for girls and women because there is no direct physical contact between opponents. Therefore, the necessity of athletes to present themselves as feminine, even hyper-sexy-feminine, is present even in traditionally acceptable sports for females.

How a girl or woman defines feminine bodywork for herself is an individual choice that is impacted by family, peers, media, race, class, socialization, and other agents of importance in her life, such as teachers, coaches, role models, and icons. Compliance with or resistance to the trappings of femininity *du jour* can be difficult to ascertain because whatever is "in" often changes on a whim within the fashion or music industries, the media, and internet blogs and with resistance to parental expectations, on social or political movements, and so on. The impact of these whims is generally greater on girls and women than on boys and men because the limits of what is outwardly and acceptably masculine are kept fairly rigid. Because what is feminine is what is not masculine, attention to the ever-changing trappings of femininity and feminine presentation of self requires a measure of vigilance.

DECORATING THE BODY

Using the body as an ornamental surface is common to females as well as males within every culture on the planet. How the body is decorated has often been strictly safeguarded by sex, status, and group affiliation (both in-group and out-group) or rebellion. The types of decorations vary within and across cultures and generations.

BOX 7.2

Tattooing is an increasingly common form of body adornment that is being adopted by women today. Among young women, including many female athletes, the practice of tattooing the body is obviously not seen to be an extreme form of bodily modification (Daniels, 2002). The popularity of marking the body is increasing among women of various ages, races, and ethnic backgrounds. Whether it can be accepted as feminine in common-sense understandings of the concept is yet to be seen!

It is likely that tattooing, like muscles, has become a more accepted component of feminine display. However, there is still an invisible and un-defined line that, if crossed, removes the female body from the feminine to the masculine or, in the case of tattooing, from the feminine to the bizarre.

> No form of skin modification is as layered with meaning as tattooing. As a largely representational, symbolically charged permanent mark it tells stories about female experience and triggers reactions that underscore cultural expectations of women.... Even after decades of feminist progress, however, women who mark themselves with tattoos commit a transgressive act whose shock value lingers on in some quarters today.... Tattoos appeal to contemporary women as both emblems of empowerment in an era of feminist gains and as badges of self-determination at a time when controversies about date rape, abortion rights, and sexual harassment have many women thinking hard about who controls their bodies—and why. (DeMello, 2000, p. 7)

The tattoo has always carried the significance of difference. It has been worn to signify power, status, group affiliation, or accomplishments that are not available to everyone. Generally, the tattoo has been a visual signifier of traditional masculinity (Atkinson, 2002). The decision of female athletes to get tattooed is often practiced as a group-based ritual to commemorate or celebrate a significant sporting achievement, such as winning a national championship or making an Olympic team (Daniels, 2004). Marking the body literally signifies affiliation with a group or commemoration of an important goal, or may represent an aspect of identity. With respect to the adornment of the female athlete's body for the purpose of adhering to compulsory femininity, there are some indications that athletes do practice self-surveillance in this regard, but that they also set their own rules.

Hairstyle has been an obvious signifier of feminine presentation for centuries, although differences in style for various social classes, ages, races, and ethnic groups have existed simultaneously. Even with these differences, the dominant cultural norm for hairstyle, and even colour, rapidly changes at the whim of fashion design and other social conditions. Hairstyle might be one of the most enduring and obvious indicators of compliance and non-compliance to a feminine presentation. Daily requirements for hair care—shampooing, brushing and blow-drying, styling, and periodic "repair"—is an obvious aspect of feminine bodywork that requires time for the daily attention it demands and money for the countless products needed to get the right look. A bad hair day is somewhat of a cliché, but as with all stereotypes there is some truth behind it.

For North American female athletes, the ponytail is worn in such overwhelming numbers that it seems to be a mandatory requirement for participation in most sports. Regardless of the feminine or masculine designation of the sport or activity, the ponytail is present in a number of forms such as braids, French braids, or a free-flowing horse tail. It often seems that nearly everyone playing on a specific team has an identical hairstyle on the field, making this feminine signifier appear to be a part of the team's uniform. It is as if the ponytail was ordered from a catalogue along with the rest of the uniform.

Because knowing the gender of a person influences how one might react to or treat that person, being able to distinguish between females and males is central to our interpersonal relationships and evaluations. Sometimes the only way to determine the gender of a group of athletes is by their hairstyles. There are some male athletes who wear their hair long. This sets them apart from the majority of their team mates. Long hair on a male athlete invites a quizzical gaze. It draws attention to the athlete, but the sporting of this female signifier is unlikely to call forth any question of the male athlete's sexuality. The absence of this near-universal femininity signifier on a female athlete, however, is often taken to be an indicator of lesbianism, especially if she participates in a traditionally masculine sport.

Female athletes who compete in the most obvious of masculine sports, such as boxing or rugby, have consciously crossed a line to become gender resistors or to be seen as polygendered individuals. They are more than passingly aware that their choice to engage in a particular sport invites criticism of their gender and their sexuality. What has changed in the mindset of these female athletes and others of their generation is that they do not question their right to be involved in any sport they choose in the first place. As females, they do not see sport and physical activity as a questionable performative aspect of their being. They elect to learn the skills necessary for participation in their sport of choice and to be involved in rough-and-tumble, contact-based activities. The physicality of many of the sports they choose is the reason they pick them.

This is not to say that these athletes reject their femininity or themselves as feminine individuals. To the contrary, female athletes today may be more aware of the duality/multiplicity of gender than their predecessors who engaged in "apologetic" behaviours only a generation ago. Those first Title IX-era athletes were challenging the belief that females did not belong in "real" (read: masculine) sports at all. Once a critical mass of females (and their parents!) had embraced the notion that sport was for girls as well as for boys, the barriers changed from "you do not belong here at all" to "you can be here, but you'd better look like what a woman should look like." In that admonition, what a woman should look like is a feminine, heterosexually attractive female.

There are female athletes who consciously challenge this constraint. In a narrative about herself as a high-performance rower, Tosha Tsang (2000) wrote: "You see, I am female. More precisely, I am a Canadian female—and I am a Canadian female with hairy legs" (p. 48). She reported that some of her team mates and competitors may not have been comfortable with her conscious rejection of an obvious compliance to a feminine presentation, but that she resented the pressure put on female athletes to conform to a "story of gender ... a beauty standard" (p. 49) that they are expected to play out on their bodies. Tsang stated that she felt "a slight resentment at being pressured to change something about myself that has been a choice characterized by struggle" (p. 49). She goes on to declare that it is important to her to resist the demand to conform.

There is no way to know how many female athletes feel this same way, but cave under the pressures to conform. It is likely that many transgender and transsexual athletes would endorse this kind of resistance. Until there is a critical mass of female athletes who have the conviction to live in and present their bodies as they choose, we are unlikely to see many who resist adorning their bodies in a way that is expected of feminine women.

Women have won a hard-fought battle to be able to engage in any sport they choose. The price that has been exacted for that privilege is clearly stamped on their bodies. The media perpetuates the requirement that for sport to be acceptable for women, its representatives must be media-genic glamazons. This makes invisible or challenges the heterosexuality of any female athletes (most especially those in traditionally masculine-identi-fied sports) who do not femme-inize their bodies to meet demands that are unfair and incongruent to a naturally polygendered individual.

The dilemma of presenting an acceptably feminine body is further complicated for female athletes who come from outside of the dominant cultural group. "Gendered (along with 'raced' and 'classed') bodies cre-ate particular contexts for social relations as they signal, manage, and negotiate information about power and status" (Martin, 2003, p. 220). Commentary on the body is one of the most obvious indicators of the du-al-gendered cultural understanding of sport. The gendering of sport must end altogether or the polygendered nature of all athletes, male as well as female, must be accepted as ordinary. Until the female athlete can throw off the label of being gender-incongruent (and therefore masculine), her physical appearance will remain central to the evaluations made of her. She will be seen using hegemonic femininity markers in competitive situ-ations and in her everyday life, even if they do not fit who she sees herself to be. The contrast between contemporary requisite femininity and the supposedly masculine somatotype of the female athlete underlies the desire/need of some competitors to visually attach feminine signifiers to their sport and to themselves.

Chapter 8

THE END GAME:
A NEW POLYGENDERED BEGINNING

> Words act so much like human beings that sometimes
> it is hard to tell them apart. Their lives follow the pat-
> tern of our own life histories. Some are born over on
> the wrong side of the railroad tracks—dirty words or,
> at the least, vulgar ones that are barred from better
> society. They have a grubby childhood and ragamuf-
> fins for companions. Other, lucky ones are born in the
> Mayfair district with a silver spoon in their mouths.
> (Funk, 1950, p. 51)

Words are powerful. They can take on a meaning much larger than their
use as communication tools. A single word can embody a concept greater
than its part of speech or definition ever intended. The perception attached to a word can change and grow until a particular arrangement of
letters takes on the clout to control a person's life or beliefs. There have
been many such words over time. Some words have become so offensive
that their use today generates immediate condemnation of the user. Other
words become passé, for they are too old-fashioned or no longer describe a
concept, technology, or belief system that has any use in today's cultural
consciousness. One of the purposes of this book is to stage a coup and de-
throne the words gender and femininity or, if they cannot be designated
as passé, to at least reduce their conceptual power. The reason for this is to
remove some of the barriers that girls and women face in achieving their
potential and celebrating themselves as persons.

One arena in which gender is responsible for constructing numerous barriers to girls' and women's growth is sport and involvement in
physical activity. "A positive self concept is an important part of human

development and sports participation has been known to contribute to it" (Klomsten, Skaalvik & Espnes, 2004, p. 119). The results of a study by Angelini (2008) showed that females feel a positive sense of arousal and dominance when watching female athletes on television that does not occur when they watch male athletes. Obviously, numerous aspects of involvement in sport are empowering for women. However, hegemonic masculinity, and its absence (femininity), has the power to reduce the contribution of sport in the development of a strong self-concept in some girls and women.

The judgment that often befalls a female who underperforms her femininity is swift. Girls and women whose gender performativity is seen to be as more masculine than feminine because of their involvement in particular sports very often face a strong and swift critique of their gender adherence and/or sexuality. I challenge the notion of a feminine essence that all women must possess or that some women have more than others. Femininity "is rather a product of discourses, practices, and social relations that construct the situation of women in particular societies in ways that typically disable women in relation to men" (Whitson, 1994, p. 355). Thus, gender and femininity are two words for which common-sense understandings have grown to include a power that impacts the lives of girls and women on a daily basis, generally in a negative way, as they remove many of the individual's choices about how to be whomever she chooses.

The implications of gender and femininity are extensively misunderstood and misapplied. Their ever-changing meanings are based on shifting medical, scientific, and human constructs of existence for female members of the dominant cultural race and class, although they are used to scrutinize and judge all women in that culture and others (Roszak, 1999).[1] Even though the majority of women are not permitted the power or privilege of the women for whom these concepts were originally created or intended, they are nonetheless impacted by them.

The concept of gender has come to be synonymous with biological sex, although from the perspective of biomedical history the reverse was once the held to be true (Fausto-Sterling, 2000). Today, the foundation of one's gender is one's body (Bem, 1993; Rudacille, 2006). In other words, the body that one is born into is seen to completely determine one's abilities, behaviours, and interests because these are the socially determined components of gender. Although it can be accepted that some abilities, behaviours, and interests seem to be more strongly seen or developed in females or males, none of these factors is found solely in either sex (Roszak, 1999). "Deeply rooted assumptions about our bodies keep us locked into the belief that there are only two sexes—male and female—and that the sex of the body is always consistent with the sex of the brain" (Rudacille, 2006, p. 9). Hormonal influences on the hard-wiring of the brain do have some legitimacy in predicting differences between the sexes, but these are biological and only rarely apply exclusively to one sex or the other except in the area of reproduction. Culture and socialization also strongly effect the development of human beings and, therefore, gender.

FEMININITY: A SOCIAL CONSTRUCT

Femininity has come to be understood as the natural condition of all people born with female bodies. One problem with this designation is that science and medicine have clearly determined that the two-sex model of human beings (female and male exclusively) is incorrect, or at least incomplete (Fausto-Sterling, 2001). Even so, the most accepted solution to dealing with bodies that do not match accepted conformations, or bodies and brains that do not seem to match each other, is to medically and/or psychologically intervene in order to match the individual to the two-sex binary (van der Wijngaard, 1997). Even though many individuals are born outside of the XX or XY chromosomal conformation, with ambiguous genitalia, or as pseudo-hermaphrodites/intersexed individuals, the medical establishment defies its own findings by attempting to normalize these bodies to be exclusively female or male, and consequently feminine or masculine by default.

"The very attribution of femininity to female bodies as if it were a natural or necessary property takes place within a normative framework in which the assignment of femininity to femaleness is one mechanism for the production of gender itself" (Butler, 2004, p. 10). If gender cannot be eliminated as an artificial and limiting construct, acceptance of the polygendered nature of all humans could go a long way to eliminating the extreme measures that may be undertaken to match people to an artificial (or at least limiting) gender paradigm. Intersex, transgender, transsexual, and other self-designated queer persons would certainly applaud the freedom that would come with the elimination of a single, bipolar gender assignment. Accepting the polygendered state in all of us would enrich all of our lives.

Children who demonstrate significant cross-gender behaviours (including some girls who display tomboy characteristics and want to participate in traditionally masculine, rough-and-tumble activities, including sports) are often suspected by parents or other adults of having gender dysphoria—a condition of discomfort with one's assigned gender (Gottschalk, 2003). The children themselves often feel perfectly comfortable with who they are. There is probably no pathology in the overwhelming majority of children who make and enjoy cross-gender choices.

In extreme cases children can be diagnosed with gender identity disorder, which can be interpreted as a precursor to homosexual behaviour and, therefore, a condition that requires intervention. "Within social sciences, and particularly psychology, there is a long history of assuming that so-called cross-sex behaviours and preferences (e.g. athleticism among females) were indicators of emotional disturbance or sexual deviance" (Hall, 2002, p. 8). What a strange leap in logic to classify someone as having a psychological disorder "simply because someone of a given gender manifests attributes of another gender or a desire to live as another gender" (Butler, 2004, p. 5). This is particularly true when we see so much diversity in abilities, interests, and behaviours of individuals who are all assigned to a single sex/gender category.

There is no question that gender has a tremendous impact on how we live our lives and the choices that we make as females. But, on a daily basis, female/male differences may take on far too much power in defining and restricting individuals. The similarities among all types of people need to be recognized as also having a great influence on our day-to-day lives. The more we can celebrate our strengths, regardless of how these fit into an arbitrary gender binary, the happier and more confident we can all be as individuals.

Certainly, from a social perspective, being simply female/feminine or male/masculine is an easier state of being than attempting to negotiate social customs and conditions as something other than one of the two well-accepted alternatives. Wanting to be an athlete, especially if one is female, challenges this simplicity in a most profound way. The female athlete who trains hard to develop a muscular and strong body for participation in her sport demonstrates intense, intentional, focused work. This is a sign of socially defined masculine instrumentality, not feminine passivity. However, this desire and its obvious physical outcomes can become a site of conflict and ambiguity that is often not understood or accepted (Schulze, 1990).[2] "It is a privilege not to have to think about how you are embodied," wrote historian Susan Stryker, comparing gender privilege to race privilege and pointing out that culturally normative gendered people do not have to think about gender "in the same way that white people never have to think about race" (as quoted in Rudacille, 2006, p. 19). However, abilities, behaviours, and interests cannot be divided into the exclusive domain of either females or males (or any race, class, or ethnic group for that matter), especially when sport is added to the mix in the 21st century.

THE IMPORTANCE OF SPORT-FOR-ALL

Involvement in organized sport and physical activity is as much a part of the childhood and life path of girls and women today as it has been for boys and men for over a century. A polarized gender binary serves to keep sport in a masculine domain, which makes very little sense in today's North American culture. Even though girls today are socialized to accept sport and physical activity as an important part of their lives, it cannot be overlooked "how differently the childhoods of girls and boys come to be structured: by discourses of femininity and masculinity and by gendered practices of play that teach us to inhabit and experience our bodies in profoundly different ways" (Whitson, 1994, p. 353). The female athlete, especially in those sports that are most associated with the masculinity and (hetero)sexuality of males, is stigmatized and seen to be non-conforming to a feminine performance. This makes her body an anomaly within the realm of both sport and gender (Veri, 1999). Females are constantly forced to negotiate the mixed messages that they receive about being female, feminine, and athletes.

The meanings about bodies and sport that are learned by both boys and girls have importance beyond a simple defining practice of what boys do and what girls do, because boys and girls do many of the same things—including sport. This has become a reality, most particularly, in the post-Title IX era. The entrance of girls, in astonishing numbers, into organized sports that have been traditionally reserved for boys should have changed the meaning of both sport and gender. However, these messages and their big-picture meanings have not been and are not necessarily well-integrated into the individual or the larger social fabric.

The position of women has changed in all aspects of society. There has been a tremendous backlash to this emancipation because it challenges traditional gender stratifications and power relations. Women can no longer be defined as weak or dependent. Through their participation in numerous sports, we can see that women display "physical strength and endurance, competitiveness and risk-taking behaviours" (Lenskyj, 1995, p. 45). To reassure people that female athletes, especially high-performance female athletes in traditionally masculine activities, are still women "it became important to send out reassuring messages that, underneath their tough exteriors, they were just like 'the girl next door,' interested in frilly clothing and jewellery, sewing, cooking and boyfriends—in other words, heterosexual" (Lenskyj, 1995, p. 45). However, the female athlete is unlikely to still be the girl next door with the ponytail and fresh, innocent look. She probably still has the ubiquitous ponytail, but her look may be one of obvious fitness and muscle beyond others' comfort level. She may be more confident and outgoing than some people think girls should be. She may feel that sweating or getting dirty and bruised in practise is more important than cultivating a look that is certain to get her a date for the graduation ball.

The sporting gender order can only be maintained if the presentation of self of the female athlete can be criticized and understood to be not feminine. The appearance of a muscular, confident, physical female athlete underlines the falseness of a gendered embodiment that is socially constructed and highly restricted. "What makes this fully developed body so terrifying is the possibility that, taken to the very limits of biology, gender confusion becomes gender eradication" (Gaines & Herzog, 1990, p. 9). Sport has the potential to empower girls and women by teaching them to effectively use their bodies in physical activity (Veri, 1999). Hegemonic gender ideology has the potential to take that away. Accepting being polygendered has the potential to allow it. It is important that the absences and gaps in our knowledge and understandings of the capabilities of female and male bodies are investigated and represented fairly if both the rigid gender binary and its application to sport are to be upgraded in the 21st century.

IT'S TIME TO END THE BATTLE OF THE SEXES

Throughout this book, I have attempted to clarify some of the historical and scientific bases (and biases) of influence that have contributed to contemporary understandings and misunderstandings of gender and its two distinct and limited conditions: feminine and masculine. The four primary common-sense understandings of gender are: 1) it is a natural condition; 2) it is linked to the biological sex (male/female) of the individual; 3) masculine and feminine are polar opposites (with feminine defined as what masculine is not); and 4) masculinity is natural/essential to male bodies exclusively and femininity is natural/essential to female bodies exclusively. These understandings are all false to some extent. The one that has the most validity is that femininity is defined by what masculinity is not (Bem, 1993; de Beauvoir, 1952; Hall, 2002). This has little to do with naturalness or with biological sex (in which case the differences need to be identified as sex differences not gender differences), but a great deal to do with the historical patriarchal structures that underlie most of Western civilization and the androcentric lenses through which we view and analyze our social constructions and cultural forms.

Masculinity, and therefore femininity, has much more to do with social conditioning and androcentrism than biology. "Woven into these sex and gender divisions is the heterosexual imperative that privileges particular expressions of masculinity above others, and above all types of femininity" (Brackenridge, 2001, p. 81). The hierarchical stratification of masculinity over femininity furthers compounds notions of gender and moves any analysis from one of difference to one of power. This positioning also makes invisible many differences in physical capabilities, which during numerous eras have resulted in females of certain races and classes performing strenuous physical labours that have never been seen to detract from their femininity or increase their masculinity, as would be a requirement of a biologically gendered body.

When sport is situated in the masculine realm, the female athlete is placed front and centre into an obvious, if not conscious, resistance to her traditional gender order and its arbitrary restrictions. "The athletic performance of gender is a special case, for women's sport in particular has shown us in the last few decades just how radically gender norms can be altered through a spectacular public restaging ... as challenges to the norm that effectively unsettle the rigidity of gendered expectations and broaden the scope of acceptable gender performance" (Butler, 1998, p. 108). This is not yet a well-accepted adjustment to contemporary notions of gender in general or femininity in particular. Thus, when high-performance female athletes are seen to surpass the athletic abilities of the majority of males, the primary strategy for pushing back against this obvious challenge to the essential nature of gender is to attack the femininity of all female athletes, regardless of level of sporting involvement or success.

Even with such obvious challenges to the essentialist nature of gender, understandings of femininity are still "grounded in a mixture of biology and 19th-century middle-class views" and "have not disappeared from contemporary Western culture" (Weedon, 1999, p. 5). Even if biological and neurological studies one day more substantially confirm a natural connection between sex and gender (which will also likely support multiple sexualities and genders rather than just two), there will still be more similarities among females and males (and other sexual designations) than differences. After all, we are a single species of fairly highly developed mental abilities and adaptabilities. The potential for the development of all individuals increases when we focus on recognizing each other's strengths rather than each other's weaknesses or, in the case of a gender binary, one's absences. We need to view "absences" as differences rather than deficiencies (Lenskyj, 1994a). The other important piece to this solution is to not privilege particular strengths over others, but to recognize and celebrate the myriad contributions that people make to all aspects of our social structure and culture.

Separating or at least understanding natural (scientific) conditions from social (cultural) influences has been part of an ongoing debate since the mid-20th century. The nature versus nurture argument has still not been resolved relative to human development and behaviour. One of the underlying causes of this lack of understanding is the constantly changing understanding of vocabulary and the traditional, but misapplied, notion of the objectivity of science (Roszak, 1999). For example, "if we simply look at the facts as they are, a universal dividing line between the sexes never existed in nature. Anne Fausto-Sterling[3] proposes to distinguish five sexes instead of two, in order to make it possible for people with more ambiguous sex to live a more human life" (van der Wijngaard, 1997, p. 3). Accepting a multi-sex model requires that we also accept a multi- or poly-gender model or get rid of the concept of gender altogether.

More contemporary scientific studies often look to prenatal hormonal influences and their impact on the development of the brain to explain differences between females and males, heterosexuals and homosexuals, and other "apparent" human binaries. What must be considered, though, is whether preconceived expectations of behaviours and abilities that are adopted by children in order to match parental expectations and socialization pressures can be interpreted as conclusive evidence of the essentialist nature of femininity and masculinity based exclusively on the apparent sex of the person. "Gender difference ... is not naturally given but is an effect of relations of knowledge and power which permeates all areas of life. Moreover, the ways in which gender difference is defined are far from neutral" (Weedon, 1999, p. 5). It is not just gender that can be read as an indicator of power imbalances among people. We must also look to the relationships of class, race, and sexuality in the separation and classification of people. Through the stratification of a white, patriarchal social structure, women in general, non-Caucasian women and men, and other groups on the outside of a privileged position are deemed inferior. "Differences can be categorized in various ways, for example as social, political, cultural, or natural. How differences are defined has implications for whether they are seen as desirable, changeable, or fixed" (Weedon, 1999, p. 5).

What happens when individuals with ambiguous sex designations at birth have a particular body surgically designed for them whether or not it matches the hormonally constructed brain they were born with? Or what happens when a hormonal abnormality called 5-alpha-reductase deficiency (which inhibits the development of male external genitalia in utero) occurs and babies that are apparently female at birth begin to develop as males at puberty? How do we explain the apparent increase in transgender individuals? It must never be overlooked that strict adherence to a two-sex model, and therefore a two-gender model, is the means "by which bodies become identifiable, recognizable, and intelligible" (Butler, 1998, p. 107) as only one of two choices, regardless of the evidence that exists to support the speciousness of this conclusion. Whatever other conditions exist to challenge the gender binary, the physically active and strong female athlete is a direct challenge to hegemonic notions of female frailty, especially as they are applied to white, middle- and upper-class women (Lenskyj, 1994b).

What a strict gender binary does not explain is the enormous overlap in abilities, behaviours, and interests among female and male individuals or how these same abilities, behaviours, and interests are applied differently to females and males in various cultures. Once again, we are confronted with the same questions that were disregarded by Terman and Miles nearly a century ago.

One consequence of the first-, second-, and third-wave feminist movements over the past two centuries is that many of the biological and cultural conditions that functioned to reinforce beliefs about sex or gender differences disappeared. Women did not suffer from being educated or getting the vote. Women were found to be just as capable as men of becoming skilled and employed in every occupational field. Men were found to be loving and successful caregiver parents to their children. And girls and women became successful athletes. The underlying reasons for these changes were education, training, and opportunity. Resistance to traditional restrictions laid out in sex-role and gender-appropriate belief systems has contributed enormously to the changes in social structures that have permitted these circumstances of human growth to occur. From this, it is important to stop seeing femininity and masculinity—however they are manifested or performed by individuals—to be binary opposites that are applied exclusively to female and male bodies, respectively.

Certainly, there are biological differences between women and men (and other sexes, whether they are recognized or not). The greater differences between women and men can be attributed to the lives we live through socialization pressures to behave and present ourselves in particular ways. Recently, the popular media has paid a great deal of attention to "trans" persons.[4] Magazine and television stories have generally been about people who strongly believe that they were born into the "wrong" body. The heart-wrenching and at times tragic stories of these individuals might stop being heart-wrenching and tragic if the rigid gender binary were eliminated or broadened to include greater variety, which would more appropriately make room for all individuals.

Natural female/male differences obviously do exist within a biological framework and possibly also within a psychological one. How much and to what extent these differences truly impact female/male divergence is not known and may not be known for a long time. What will always be more important than any differences in how these variations manifest themselves is a resistance to putting a value on the variant that will function to maintain a hierarchical, hegemonic, and limiting relationship among people. Along with homophobia, genderism is one of the last acceptable biases. Embracing the polygendered nature of all people is a timely concept in removing any limitations that single gender designations bring.

In the domain of sport, most female/male differences in performance have been eliminated. This is not to say that, in absolute terms, the fastest or strongest person in the world is likely to be female. But the well-trained female athlete is likely to be, in relative or absolute terms, faster and stronger than the great majority of males, especially if the female has had more physical training. This cannot be attributed to some sudden or miraculous change in female physiology. It has come about since the last third of the 20th century, when girls and women were suddenly (and, in many cases, miraculously) given more equitable access to sport programs, highly trained coaches, excellent facilities, and competitive experiences, and a social shift through which the term "female athlete" has become legitimated and increasingly celebrated. Thus, many of the beliefs regarding the differences between women and men in a sporting perspective, "and in this context between masculine and feminine sports, are constructs of social reality that reinforce inequities between genders, which include the concepts of masculine dominance and feminine inferiority" (Angelini, 2008, p. 128). They are not a reflection of the actual physical abilities of people who train to be athletes.

THE NEW SPORTING REALITY

This is becoming a far more recognized and accepted reality in the general population, where family members, friends, peers, and fans cheer on female athletes with all the enthusiasm and support that used to be reserved for males. "Cultural norms legitimated in a society are constantly reinforced until the values are experienced as reality" (Fusco, 1998, p. 89). Conscious resistance to the normative cultural beliefs about sports as a masculine domain have made, and continue to make, a huge impact on the growing acceptance of a new sporting reality that includes girls and women. New values that reflect the reality of 21st-century sporting and physical activity practices should, by now, be accepted and reinforced in all realms of our culture. Educational institutions, sport governance and delivery systems, and all forms of the media need to embrace and promote this new reality because it leads to a healthier population in general and greater self-esteem in individuals.

The cultural shift toward universal acceptance of sport-for-all is still in progress. Male experiences in sport continue to be the standard by which human sporting excellence is measured, especially as it is presented in various forms of the media.[5] The essence of masculinity is seen to be performance, and sport legitimizes this way of being male. Sport performance is one of the most visual and appreciated forms of masculinity. Even as girls and women challenge this traditional gender designation, arguments continue to be made that the best athlete in this or that sport or event will always be male. The obvious response to this challenge is "who cares?"

Most males, like most females, will never be successful enough as athletes to come anywhere close to the standard required to be the best (or even highly competitive) in most organized sport structures. This reality is never used to keep boys and men from playing because the common-sense belief is that through sport at any level, they will learn to be men/masculine. The bigger problem is that when all males are assumed to be more naturally athletic than all females (by reason of essentialist beliefs about hegemonic masculinity and femininity), then females are seen to be deficient. This deficit, measured from what males supposedly have naturally, confirms definitions of femininity and places it in a constructed position of inferiority relative to masculinity.

Conversely, participating in sports does little to teach young girls about being women/feminine. Even as most young girls participate in some form of organized sport these days, many still experience a cognitive dissonance between how they see themselves as active females and the messages that bombard them regarding what it is to be a feminine woman. This can be explained through aspects of social identity theory, which supports the concept that "being exposed to stereotypical portrayals of a group will only reinforce an individual's previously held stereotypical beliefs, and how members of the stereotyped group can begin to believe the stereotypes" (Angelini, 2008, p. 129). Even though many females are now participating in organized sports and recreational physical activities, the structures and organization of sport are still androcentric. In addition, the majority of images that endorse active females still promote a hetero-sexy, thin, beautiful visual as the only socially acceptable presentation of a female as feminine for girls and women.

Focusing on who is the fastest, strongest, or best is harmful to all children and adults, who should be able to get the most that they can out of any sporting or physical activity. The underlying meaning of "the best" refers only to the outcome of an event—not participation in it. For most people, females and males of all ages, the process of sport, the effort of using one's body to accomplish a goal, the sensuousness of myriad feelings while being active, and the connection to others or to nature is ultimately what needs to be given greater appreciation in sport participation (Lenskyj, 1994b). When we focus on "the best" we are limiting our analysis to a miniscule number of people on the planet, male or female, who can compete at the highest levels. When the best is assumed to be referring to a masculine male then sporting participation can be further restricted, particularly for females. "... Popular understandings of empowerment and the powerful body must move away from the traditional masculine preoccupation with force and domination toward a new emphasis on personal experience of skill and of pleasure in motion, and on sharing these experiences with others" (Whitson, 1994, p. 360). The general health of the population also depends on this. All of the fitness components needed to be physically active are important for all individuals, regardless of their assumed sex or assigned gender.

Many of us enjoy watching high-performance and professional sports. This sensual experience is often what drives us to take up a new sport or activity, even though we are well aware that we will probably never come close to the skill level of those who motivated us. Most of us do not care about that level of achievement, but continue to practise and play because of how it makes us feel. It is also quite likely that while we play, we pay little or no attention to the appropriateness of our play to sex roles or gender restrictions.

Almost all women will be judged as deficient when set against a model of being the best. Those women who overcome their "deficiencies" of being women are still likely to be seen as trespassing into masculine territory and sacrificing their femininity. The traditional outcome of this is to label those women as unfeminine, mannish, or lesbian. In other words, they are declared to be heterosexually unattractive to males. In this discourse, "*her* body must work to enhance *his* sexual pleasure" (Schulze, 1990, p. 62; emphasis in original). Thus, the dilemma of femininity and the female athlete becomes one that must be faced and dealt with by the majority of female athletes, often beginning when they are young girls.

As presented earlier, training for participation in sport and physical activity changes the physical body (not to disregard the psychic and spiritual bodies) in myriad ways. Depending on the sport and its performance demands, the optimum body size and shape may be very different from the accepted and acceptable body morphology required by hegemonic gender practice. Female athletes are more likely than male athletes to develop their bodies in ways that will be unrecognizable as "appropriately" feminine.

Normal physiological processes in males generally produce a body that is taller and bigger than female bodies and more approaches the masculine ideal. This is celebrated in our culture. On the other hand, many girls and women abhor the normal physiological processes of their bodies, which may produce a mature female body that looks very different from the images of the media-genic glamazon with which they are bombarded on a daily basis. Disordered eating practices and poor body images are a far cry from anything celebratory. At any point in time, one in every two women is on a "diet." The impact of weight beauty is felt by girls as young as eight or nine years old, who worry about being fat or not pretty enough (Bordo, 1993). It would be such a better way of living if these young girls were more concerned about perfecting that new skill, increasing their speed and endurance, or scoring a personal best in their next competition with the most appropriate body for achieving those goals.

For many female athletes, the difference between the ideal feminine body and the ideal sporting body can be overwhelming. This can be due to an athlete interpreting her athletic actions with a gendered analysis and seeing her training and performance as "emulating the values and practices of conventional masculinity" (Lock, 2006, p. 160), rather than as a celebration of the range of her physical and mental capabilities as an athlete. Her sporting body, which she has worked hard to create, train, and discipline, should be a source of pride and accomplishment. Problems arise when she is seen to pay more attention to her athletic body than to her "appropriate" feminine one. "The deliberately muscular woman disturbs dominant notions of sex, gender, and sexuality, and any discursive field that includes her risks opening up a site of contest and conflict, anxiety and ambiguity" (Schulze, 1990, p. 59). The feminine woman will find it difficult to take pride in the achievement she has accomplished in the intentional creation of this athletic body. The polygendered woman will know that her bodily accomplishment is one in which to take pride.

CELEBRATING ALL WOMEN AS ATHLETES

Although North Americans have had a love–hate relationship with many of their most successful female athletes over the past century, we cannot ever forget that the majority of female athletes will always be young girls, teenagers, young women, middle-aged women, and senior citizens who train, participate, and compete for the love of the games they play. Many will win ribbons and trophies. Many will be awarded athletic scholarships and places on championship teams. Many will win local tournaments or club championships. Only a minuscule few will ever see the inside of a professional locker room, a world championship venue, or an Olympic podium from the perspective of an athlete.

We need to understand the damage to self-esteem and to bodies when the joy and health of sporting participation are removed from the socially embedded notions of femininity that are still so powerfully projected in our culture.[6] Regardless of the level of sporting accomplishment that a woman attains, all of the dedication and hard work that took her there needs to be seen as an important part of who she is as a whole person, and not as a masculine pretender. "Muscle mass, its articulation, and the strength and power the body displays, is clearly an achievement, the product of years of intense, concentrated, deliberate work in the gym, a sign of activity, not passivity" (Schulze, 1990, p. 70). In a polygendered state, this bodywork would be accepted in the realm of the female as completely natural.

When any physical training process or outcome is deemed to be unnatural the sporting achievements of everyone are compromised. Flexibility is absolutely essential for movement and to help in the reduction of injury. However, flexibility is defined as a feminine characteristic. This is because girls have a tendency to be more flexible than boys. It may also be an effect of the games and activities that girls are taught and encouraged to play. But can you image the disaster for every male athlete who does not develop his flexibility to an appropriate level for his sport? The same can be said for strength. Males have a tendency to be stronger than females. The activities that are designated as gender-appropriate for boys also require them to develop greater amounts of strength in order to be more effective players. Although strength is equally important for girls, the girl who trains to develop her strength will not be viewed in the same way as a boy who trains to develop his flexibility. Although both physical attributes are essential for sport participation (not to mention everyday movement), strength, which often comes with increased muscle size, is deemed to be wholly masculine. The woman with obvious muscles is somehow less than a woman. She is often perceived to be mannish or a lesbian. It is time to stop adding two and two and coming up with something other than four. Muscles do not make a woman less than a woman. Even if muscles maintain a masculine designation, they will be completely appropriate for all polygendered people.

Homophobia and homo-negative practices are among the most traditional and easy methods of labelling a woman as not feminine. The image of a female athlete (particularly one from a traditionally masculine-designated sport) is very similar to the stereotype of the butch lesbian. The image of the masculine male and the prototypical athlete are one and the same. Unfortunately, a description of the proto-typical lesbian and the female athlete are also the same. This interpretation renders invisible or unimportant femme-inine lesbians and female athletes in gender-appropriate sports for females. The effect, however, is one of labelling all female athletes as deviant. For over a century, the white, upper- or middle-class female athlete who did not project a prototypical feminine image and demeanour was sexually suspect. Working-class women were often overlooked in this analysis unless they were exceptionally famous, such as Babe Didrikson Zaharias, and even she did not attract this negative attention until she became one of the top female golfers—a game traditionally restricted to upper-class women. Female athletes of colour were also frequently ignored in this analysis, but the homophobic fallout did affect them in the same ways that it impacted all girls and women who wanted to be athletes.

The only acceptable way for a woman to be an athlete was to present herself as feminine and to participate within the confines of traditionally gender-appropriate games and sports. Another difficulty with this equation is that what was gender-appropriate for girls and women changed as often as the characteristics that defined them as feminine.

Lesbian labelling has always been a fairly easy way to control women in sport. It has been used as an intentional strategy to do just that for over a century. "The homophobic agenda is clear: sportswomen, already seen as nonconforming, should at least present themselves as unequivo-cally heterosexual, and this hyper-feminine image is seen as an effective marketing strategy for female sport" (Lenskyj, 1994b, p. 359). The sport media, in all its forms, is an obvious user of this approach (Carty, 2005). When a female athlete appears in an advertisement, she is usually among the most attractive of women from any cultural area. She is just as made-up and air-brushed as any rock star or Hollywood celebrity. She is often unidentifiable as an athlete because she is rarely seen dressed in her sports gear or participating in her activity, although this is beginning to change. Her feminine and sexually appealing characteristics are highlighted in order to sell whatever product she has been selected to shill. Thus, the message is put forward that female athletes must attend to the rules of femininity, even though it is difficult for many female athletes to present a feminine ideal and remain competitive in their sport (Klomsten et al., 2004).

In the current post-Title IX era, many female athletes intentionally reject the ideals of the feminine presentation of body/self that are seen to be the appropriate gender performativity for women in her culture. Other female athletes are more than aware that they are being constantly scrutinized, and they actively participate in their own self-surveillance and maintenance of their feminine presentation to avoid critique or even potential harm to their sporting careers because they do fit the feminine ideal (Shogan, 1999; Veri, 1999). In the 1970s, feminist sport researchers often referred to the dilemma felt by the female athlete who also wanted to see herself as feminine as a "role conflict." In itself, this was a kind of acceptance of the social position that sport was masculine and that females were cautiously welcomed visitors, but who were expected to know their proper place and deportment. More recent research has indicated that role conflict appears "to be relatively low among female athletes" (Allison, 1991, p. 49). Even Terman and Miles found that the university-aged female athletes they tested in the 1920s and 1930s were very well-adjusted females, even though they scored high on the masculine personality scales!

Many contemporary female athletes certainly face a dilemma relative to their understanding of themselves as feminine beings. I suggest that the problem is not with the female athletes themselves, but with a system of gender assignment that has outlived its usefulness within the functioning of a 21st-century, North American cultural tapestry. There are myriad forms of self-expression. To designate specific interests, behaviours, or physical appearance factors as either feminine or masculine and then to sanction individuals who choose to cross this indefinite line, either intentionally or unintentionally, is a clear path to lower self-esteem, poor body image, and/or restricted personal choices.

In the case of sport and physical activity, this path can also lead to health risks. Young girls are clearly receiving mixed messages. Their parents enrol them in soccer, hockey, and baseball leagues. The girls learn how to use their bodies in productive and fun ways. They learn all of the valuable skills and advantages that sport has supposedly been teaching to boys for decades. As they get older, however, the messages that they receive about what it means to be a girl may no longer include being strong or fast. More and more girls are rejecting these messages because of the importance of sport to them. Many more girls are heeding these warnings, however, and obesity and inactivity are two critical health concerns among girls and young women. A ponytail may not be enough to overcome the negative messages that many females are receiving about their proper performance of gender.

Sport, muscles, training, competition, and the positive attention that might come from sport participation are not seen as masculine by the females who have celebrated these things as a part of their lives. Or, if they learn that these attributes are designated as masculine, they do not care. Female athletes are not choosing to be masculine; they are choosing to be athletes. Young girls and women today have grown up in a poly-gendered state that many celebrate, although they would have little or no awareness of this concept. Pat Griffin, a coach, Master's athlete, and critic of sport and its misogynistic and homophobic foundations "argues that intolerance for gender and sexual diversity are a form of oppression and, therefore, must be considered a social justice issue" (Veri, 1999, p. 356). Restricting the freedoms of individuals based on bias, customs that no longer serve the culture or its individuals in the traditional ways, and practices that limit human growth and potential need to be carefully examined. There is no problem with girls wanting to display themselves as "feminine," as long as it is a choice and not a requirement. The problem lies in the ways in which femininity is constructed and the negative impact it has on those persons who are seen to need to be feminine and not masculine, as if these constructs are completely natural.

As a female who plays sports, who studies the social and cultural structures and meaning of sports, and who advocates for change in sport, I believe that sport is an avenue of transformation for all who engage in it. I learned, first hand, about gender through sport. I learned the positives as well as the negatives of being involved in a number of sports as an athlete, coach, official, and administrator. The positives have almost always outweighed the negatives. For me, the largest remaining negative for girls and women in sport and physical activity is the artificial gender binary of femininity and masculinity and the tie-in this has to one's sexuality.

It is time to celebrate the physicality of girls and women in the entire world of sport, and not just in those activities that enhance traditional ideals of femininity and heterosexual attractiveness. "Indeed, women's sports have the power to rearticulate gender ideals such that those very athletic women's bodies that, at one time, are considered outside the norm (too much, too masculine, even monstrous), can come, over time, to constitute a new ideal of accomplishment and grace, a standard for women's achievement" (Butler, 1998, p. 104). It is time to celebrate the polygendered nature of all individuals.

Notes

1. See, for example, the works of Bem, 1993; Butler, 1990, 1993, 2004; Fausto-Sterling, 2000; Money & Ehrhardt, 1972; Roszak, 1999; Rudacille, 2006.

2. Acceptable sports and activities for girls in the 1950s and 1960s varied greatly according to race, class, and the locations (urban/suburban/rural) in which they lived. Remnants of these differences continue to exist today.

3. See the detailed reports tracking the changes resulting from Title IX by Carpenter and Acosta (2005), including their website at www.acostacarpenter.org.

4. See, for example, Messner, 1994; Miller, 2001.

5. "... deterritorialization refers to a situation in which a cultural practice is borrowed from its original context and is assigned, or recoded with, a new meaning. In this formulation, the cultural form is freed of its original significance and once freed it can be reinvested with an entirely new meaning, all the while keeping the external form basically the same" (DeMello, 2000, p. 12).

6. Even though a professional football league for women exists in the United States, it is not well known, gets almost no media coverage outside of limited markets, and, of course, does not pay a living wage let alone a celebrity salary to the players. The same is true of Canadian professional ice hockey leagues for women.

7. It is interesting to note that the only Olympic athlete ever to masquerade as a different sex was actually a German man in the women's high-jump event of the 1936 Olympic Games. "Dora" Ratjen, who finished fourth behind three female jumpers, is the only athlete ever to be caught attempting to pass as a different sex. Although the International Olympic Committee established the requirement of "sex testing" to catch athletes who were attempting to compete as a different sex, only those competing as females have ever been tested. This translates to the belief that no

woman could ever beat a man in Olympic competition, so there is no need to test the competitors in men's events.

CHAPTER 1

1. It is becoming increasingly common to find a "gender" box on many application forms, questionnaires, and other database entry forms. This "gender" box offers the choices of female and male. Thus, these boxes ought to be labelled "sex," not gender. The frequency of seeing a choice for gender where sex is actually the desired information has contributed much to the growing misunderstanding of the precise terms "sex" and "gender," and the conflation of stereotypical understanding of the differences between sex and gender.

2. There are a number of sports, such as gymnastics, swimming, and tennis, that are considered to be gender-appropriate for females. In general, however, sport is still considered to be a male domain. See, for example, Messner, 1994; Miller, 2001.

3. See, for example, de Lauretis, 2007; Fausto-Sterling, 2000; Rudacille, 2006; Tarrant, 2006.

4. There is one notable exception to this. Princess Anne, of Great Britain, was the only female Olympian (1976; British Three Day Event Team) not to undergo sex testing during this period. She was royalty, and would become a member of the International Olympic Committee in 1983. She also competed in equestrian events, the only Olympic sports where women and men compete on the same teams and head-to-head. With this in mind, it is curious that any female equestrians would need to be tested.

5. See, for example, Carlson, 1991; Daniels, 1992.

6. See, for example, Bem, 1993; Butler, 2004; Fausto-Sterling, 2000; Hester, 2004; Money & Ehrhardt, 1972; Rudacille, 2006.

7. See also Hamilton, 2005.

8. Sexuality is a highly complex topic and cannot be fully investigated in this book. The material provided here is a general introduction to certain aspects of heterosexuality, hetero-normative assumptions, and lesbian, trans, and queer aspects of sexuality as they are sometimes applied within a sporting context.

9. Butler (1993) proposed that gender is a factor that is *performed* by females and males to display the local and cultural dimensions of what it means to be a girl/woman or boy/man. The performative nature of gender is one

that is learned through socialization processes of family, educational and religious institutions, peer pressure, and certain governmental concerns. Cultural sanctions, to varying degrees, are often used to discipline children and adults who do not conform to contemporary standards or restrictions of gender. Simone de Beauvoir (1952), in her book *The Second Sex*, wrote that "one is not born a woman, but one becomes a woman."

10. See, for example, Griffin, 1998; Hall, 1996, 2002; Kolnes, 1995; Krane and Barber, 2003; Lenskyj, 1999.

11. There was a belief at this time that menses and the initial development of the uterus were simultaneous functions. This was not seen to be an issue with males because the fully formed penis was obvious at birth. In addition, men were obviously not negatively affected by education because educated men were generally successful in fathering children.

CHAPTER 2

1. Later chapters discuss in more detail the idea that muscular strength is one of the primary signifiers of masculinity and is thus not appropriate for the female/feminine. Our limited knowledge about strength development in females comes partly from this gendered perspective.

2. I suggest that their work might have been *the* earliest published, as the majority of the studies they cite in this book are their own previous research projects.

3. These are both actual test items from Terman and Miles' M-F (masculine/feminine) test instrument.

4. In her work *Gender Trouble* (1990), Butler coined the words "performative" and "performativity" to illustrate how, in contemporary North American culture, women and men demonstrate an understanding of their specific genders through self-expressive means. How people dress, behave, and present themselves in public venues all reflect how they perceive their own gendered state and perform it for others. Butler's position is that gender is not only learned, but is also acted out in particular ways to meet the contemporary demands for compliance to femininity by females and masculinity by males.

5. It is interesting to note the androcentric nature of the quantitative results, with masculine designated as positive and feminine designated as negative relative to the masculine.

6. Terman and Miles were attempting to find a way to measure deviance in the masculine and feminine personality types. They were adamant that

deviation across masculine and feminine test scores, what today would be called the gender divide, was not to be interpreted as an indicator of homosexuality in either feminine males or masculine females. They wrote: "Most emphatic warning is necessary against the assumption that an extremely feminine score for males or an extremely masculine score for females can serve as an adequate basis for the diagnosis of homosexuality, either overt or latent. It is true as we shall show, that male homosexuals *of the passive type* as a rule earn markedly feminine scores, and that the small number of female homosexuals *of the active type* whom we have tested earned high masculine scores. That the converse of these rules is in accord with the facts, we have no assurance whatever; indeed, our findings indicated that a majority of subjects who test as variates in the direction of the opposite sex are capable of making a perfectly normal heterosexual adjustment" (Terman & Miles, 1936, p. 9; emphasis added).

7.   This means that as males age their masculinity rating actually goes down. Relative to the test items chosen by Terman and Miles, this translates to mean that as men age they are more drawn to those interests or beliefs that Terman and Miles determined were measures of femininity.

8.   In their work, Terman and Miles use the abbreviation "M-F" for masculine/feminine as it relates to personality types they are examining, not male/female persons.

CHAPTER 3

1.   These may not be the exact terms that my students have used, but the gist of the labels contained in Helgeson's data is apparent.

2.   I first came across the term "glamazon" in M.A. Hall's book, *The Girl and the Game* (2000), but am unsure of when this term was coined or by whom.

CHAPTER 4

1.   See, for example, Halberstam, 1998; Williams & Bendelow, 1998.

2.   Female to male transsexuals who undergo sex-reassignment surgery would be an exception to this. However, some critics of this personal choice might never accept that the person is now actually male, regardless of the anatomical markers. No matter how well the female to male transsexual

is able to embody masculinity in his everyday presentation of self and demeanour, some will refuse to acknowledge this person as anything but a deviant female. The transgender female retains his female body, but dons a masculine performativity to whatever degree suits his personality and life circumstances. In later materials, I go into specific details regarding gender, transgender, and transsexuality relative to female athletes.

3. I recently received an invitation to a reception. The indicated dress for the evening was "casual chic." I had to inquire what this meant in general and what it meant specifically for the city and people who were having the party. Another example of this was a wedding invitation that indicated "Dallas casual" as the requisite attire. One not coming from Dallas or even used to socializing with the sub-culture of Dallas residents throwing this party may not have had any idea what this style of dress actually means. To be overdressed or underdressed can be a catalyst for femininity stress! A reception that requires business attire does not mean that construction workers, farmhands, or stay-at-home moms are invited to wear their "business" attire. Our language is also based on hierarchical and patriarchal meanings.

4. She will also have many physical attributes designated as feminine, such as flexibility, agility, balance, and grace. Male athletes are also required to have these attributes as they are integral to successful motor-skill acquisition and execution. However, these physical aspects of movement are often overlooked altogether as they are signifiers of appropriate feminine comportment. All feminine attributes are devalued in the male-stream analysis of sport.

5. To emphasize the assigned femininity of these sports, the participation by boys and men in these activities has traditionally been suspect. Although gymnastics has become widely acceptable as a men's sport, the differences in artistic gymnastics equipment and events for men are designed to highlight men's upper-body strength. Male figure skaters frequently have their sexuality questioned because of their participation in a feminine-designated sport.

6. This may be particularly true for specific national or ethnic sub-cultures.

7. It might be suggested that the concept of misogyny, as it was created by the ancient Greeks, actually has very little to do with the hatred of women, but rather the hatred of anything womanly or feminine in men themselves. Most men love, or at least like, some women in their lives—mothers, grandmothers, aunts, sisters, cousins, teachers, girlfriends, wives, or daughters. So why is misogyny still such a powerful force to keep women

as second-class people? I doubt that misogyny has very much to do with women at all, but rather those natural and present-in-everyone character-istics that are deemed womanly or feminine. Misogyny is also likely the same concept that causes such negative reactions to anything seen in a woman that can be deemed masculine. If women are/can be masculine then men are/can be feminine. Acceptance of the polygendered nature of all people might go a long way to healing this centuries-old divide.

CHAPTER 5

1. See also Shogan, 1999.
2. See also Tsang, 2000.
3. Long hair has always been seen to be a more appropriately feminine style. The short bob of the 1920s flapper, which was worn to show a state of liberation for women, was as shocking to many people as the dress and behaviour of the flappers. Hairstyles that are very short are considered masculine or butch. Some players in the All-American Girls Professional Baseball League were fired from their teams and sent home for having had their hair cut too short. Short hair is frequently seen to be "proof" of a female athlete being a lesbian; thus all the ponytails seen adorning North American female athletes.
4. This aspect of the presentation of self will be discussed further in Chapter 7.
5. These promises include marriage, security, and legitimacy for her children. These are all acquired through the man, and not through the efforts of the woman herself—or at least not without some criticism if she acquires these things by herself or with a female partner. The general perception is that none of these can really be achieved without a man. Traditional practices such as a woman taking her husband's last name at marriage and the chil-dren from a previous marriage carrying the last name of the father, even if the mother has changed her own name, reflect the traditional position of marriage as one of property ownership not companionability. The cur-rent debates regarding same-sex marriage are challenges to not only the man/woman definition of marriage, but also to the notion of the wife/children as property of the husband. The legitimacy of a woman is often confirmed through her relationship with a man. Many unmarried women are often asked "When are you going to get married?" The assumption is that all women desire marriage, and that a woman's value is somewhat diminished without it.

6. This statement was made by Baron Pierre de Coubertin, founder of the modern Olympic movement. His disdain for female athletes was obvious, and his impact on women's sporting participation since the end of the 19th century is still being felt.

7. Judged sports such as gymnastics, figure skating, and synchronized swimming do have unwritten requirements for the physical presentation of the body. How these athletes look can have an impact on the scores given by a judge—either positively or negatively. The athlete's concern regarding the visual femininity of her body may have much less to do with achieving a feminine-looking body than with sculpting an appropriately feminine-looking body that is representative of the top performers in her sport. These athletes not only have acceptably feminine bodies, but they are using them in traditionally feminine-designated sports. Even so, or possibly especially so, eating disorders are more common among these athletes than among any other sport participants.

8. In the realm of recreation and exercise participation "good fit" becomes—or ought to become—a moot point. Any girl or woman of any size, shape, and (dis)ability can learn at least the basics of almost any position or event in any sport or physical activity. Her participation in a physical activity to a level that suits her is a matter of choice rather than one of "good fit" for her body and possession of the physical fitness characteristics necessary for high-performance success. This reality, however, often does not exist. Teachers/coaches may discourage girls and women with less than "good-fit" body types from entering into a particular activity, even if fitness and general involvement in a physical activity, not excellence, is their goal. In addition, a goal of health, well-being, social involvement, and fun does not necessarily free women from the self-surveillance of their bodies as a social construction.

9. Signifiers can be things such as hairdos, hair ribbons, jewellery, nail polish, and make-up. These non-verbal signs are easily recognizable as appropriate for females, and thus feminine, within a North American setting.

10. Success in sport can be defined in many ways. For my purpose here, I am looking at the body as an instrument used in acquiring certain motor skills. As I define it here, successful performance of motor skills relates to the ability to execute the movement patterns and actions required to participate in an activity to a consciously repeatable utilization level. Performance at a utilization level means that the performer can successfully execute the skill in a number of game-like circumstances with normal game-like challenges, without the athlete being at risk of injury due to

having too low a skill level or having the skills fall apart. Success, in this context, does not refer to making a team or personal-best performance. It merely defines the correct mechanical process necessary to execute desired motor skills.

11. An example of female athletes with good body-to-sport fit would be the finalists in the discus competition at the 2008 Beijing Olympic Summer Games. These 12 women averaged 181 cm/5'11" in height and 92.5 kg/203.5 pounds in weight (http://results.beijing2008.cn). Generally, women with these dimensions are likely to be considered outside the limits of a feminine body. But I am certain that Stephanie Brown Trafton would not trade her gold-medal-winning performance in Beijing for a different body that would not have produced the successful throws that brought her a medal.

12. In the all-around competition in Munich, the gold medal was won by 20-year-old Ludmila Tourischeva, the silver by 20-year-old Karin Janz, and the bronze by 18-year-old Tamara Lazakovich. By the next Olympic Summer Games, held in Montreal in 1976, 14-year-old Nadia Comaneci was the all-around gold medal winner. It has been over 30 years since the winner of an Olympic or World Championship all-around gold medal was over the age of 20!

13. The *Code of Points* is the rule book for all gymnastics competitions. It contains a list of all of the elements that can be awarded difficulty points by the judges during a competition. If a new element is not included in the *Code of Points* then a coach/country can submit the element(s) for evaluation prior to a competition in an attempt to increase the difficulty level of a routine performed by one or more gymnasts. A jury of judges determines whether the moves are "legal" within the regulations of the event, and either refuses to assign difficulty at all or appropriately rates the difficulty of the element. Refusing to assign difficulty does not prevent a gymnast from including those elements in her routine (unless they somehow violate a rule and would then incur a penalty), but she would add no extra difficultly points to her score. The introduction of new moves is one way in which elements become named after the gymnasts who first perform them in competition. In the case of the Russian delegation in 1972, no difficulty values were assigned to the elements proposed and eventually performed by Korbut.

14. In 1970, 18-year-old Cathy Rigby won a silver medal on the balance beam at the World Championships. This was the highest-ever placing for an American woman in international competition at this level. Rigby's pixie-like looks and stature (4'10" and 89 pounds) and 16th all-around placing

at the 1968 Olympic Summer Games in Mexico City made her an instant media star. It was partly the success and popularity of Rigby that caused such interest in the 1972 Munich broadcast, which allowed so many viewers to witness Olga Korbut's controversial but exciting routines.

15. One outcome of the infantilization of women's gymnastics is the early retirement/burnout of young competitors. When artistic gymnastics was a women's sport, competitors could look forward to competing in gymnastics in countless university programs in Canada and the United States. As gymnasts became younger and younger competitive programs became situated in private clubs rather than schools. There were fewer gymnasts remaining in the sport through their high-school years and beyond. Although many American universities still support strong women's gymnastics teams, the sport disappeared from Canadian universities in the 1990s and can rarely be found in any Canadian high schools today.

16. See also Miller, 2001.

17. Even the close head-to-head competitions of the lead male figure skaters—often assumed to not be heterosexually masculine due to their participation in a culturally normative feminine activity—are labelled with masculine signifiers, such as "the *battle* of the Brians" between Brian Orser and Brian Boitano, which took place in Calgary in 1988.

18. See, for example, Dworkin, 2003.

19. The "soma" or "somatotype" is a representation of the anatomical body structure of a person. For example, a "mesomorph" presents a uniformly muscular body, while an "ectomorph" presents a thin body structure.

20. Ergogenics is a collection of natural and/or artificial aids that can be used to enhance the natural physical aspects of the body. Proper nutrition and carefully constructed training regimes can be defined as ergogenic aids, as can vitamin supplements or banned substances such as steroids or other designer drugs that have been used by athletes to improve aspects of their performance.

21. The least common denominator, participation in sports at the highest levels such as the Olympic Games, World Championships, or professional sports, is often one indicator of the appropriateness of participation in a sport by females. If women are prohibited from competing in a sport at the Olympic Games then there is a tacit understanding that this activity would be inappropriate for girls at the playground level.

22. These activities vary by country or region. In some countries these activities may be played exclusively by males, while in other countries the participants are exclusively female. This functions to further confound the

defined gender-appropriateness of certain activities, but because the rule is disproved in another country the result may never be felt in, for example, North America.

CHAPTER 6

1. Sports that are seen as masculine or gender-appropriate for males are not only those sports and activities that have traditionally been played (or been seen to be played) by boys. They also include the team and individual sports that are seen most often in various media forms. Television, newspapers, sport-related magazines, and many internet websites are generally directed toward professional team and/or individual sports or amateur sports played in high schools, colleges, and universities. The majority of the coverage is directed to men's teams and male athletes. Although there has been a significant increase in the amount of coverage for women's sports at all levels, less than 10% of all media focus is directed to women's sports or female athletes (Duncan & Messner, 2005). In addition, the majority of this coverage tends to be in those activities that are gender-appropriate for females or directed toward female athletes who possess the requisite hetero-sexy presentation that often portrays the athletes as first feminine females and second, even incidentally, as athletes. The issue of gender is not the only consideration when designating certain sports as gender-appropriate for women. Class and race underline those activities that get the most coverage—especially on television. Women's golf and tennis generally get the most coverage of any professional sports for women. These sports have a history of being "country club" sports that were reserved, almost exclusively, for the wives and daughters of white, upper-class men. The race and class base of the participants in these sports restricted access to the general public until the second half of the 20th century. Because the "masses" were not able to participate in these activities, their appropriateness for white, upper-class women was secured. The gender of the participant was less a restriction than the race and class of the players. Although both tennis and golf have a far more universal appeal today, their upper-class ancestry protects, to some extent, the assumed femininity of the female players. Other times of increased coverage of women's sports are during the Olympic Summer and Winter Games or during some World Championships, such as those for figure skating or gymnastics. During these times, national pride trumps gender. However, the sports that are

highlighted during these events still reflect a strong culturally embedded notion of appropriateness for female competitors.

2. All sports-related motor skills require a combination of performance variables that are made up of masculine (i.e., power, strength, speed) and feminine (i.e., flexibility, balance, agility) designated factors. To ignore any one of the requisite variables will cause the skill to be impossible to learn or execute most efficiently.

3. It ought not to matter that an activity is designated as masculine or feminine. What matters is that this designation does not place the activity into an exclusive realm for males or females. The necessary incorporation of "masculine" and "feminine" performance factors in all sports makes them all polygendered. This ought to make all sports appropriate for all people who choose to learn and play them.

4. This statement is qualified by the fact that many individuals are "dis"abled or "un"abled in myriad ways and ought not to be taken as able-ist in interpretation or intent. At certain times of their lives, people who are able-bodied may enter temporarily or permanently into a different state of "able," which may or may not negatively impact on their ability to acquire or execute various natural or learned movements. What is wonderful about the human body, regardless of its assumed or assigned sex, is that individuals with various differences from the assumed norm in anatomy and/ or physiology have the ability, if not the opportunity, to engage in sport and physical activities at the highest elite levels. The Special Olympics and the Paralympic Games are examples of the how gestures and movements are not reserved for particular kinds of bodies or bodies of various sexes. An additional difference here is that many "dis"abled athletes are also desexualized as people. To comment on the sexual attractiveness of, say, a Special Olympian with Down syndrome or cerebral palsy would be considered, in most cases, to be inappropriate. Because the sexuality of these athletes is made invisible or non-existent the apparent sex of the athlete becomes a non-issue and, therefore, so does the analysis of femininity or masculinity of their bodies. In this situation, the gender of the athlete and the designation of the sport become non-issues as well.

5. The United States does not have an officially designated national sport. Historically, baseball has been accepted as the country's "national pastime." Basketball and American football, it might be argued, have overtaken baseball in popularity, but neither is officially designated as the national sport. It is interesting to consider that all three of these sports have longstanding professional leagues and may be more popular with

spectators than participants—especially after graduation from high school or college/university. Although girls and women play all of these sports in various forms in increasing numbers, the only nationally recognized professional league for women in any of these sports is the WNBA (basketball), although there are smaller leagues for women in both baseball and football. In any case, the official declaration by a government or government agency of a sport as "the national sport" can be seen to reflect traditional ideas about sport being a masculine activity and more appropriate for males than for females. If this were not the case, the national sports of Canada might be skiing/snowboarding and canoeing!

6. It must be remembered that the rating system created by Terman and Miles rated all of these team sports as highly masculine, even though girls and women of various classes and races were participating in them. The ratings of these sports contributed to the higher than average masculine scores achieved by females who participated in these activities.

7. Various dance activities, including tap, ballet, and jazz, are still popular activities for young girls. Adult participation in dance activities and the popularity of ballroom and competitive dance has been boosted through television series such as *Dancing with the Stars* and *So You Think You Can Dance*. However, even though high-performance competition exists in the dance world, most people would not classify dance as a sport. There has been organized opposition to the inclusion of ballroom dance in the Olympic Summer Games even though ice dance, regardless of its tarnished reputation, continues to be a part of the Olympic Winter Games.

8. Competitive jump-rope activities have become very popular in school physical education programs and among certain urban groups of girls and boys. The cost of equipment is low and the space required to participate is smaller than many other team-game requirements. The fitness level of competitive jumpers is obvious and is promoted through programs such as Jump Rope for Heart. However, jumping rope, regardless of the level of the participant/competitor, would rarely be recognized as a "sport" by most individuals or sports governing bodies.

9. It is interesting to note that women now participate in all of these individual activities in the Olympic Games. With respect to team sports, except for volleyball most of the popular team sports played by college and university women at this time were not yet acceptable at the Olympic level. Field hockey, played only by girls and women in North American schools, did not become an Olympic sport for women until 1980; seventy six years after the first men's field hockey events (1908). Basketball was added to the

Olympic roster of women's sports in 1976. This was 40 years after men's basketball became a medal event in the Olympics. Soccer and softball were added to the Olympic schedule for women for the 1996 summer games in Atlanta. Men's football (soccer) was an exhibition sport in 1900 and 1904. It became a medal sport in 1908. Baseball was added in 1992. Women's ice hockey was a more contentious addition to the 1998 Olympic Winter Games. Volleyball, the first team sport accepted by the IOC for women (1964), was acceptable because a net separates the teams and prevents any physical contact between members of opposing teams—a factor not representative of any other Olympic team sport. This is one reason that volleyball continues to be an acceptable gender-appropriate team sport for girls. It was discussed earlier that volleyball was the earliest instance of a team sport to be added to the Olympic schedule for both women and men at the same time.

10. Golf was one of the original sports of the modern Olympic Summer Games, but was later removed. Archery is now an event for both men and women in the Olympic Summer Games.

11. Fencing, badminton, and tennis have also been added to the Olympic Summer Games events that are open to women.

12. This was not an overnight or easy transition. Myriad lawsuits in the United States and Canada have challenged the restrictions to girls' and women's involvement in sports both within and outside of the school setting. Many challenges in the United States have been filed using violations of Title IX as the grounds for the suit. In Canada, the Canadian Charter of Rights and Freedoms has been used in lawsuits to support the position that the civil rights of girls and women were being denied in the domain of sport. One example of a blatant civil rights abuse was brought to light in a Canadian lawsuit in which a young female hockey player, Justine Blainey, challenged a section of the Ontario Human Rights Code when she was denied the right to play ice hockey for a boys' team. She had been selected in a try-out in which she beat a number of boys for the position. Section 19.2 of the Ontario Human Rights Code stated that "there shall be no discrimination based on sex *except in sport*." Her case was easily won, but a challenge to the decision by the Ontario Minor Hockey Association forced the case to the Canadian Supreme Court. Blainey won her case again. The highest court had determined that the Ontario law was unconstitutional. However, as the wheels of justice grind slowly, Blainey was too old to play hockey in that league by the time the case was won. Fortunately, the girls who come behind her in the national sport of hockey, and in all other sports in the

province of Ontario, will not have this roadblock to their right to play sport. Challenges to Title IX are still being filed and opponents in Congress have written bills to have it repealed. Challenges for the inclusion of additional sports and events for women in the Olympic Summer and Winter Games also continue. There is currently, for example, worldwide pressure on the IOC to add women's ski jumping to the program for the 2010 Vancouver Olympic Winter Games.

CHAPTER 7

1. See, for example, Atkinson, 2002; Daniels, 2004.
2. This legitimacy of the female athlete may also contribute to a change in the perception of the sports. If a sport or physical activity has a traditional representation/reputation as a masculine sport, any perceived threat to the masculinity of the sport or the male athletes who participate in it may increase any barriers that exist to women's participation. However, if the gaze directed at female athletes in the sport perceives appropriate femininity and heterosexual appeal, and the women are not seen to pose a threat to the masculinity of the male athletes in the activity, this may mollify detractors of women in the sport.
3. As a former gymnastics coach and judge I know this to be true first-hand. While coaching a high-school gymnastics team, I had one girl who was 6' tall. She was awkward at times (who isn't?) and had to work harder than any of her team mates to acquire and execute her skills—most of which were very basic and without performance difficulty. Judges at our meets often commented that she had no right to be on a gymnastics team. One of my college gymnasts stood at about 5'2" tall and over 180 pounds. I was always aware of the judges commenting negatively about her as she waited her turn to mount the balance beam. But once she was up there, her movements were graceful and light. Generally, she was my most consistent and highest scoring gymnast on the beam. As a judge, I often had to argue with fellow judges on the panel who made random deductions because a gymnast's hair was messy or her leotard did not fit right. For the most part, these gymnasts were young girls who just wanted to do gymnastics and compete for their schools or clubs. They were not going to the Olympics or even the regional championships—let alone nationals. But they were still victims of the body judgments that are rampant in many of the gender-appropriate sports for girls.

4. This reality also exists for women who want to be coaches, officials, or administrators in almost all levels of the sport-delivery system.

5. This compartmentalization may also be in place for male athletes who participate in traditionally gender-appropriate sports for females. Although it is often applied to a lesser extent, the sexuality of these male athletes often enters the assessment of them as athletes and as men.

6. Examples of this sort of supervisory practice can be seen in *A League of Their Own* (1992), a film about a professional women's baseball league in the 1940s. Uniforms, hairstyles, manners, poise, and demeanour were all carefully monitored by those in power in the league. I can attest to personal experience with some of these requirements as both an athlete and a coach in the pre-Title IX years.

CHAPTER 8

1. Some physical and cognitive disabilities may even remove some women from the common-sense possibility of being seen as sexual beings. If they are removed from the realm of heterosexual desirability or attractiveness then their compliance with the "rules" of femininity may be seen as moot or unimportant in a general sense. This is probably not truly the case for the particular women, but if a social construction of these women removes or disregards their sexuality or sexual attractiveness based on a disability or disfigurement, the absence of compliance to a feminine presentation of self might be completely overlooked.

2. Lois Gould's short story, called *X: A Fabulous Child's Story*, tells the tale of a "Secret Scientific Xperiment." Parents had to be found who would not reveal anything about the sex/gender of Baby X. The story goes on to reveal the frustration that people had in not knowing how to treat or talk to a baby whose sex/gender they did not know. Children picked on and bullied X, but no one ever revealed X's true sex/gender! Eventually, X's teachers learned that there were ways of lining up children other than by girl lines and boy lines. When X won a baking contest, all the girls claimed X. When X won a race against boys, all the boys claimed X. In the end, both girls and boys wanted to be more like X because X could do whatever interested X and X was good at. The Xpert scientists finally declared X the least mixed-up child ever! Gould's story has a wonderful, happy ending, but the initial sadness of the child for being picked on and ostracized and the anger of people who could not learn

the sex/gender of the child is a more likely scenario than Gould's happy ending. Unfortunately.

3. From Fausto-Sterling, 1993.

4. There is a growing interest in "trans" factors in research in a number of academic areas that span social science and natural science disciplines.

5. Over 90% of all television and newspaper sport coverage is of men's sports events. The overwhelming majority of this coverage is of professional sport. This skewing of the media reinforces masculine performance as natural and the epitome of sport. The primary coverage of women's events is restricted to gender-appropriate activities for girls and women such as tennis and golf (traditional upper-class sports), figure skating, and gymnastics. The women's "team" sport with the greatest network television broadcast time is beach volleyball, which draws large numbers of male spectators due to the beauty/sexuality of the players and their uniforms. Most access to women's sport broadcasting is through cable or satellite delivery, which involves high financial costs. See, for example, Alper & Jhally, 2002; Duncan & Messner, 2005; Wright & Clarke, 1999.

6. See, for example, Blinde, Taub & Han, 1994; Kane, 1995.

References

Abbott, E., Greenhut, R. (Producers), & Marshall, P. (Director). (1992). *A league of their own* [Motion picture]. United States: Columbia Pictures Industries.

Adams, M. L. (1997). To be an ordinary hero: Male figure skaters and the ideology of gender. *AVANTE, 3*(3), 93–110.

Allison, M. T. (1991). Role conflict and the female athlete: Preoccupations with little grounding. *Journal of Applied Sport Psychology, 3*(1), 49–60.

Alper, L. (Producer), & Jhally, S. (Director). (2002). *Playing unfair: The media image of the female athlete.* Northampton, MA: Media Education Foundation.

Angelini, J. R. (2008). How did the sport make you feel? Looking at the three dimensions of emotion through a gendered lens. *Sex Roles, 58*, 127–135.

Atkinson, M. (2002). Pretty in pink: Conformity, resistance, and negotiation in women's tattooing. *Sex Roles, 47*(5/6), 219–235.

Bartky, S. L. (1988). Foucault, femininity, and the modernization of patriarchal power. In I. Diamond & L. Quinby (Eds.), *Feminism and Foucault: Reflections on resistance* (pp. 61–86). Boston: Northeastern University Press.

Bem, S. L. (1993). *The lenses of gender: Transforming the debate on sexual inequality.* New Haven, CT: Yale University Press.

Bishop, P., Cureton, K., & Collins, M. (1987). Sex differences in muscular strength in equally-trained men and women. *Ergonomics, 30*(4), 675–687.

Blinde, E. M., Taub, D. E., & Han, L. (1994). Sport as a site for women's group and societal empowerment: Perspectives from the college athlete. *Sociology of Sport Journal, 11*(1), 51–59.

Bordo, S. R. (1989). The body and the reproduction of femininity: A feminist appropriation of Foucault. In A. Jagger & S. R. Bordo (Eds.), *Gender/body/knowledge: Feminist reconstructions of being and knowing* (pp. 13–33). New Brunswick, NJ: Rutgers University Press.

Bordo, S. R. (1993). *Unbearable weight: Western culture and the body.* Berkeley, CA: University of California Press.

Brackenridge, C. H. (2001). *Spoilsports: Understanding and preventing sexual exploitation in sport.* London: Routledge.

Brown, D. (2006). Pierre Bourdieu's "Masculine Domination" thesis and the gendered body in sport and physical culture. *Sociology of Sport Journal*, 23(2), 162–188.

Butler, J. P. (1990). *Gender trouble: Feminism and the subversion of identity*. New York: Routledge.

Butler, J. P. (1993). *Bodies that matter: On the discursive limits of sex*. New York: Routledge.

Butler, J. P. (1998). Athletic genders: Hyperbolic instance and/or the overcoming of sexual binarism. *Stanford Humanities Review*, 6(2), 104–111.

Butler, J. P. (2004). *Undoing gender*. New York: Routledge.

Cahn, S. K. (1994). *Coming on strong: Gender and sexuality in twentieth-century women's sport*. New York: The Free Press.

Caldwell, M. (1993). Eating disorders and related behavior among athletes. In G. L. Cohen (Ed.), *Women in sport: Issues and controversies*. Newberry Park: Sage.

Cann, A. (1993). Evaluative expectations and the gender schema: Is failed inconsistency better? *Sex Roles*, 28(11/12), 667–678.

Carlson, A. (1991). When is a woman not a woman? *Women's Sport and Fitness*, 13(2), 24–29.

Carpenter, L. J. & Acosta, R. V. (2005). *Title IX*. Champaign, IL: Human Kinetics.

Carpenter, S. (1994). Characteristics of gender subtypes: Group and individual differences. *Sex Roles*, 31(3/4), 167–184.

Carr, C. L. (2005). Tomboyism or lesbianism: Beyond sex/gender/sexual conflation. *Sex Roles*, 53(1/2), 119–131.

Carty, V. (2005). Textual portrayals of female athletes: Liberation or nuanced forms of patriarchy? *Frontiers*, 26(2), 132–155.

Caudwell, J. (2006). Femme-fatale: Rethinking the femme-inine. In J. Caudwell (Ed.), *Sport, sexualities, & queer/theory* (pp. 145–158). London: Routledge.

Choi, P. Y. L. (2000). *Femininity and physically active woman*. London: Routledge.

Comfort, A. (1963). *Sex in Society*. Carol Publishing Corporation.

Connell, R. W. (1995). *Masculinities*. London: Polity Press.

Crocker, R. E., Snyder, J., Kowalski, C., & Hoar, S. (2000). Don't let me be fat or physically incompetent! The relationship between physical self-concept and social physique anxiety in Canadian high performance female adolescent athletes. *AVANTE*, 6(3), 16–23.

Daniels, D. B. (1992). Gender (body) verification (building). *Play and Culture*, 5, 370–377.

Daniels, D. B. (2002). Woman/athlete: Can you tell one when you see one? *Canadian Women's Studies/les cahiers de la femme (Special Issue on Women and Sport)*, 21(3), 64–72.

Daniels, D. B. (2004). The mark of an athlete. *Women in Sport and Physical Activity Journal, 13*(2), 51–64.

Daniels, D. B. (2005a). Lesbianism. In D. Levinson & K. Christensen (Eds.), *Berkshire encyclopedia of world sport* (Vol. 3, pp. 926–932). Great Barrington, MA: Berkshire Publishing Group.

Daniels, D. B. (2005b). "You throw like a girl": Misogyny on the silver screen. *Film and History: An Interdisciplinary Journal of Film and Television Studies, 35*(1), 29–38.

Daniels, D. B. & Winter, W. G. (1989). The myth of female frailty: The reality of females and physical activity. *Recent Advances in Nursing, 25*, 1–19.

de Beauvoir, S. (1952/1974). *The second sex.* New York: Knopf.

de Lauretis, T. (2007). *Figures of resistance: Essays in feminist theory.* Champaign, IL: University of Illinois Press.

DeMello, M. (2000). *Bodies of inscription: A cultural history of the modern tattoo community.* Durham: Duke University Press.

Dinnerstein, M. & Weitz, R. (1998). Jane Fonda, Barbara Bush, and other aging bodies: Femininity and the limits of resistance. In R. Weitz (Ed.), *The politics of women's bodies: Sexuality, appearance and behavior* (pp. 189–203). Oxford/New York: Oxford University Press.

Dowling, C. (2000). *The frailty myth: Women approaching physical equality.* New York: Random House.

Duncan, M. C. &. Messner, M. A. (2005). *Gender in televised sports: News and highlights shows, 1989–2004.* Los Angeles: Amateur Athletic Foundation of Los Angeles.

Duncan, M. C., Messner, M. A., & Williams, L. (n.d.). *Coverage of women's sports in four daily newspapers.* Los Angeles: Amateur Athletic Foundation of Los Angeles.

Dworkin, S. L. (2003). "Holding back": Negotiating a glass ceiling on women's muscular strength. In R. Weitz (Ed.), *The politics of women's bodies: Sexuality, appearance and behavior* (2nd ed., pp. 240–256). New York: Oxford University Press.

Ellison, J. (2006). Model athletes: Advertising images of women in sport in Canada, 1950–2006. In A. Medovarski and B. Cranny (Eds.), *Canadian women studies: An introductory reader* (2nd ed., pp. 478–488). Toronto: Inanna Publications.

Fausto-Sterling, A. (1993). The five sexes: Why male and female are not enough. *The Sciences (March–April)*, 20–24.

Fausto-Sterling, A. (2000). *Sexing the body: Gender politics and the construction of sexuality.* New York: Basic Books.

Fédération Internationale de Volleyball. *Olympic beach volleyball tournaments specific competition regulations (as per 13.07.2004). Section 24—clothing, equipment, accessories, and marketing. Section 24.4—Women's uniforms.*

Foucault, M. (1978). *The history of sexuality, Vol. 1: An introduction.* New York: Random House.

Funk, W. (1950). *Word origins and their romantic stories.* New York: Bell Publishing Company.

Fusco, C. (1998). Lesbians and locker rooms: The subjective experiences of lesbians in sport. In G. Rail (Ed.), *Sport and postmodern times* (pp. 87–116). Albany: State University of New York Press.

Gaines, J. & Herzog, C. (Eds.). (1990). *Fabrications: Costume and the female body.* New York: Routlegde.

Geddes, P. & Thompson, J. A. (1890). *The evolution of sex.* New York: Schribner and Welford.

Gottschalk, L. (2003). Same-sex sexuality and childhood gender non-conformity: A spurious connection. *Journal of Gender Studies, 12*(1), 35–50.

Gould, L. (1980). X: A fabulous child's story. *Ms (May)*, 61–64.

Griffin, P. (1998). *Strong women, deep closets: Lesbians and homophobia in sport.* Champaign, IL: Human Kinetics.

Halberstam, J. (1998). *Female masculinity.* Durham: Duke University Press.

Hall, M. A. (1996). *Feminism and sporting bodies: Essays on theory and practice.* Champaign, IL: Human Kinetics.

Hall, M. A. (2002). *The Girl and the game: A history of women's sport in Canada.* Peterborough, ON: Broadview Press.

Hall, S. (1997). *Representation: Cultural representation and signifying practices.* London: Sage Publications.

Hamilton, R. (2005). *Gendering the vertical mosaic: Feminist perspectives on Canadian society* (2nd ed.). Toronto: Pearson Prentice Hall.

Hargreaves, J. (1994). *Sporting females: Critical issues in the history and sociology of women's sports.* London: Routledge.

Helgeson, V. S. (1994). Prototypes and dimensions of masculinity and femininity. *Sex Roles, 31*(11/12), 653–682.

Hester, J. D. (2004). Intersexes and the end of gender: Corporeal ethics and post-gender bodies. *Journal of Gender Studies, 13*(3), 215–225.

Heyman, G. D. & Legare, C. H. (2004). Children's beliefs about gender differences in the academic and social domains. *Sex Roles, 50*(3/4), 227–239.

Heywood, L. (1998). *Bodymakers: A cultural anatomy of women's body building.* New Brunswick, NJ: Rutgers University Press.

Heywood, L. & Dworkin, S. (2003). *Built to win: The female athlete as cultural icon.* Minneapolis: University of Minnesota Press.

Hult, J. S. (1994). The story of women's athletics: Manipulating a dream 1890–1985. In D. M. Costa & S. R. Guthrie (Eds.), *Women and sport: Interdisciplinary perspectives.* Champaign, IL: Human Kinetics.

Kane, M. J. (1995). Resistance/transformation of the oppositional binary: Exposing sports as a continuum. *Journal of Sport & Social Issues, 19,* 191–218.

Kidd, B. (1994). The Women's Olympic Games: Important breakthrough obscured through time. *CAAWS Action Bulletin* (Spring). Retrieved from: http://www.caaws.ca/e/milestones/women_history/olympic_games_print.cfm.

Klomsten, A. T., Skaalvik, E. M., & Espnes, G. A. (2004). Physical self-concept and sports: Do gender differences still exist? *Sex Roles, 50*(1/2), 119–127.

Kolnes, L. J. (1995). Heterosexuality as an organizing principle in women's sports. *International Review for Sociology of Sport, 30*(1), 61–77.

Krane, V. (2001). We can be athletic and feminine, but do we want to?: Challenging hegemonic femininity in women's sport. *Quest, 53,* 115–133.

Krane, V. & Barber, H. (2003). Lesbian experiences in sport: A social identity perspective. *Quest, 55,* 328–346.

Krane, V., Choi, P. Y. L., Baird, S. M., Aimar, C. M., & Kauer, K. J. (2004). Living the paradox: Female athletes negotiate femininity and muscularity. *Sex Roles, 50*(5/6), 315–329.

Leigh, M. H. & Bonin, T. M. (1977). The pioneering role of Madame Alice Milliat and the FSFI in establishing international track and field competition for women. *Journal of Sport History, 4*(1), 72–83.

Lenskyj, H. J. (1986). *Out of bounds: Women, sport and sexuality.* Toronto: Women's Press.

Lenskyj, H. J. (1994a). Girl-friendly sport and female values. *Women in Sport and Physical Activity Journal, 3*(1), 35–46.

Lenskyj, H. J. (1994b). Sexuality and femininity in sport contexts: Issues and alternatives. *Journal of Sport and Social Issues, 18*(4), 356–376.

Lenskyj, H. J. (1995). Sport and the threat to gender boundaries. *Sporting Traditions, 12*(1), 47–60.

Lenskyj, H. J. (1999). Women, sport and sexualities: Breaking the silences. In A. White & K. Young (Eds.), *Sport and gender in Canada* (pp. 170–181). New York: Oxford University Press.

Lock, R. (2006). Heterosexual femininity: The painful process of subjectification. In J. Caudwell (Ed.), *Sport, sexualities, & queer/theory* (pp. 159–173). London: Routledge.

Lorber, J. (2008). A world without gender: Making the revolution. In A. L. Ferber, K. Holcomb, & T. Wentling (Eds.), *Sex, gender, and sexuality: The new basics* (pp. 537–544). New York: Oxford University Press.

Markula, P. (2003). The technologies of the self: Sport, feminism and Foucault. *Sociology of Sport Journal, 20*(2), 87–107.

Martin, K. A. (2003). Becoming a gendered body: Practices of preschools. In R. Weitz (Ed.), *The politics of women's bodies: Sexuality, appearance and behavior* (2nd ed., pp. 219–239). New York: Oxford University Press.

Maslow, A. (1966). *The psychology of science.* New York: Harper & Row.

Matteo, S. (1988). The effect of gender-schematic processing on decisions about sex- inappropriate sport behavior. *Sex Roles, 18*(1/2), 41–58.

McArdle, W. D., Katch, F. I., & Katch, V. L. (2007). *Exercise physiology: Energy, nutrition, and human performance* (6th ed.). Baltimore: Lippincott, Williams, and Wilkins.

Merleau-Ponty, M. (1962). *Phenomenology of perception* (translated from the French by C. Smith). New York: Humanities Press.

Messner, M. A. (1994). Sports and male domination: The female athlete as contested ideological terrain. In S. Birrell & C. L. Cole (Eds.), *Women, sport, and culture.* Champagne, IL: Human Kinetics.

Metheny, E. (1965). *Connotations of movement in sport and dance: A collection of speeches about sport and dance as significant forms of human behavior.* Dubuque, IA: W. C. Brown.

Miller, L. & Penz, O. (1991). Talking bodies: Female bodybuilders colonize a male preserve. *Quest, 43,* 148–163.

Miller, T. (2001). *Sportsex.* Philadelphia: Temple University Press.

Money, J. & Ehrhardt, A. (1972). *Man and woman, boy and girl.* Baltimore: Johns Hopkins University Press.

Muscat, A. C. & Long B. C. (2008). Critical comments about body shape and weight: Disordered eating of female athletes and sport participants. *Journal of Applied Sport Psychology, 20*(1), 1–24.

Muybridge, E. (1955). *The human figure in motion.* New York: Dover Publications, Inc.

Paechter, C. (2006). Masculine femininities/feminine masculinities: Power, identities and gender. *Gender and Education, 18*(3), 253–263.

Peper, K. (1994). Female athlete = lesbian: A myth constructed from gendex role expectations and lesbiphobia. In R. J. Ringer (Ed.), *Queer words, queer images: Communication and the construction of homosexuality* (pp. 193–207). New York: New York University Press.

Powlishta, K. K. (1995). Gender bias in children's perceptions of personality traits. *Sex Roles, 32*(1/2), 17–28.

Rich, A. (1976). *Of woman born: Motherhood as experience and institution.* New York: Norton.

Roszak, T. (1999). *The gendered atom: Reflections on the sexual psychology of science.* Berkeley: Conari Press.

Rudacille, D. (2006). *The riddle of gender: Science, activism, and transgender rights.* New York: Anchor Books.

Ryan, J. (1995). *Little girls in pretty boxes: The making and breaking of elite gymnasts and figure skaters.* New York: Doubleday.

Sayers, J. (1982). *Biological politics: Feminist and anti-feminist perspectives.* London: Tavistock.

Schulze, L. (1990). On the muscle. In J. Gaines & C. Herzog (Eds.), *Fabrications: Costume and the female body.* New York: Routledge.

Shogan, D. (1999). *The making of high performance athletes: Discipline, diversity and ethics.* Toronto: The University of Toronto Press.

Simpson, J. A. & Weiner, E. S. C. (Eds.). (1989). *Oxford English Dictionary* (2nd ed., Volume VI). Oxford: Oxford University Press.

Simri, U. (1983). *A concise world history of women's sports.* Netanya: Wingate Institute for Physical Education and Sport.

Spelman, E. (1999). Woman as body: Ancient and contemporary views. In J. Price & M. Shildrick (Eds.), *Feminist theory and the body* (pp. 32–41). New York: Routledge.

Steinham, G. (1994). *Moving beyond words: Age, race, sex, power, money, muscles: Breaking boundaries of gender.* New York: Simon and Schuster.

Tarrant, S. (2006). *When sex became gender.* New York: Routledge.

Terman, L. M. & Miles, C. C. (1936). *Sex and personality: Studies in masculinity and femininity.* New York: McGraw-Hill.

Theberge, N. (1985/1994). Toward a feminist alternative to sport as a male preserve. In S. Birrell & C. L. Cole (Eds.), *Women, sport, and culture* (pp. 181–192). Champaign, IL: Human Kinetics.

Theberge, N. (1991). Reflections on the body in the sociology of sport. *Quest, 43,* 123–134.

Tsang, T. (2000). Let me tell you a story: A narrative exploration of identity in high performance sport. *Sociology of Sport Journal, 17,* 44–59.

Turner, B. S. (1984). *The body and society.* New York: Basil Blackwell.

van der Wijngaard, M. (1997). *Reinventing the sexes: The biomedical construction of femininity and masculinity.* Bloomington, IN: Indiana University Press.

Veri, M. J. (1999). Homophobic discourse surrounding the female athlete. *Quest, 51,* 355–368.

Vermillion, M. (2006). *Murder by mascot: A Mara Gilgannon mystery.* New York: Alyson Books.

Wayne, L. D. (2005). Neutral pronouns: A modest proposal whose time has come. *Canadian Women's Studies/Les Cahiers de la Femme, 24*(2 & 3), 85–91.

Weedon, C. (1999). *Feminism, theory, and the politics of difference.* Oxford: Blackwell Publishers.

Weitz, R. (Ed.). (1998). *The politics of women's bodies: Sexuality, appearance and behavior.* Oxford/New York: Oxford University Press.

Weitz, R. (2004). *Rapunzel's daughters: What women's hair tells us about women's lives.* New York: Farrar, Straus and Giroux.

Whitson, D. (1994). The embodiment of gender: Discipline, domination and empowerment. In S. Birrell & C. L. Cole (Eds.), *Women, sport, & culture* (pp. 353–371). Champaign, IL: Human Kinetics.

Williams, S. J. & Bendelow, G. (1998). *The lived body: Sociological themes and embodied issues.* London: Routledge.

Wolf, N. (1991). *The Beauty Myth.* Toronto: Vintage Books.

Wright, J. & Clarke, G. (1999). Sport, the media and the construction of compulsory heterosexuality. *International Review for Sociology of Sport, 34,* 227–243.

Young, I. M. (1980). Throwing like a girl: A phenomenology of feminine body comportment, motility and spatiality. *Human Studies, 3,* 137–156.

Young, I. M. (1990). *Throwing like a girl and other essays in feminism, philosophy and social theory.* Bloomington, IN: Indiana University Press.

Index

infantilization of, 7–8, 90, 114–16,
182–83*n*14, 183*n*15
as judged, 89, 90, 145, 181*n*7, 182*n*13,
188*n*3
male participation in, 33, 34–35,
89–90, 121, 139, 179*n*5, 189*n*5
and non-sporting activities, 7–8, 131,
186*n*7, 186*n*8
and physical movement, 131
as polygendered, 89–90
privilege enjoyed by, 148–50
and work of Terman and Miles,
60–61, 61*t*, 64, 131
femininity, 1
see also femininity/masculinity;
masculinity
and appearance, 6–7, 14, 99–102
Bartky on, 87, 98
and body size/configuration, 105–24
and bodywork, 91, 101–2, 104–5,
109–10, 120, 121, 127, 141–55
and concealment of lesbianism, 97,
142
as compulsory. *See entry immediately
below*
cultural devaluation of, 71–72
as defined by masculinity, 50–51, 163,
168
of female athletes, 88–90, 179*n*4
and female body, 87–98
and gender stereotypes, 74–85, 123–24
and gestures, movements, and postures, 125–40
and heterosexuality, 5, 6, 15, 24–25,
26, 51, 75, 82, 142
and "masculine" sports, 15–16, 17–18,
28, 70–72, 82, 88, 90–91, 92,
119–20, 121, 127, 173
media image of, 105–6

performative nature of. *See* gender
performance
as personality type, 51–65, 67–69
prototypical features of, 76–78, 77*t*,
80–82
racialization of, 102–3
sexing of, 67–85
signifiers of, 111, 143–48, 162, 181*n*9.
See also bodywork
as social construct, 159–67
in Victorian era/early 20th century,
73, 107
and view of, as threatening, 23–24
femininity, compulsory, 8, 12, 15, 70–73,
102–8, 153
see also appearance; body size and
configuration; bodywork; gestures, movements, and postures
and dress/deportment controls, 5,
133–34, 150, 189*n*6
and gender performance, 72–73,
101–2, 123, 142, 163
and heterosexuality, 5, 6, 15, 24–25,
26, 51, 75, 82, 142
and marriage/maternity, 35–40, 72,
75, 107–8, 180*n*5
and need to "fix" appearance, 82,
101–2, 105–8
and signifiers of, 111, 143–48, 162,
181*n*9
as white male construct, 72–74,
102–8, 180*n*5
as white upper-class construct, 121,
134–39, 144, 148, 155, 163, 184*n*1
femininity/masculinity
see also differences, female-male;
similarities/overlaps, female-
male; Terman-Miles research on
sex and personality

and lesbianism, 4–5, 6, 133

male coaches of, 5–6

physical movement of, 133–34

and reactions to prototypes, 80–82

as tested by Terman and Miles, 57–58, 60–61, 173

vilification of, 6

vitalism, 36–37, 75

volleyball

beach version of, 8–9, 148, 151, 190n5

body type required for, 110, 112

as girls'/women's sport, 35, 61, 138, 151

at Olympic Games, 61, 135, 186–87n9

uniforms of, 9, 148, 151, 190n5

Wickenheiser, Hayley, 8

Williams, Serena, 117, 118, 146

Williams, Venus, 117, 118

Witt, Katarina, 116

Women's Olympics/World Games, 30

women's sports

see also female athletes; "feminine" sports; *see also individual sports*

codifying femininity in, 150–51

as devalued, 7–8, 33–34, 71

eating disorders in, 90, 102, 106, 113, 121–22, 170, 181n7

as gender-appropriate. *See* gender-appropriate sports/activities

leagues of, 34, 186n5

media coverage of, 8–9, 33–34, 114–15, 116–18, 148–49, 184–85n1, 190n5

at Olympic Games, 30, 181n6, 184–85n1, 186–87n9

and race/class bias, 135–39, 148, 184n1

U.S. government funding for, 2, 5, 139–40, 187–88n12, 188n12

wrestling, 60, 130

Zaharias, Babe Didrikson, 172